THE VIEW

FROM

BREAST POCKET

MOUNTAIN

THE VIEW

FROM

BREAST POCKET

MOUNTAIN

A Memoir

Karen Hill Anton

SENYUME PRESS

Senyume Press
www.senyumepress.com

With love and respect to these mentors who've
left this world and made an enduring impression on me:

Victoria Lawrence, Rosetta Reitz, Donald Richie,
Kazuko Satoh, and Helen Yglesias.

1

———

I was nineteen and in Europe when the tenement apartment I'd grown up in burned down. In a matter of hours, my old dolls and diaries became the charred debris of a now alien Washington Heights landscape.

I imagined that warm summer day was like the ones I remembered, colored with beautiful black women in bright dresses, Fire Engine Red lipstick, gold hoop earrings from Woolworth, and bracelets from the West Indies. Sitting on their folding chairs, neighbors called out to those passing.

"How you doing today, Mr. Perry?"

"Oh, I'm coming along fine, and yourself, Mother Lee?"

"Oh I can't complain, thank you. It's hot but I can take the heat."

Then, men like my father strode down the street in shiny shoes, the taps on their heels announcing them.

Aldous Huxley said he felt clean for the first time in his life when a fire in his home left him with nothing. I didn't feel that. I only felt loss. And I knew that something, memories mostly, had been taken from me. But I didn't realize then that they wouldn't be given back. My father didn't say he felt clean, but he didn't seem to lament the loss of anything. Things were used, got old, and wore out. All things changed and all things were possible. He never said any of this, but he did say, "We never know what will come." He said it all the time. As if that cleared things up.

No one knew how or why the fire started and it didn't seem to matter. We had nothing that could be called valuable. My father only said, "It was an old building." There was no insurance to be collected and no compensation, although the city helped him find an apartment in a Harlem housing project. The place where he'd be murdered eight years later.

My father's room in our apartment was piled high with newspapers. On the floor, the table, the dresser, the foot of the bed. Turning from white to beige to yellow to brown and flaking at the edges, they disintegrated in their stacks. At the bottom of the closet in that room was an old shoebox full of photographs. The rare times I was curious about a past, I'd ask my father to take out the box so I could look at the browned black-and-white snapshots of his eight, mostly dead, brothers and sisters. "This is my father," my father would say, his voice strangely formal. In a small photograph, no bigger than a postage stamp, a black man looked at me from under his brimmed hat. His expression was meek, his eyes unassuming, and those eyes told me he had never left the state of Mississippi. There's a good chance he never left the Delta region where he was born.

There was a photograph of me in that box, too, the only one I remember of myself as a child. Taken in a photo booth, it showed me in a coat with a leopard faux fur collar and cuffs. I loved that coat, and loved that photo showing my dark eyes bright against glowing dark skin.

And there were several small copies of my parents' wedding photograph. A large tinted print of that portrait, the only framed picture in our apartment, hung on the wall in our living room during those years my days were filled with jumping rope and playing jacks. I don't remember when that picture was taken

2

down, but one day it wasn't there anymore, and the wall went on as if it had always been bare. My father was fifty when he married our mother, who was eighteen. How did that come about? I wonder about it, but now there is no one I can ask that question.

I guessed that the creamy satin wedding gown was also destroyed in the fire. That dress had been kept in the bottom drawer of a dresser full of clothes and undergarments belonging to a woman unknown to me, my mother, who was institutionalized. I found her things, musty with the smell of dusting powder, unpleasant.

One day during my last year in high school, my father pulled out the drawer as if to check if the gown was still there. "Sister, this wedding gown is here for the day you need it." "Sister" was what he, my older brother Johnny, and younger sister Mollie called me.

"Daddy, who wants to wear that old thing? Let Mollie wear it. If I ever get married, which I probably won't, I wouldn't wear that."

"Well, if you ever get married, which you probably will not, you are going to have to do something about that hair first," he said, laughing for himself.

"I think it looks good," I said, lying. I'd seen a photograph of Abbey Lincoln and Miriam Makeba and, astonished by their beauty and their short natural hair, decided on the spot I would never straighten my hair again. But after washing my hair and just leaving it, I didn't look like the magnificent Makeba or the jazz-cool Lincoln.

"You know you can't leave your hair like that."

"Why not? This is how Miriam Makeba wears it."

"She has it trimmed," my father said with authority, though I knew he'd only seen her on the cover of the album I had propped up on the dresser in my room. I'd already asked at the beauty parlor and they wouldn't do it. It was 1961 and beauty parlors straightened hair with a hot comb and curled it with hot curlers. "Girl, you better straighten that nappy head! You look like hell, and on 'em skinny legs, too," the girls on the bus taunted me. I took to walking the thirty blocks to school.

"You go up to the barber shop and tell Taylor I said to trim it for you," my father said. I didn't say anything, but I wondered why I didn't think to ask Mr. Taylor. As Daddy walked out of the room that had the mahogany dresser, he added, as he often did, "What will become of you, I do not know."

That was just something he said. I knew he wasn't worried.

My father had gone to Hampton Institute and was skilled as a tailor, but in 1950s New York City, it seemed it was never easy for him to get a job. Relief, joy, and gratitude were the feelings that filled our small kitchen when he'd return home and tell us, "Well children, I found a job today." Often he worked as a presser at local dry cleaner. We'd run up Amsterdam Avenue or down Broadway to wave at him through a tiny back room window or go in the back of the shop knowing that no matter how busy he was, he'd be glad to see us. The sweat poured off him as he stood enveloped in steam over the large presser. The sleeveless white undershirts he always worked in exposed the dark patches where his arms had been burned by the steam and presser. We invariably asked, "Can we have a nickel for a cream soda?" We were never denied. Handing over a coin to each of us in turn, with his large smile, he'd say, "Now you children run along now."

At that time, three motherless children could run around city streets freely. The clearest memory I have of running into any trouble was the time I ate some crab with Gloria Wright, who lived across the hall, and I mistakenly ate the "dead man's meat," the gills. She said it would kill me. I not only believed her, I knew it was true because we'd been warned and knew *never* to eat that part. I was afraid to sleep that night, knowing death would claim me as soon as I closed my eyes. But then I figured out that if I slept with Daddy, I couldn't possibly die. I went in the newspaper-filled room, crept into his bed, and fell asleep with my head nestled on his chest and the soft hair of his underarm. Surely death would not snatch me from the safety of my father, and it didn't.

He'd been urged to put us in foster homes or an orphanage. People said a man, and of his age, couldn't possibly raise three young children. Our mother, diagnosed as an amnesiac, was in a mental institution our entire childhood. I knew the word *amnesia* very early, and just that knowledge made me different from my friends, who didn't know words like that. If anyone asked me where my mother was, I could answer without hesitation, "She's in a hospital. She has amnesia." That's all I'd say. I could have told them more, could've said that her amnesia had something to do with the fact that she'd been so young when her children were born too close together and it was too much for her. I'd overheard my father saying this on the telephone. But I didn't let talking about my mother become a conversation. And that wasn't hard. I would say what I had to and look away.

The first word I knew how to spell was *Mississippi*, forward, backward, and fast. Gathering not only us but the neighbors' kids, too, my father set up a blackboard in our living room and taught us our "sums," spelling, and penmanship. He knew American history well, especially the period called Reconstruction, but since we weren't taught about it in school, I thought it might be something he made up, like his tales and scary ghost stories.

I don't know where along his journey he'd learned to appreciate the music of Handel, which he loved. Anything he liked he described as "fine," and once when he opened the Sunday magazine of the *Journal-American* and showed me Michelangelo's Pietà, he said, "Sister, look. This is the finest sculpture in the world." Years later, when he was long dead, I saw it in the Vatican and was overwhelmed by its beauty.

My father owned the only typewriter in the neighborhood, a heavy, black Royal he'd think nothing of carrying down our five flights of stairs and up someone else's five flights to write a letter that needed to be official. His set of Funk & Wagnalls encyclopedias was probably the only one in the neighborhood, too. He was openly seen as a resource, always called on to draw up a petition, write a eulogy, or lead a rent strike.

His personal letters were a perfect combination of wit, wisdom, and penmanship, and I loved the sound of his pen scratching across heavy bond paper, the pauses audible as he dipped the nib of the long fountain pen into a pot of blue-black ink. Angry about some injustice, he thought it was his right and responsibility to write to newspaper editors, and the papers he read daily, the *New York Journal-American* and *Amsterdam News*, must have tired of hearing from John Henry Hill, Sr. "I'm going to write my congressman!" would precede yet another fiery letter to the mythically handsome, wavy-haired, powerful politician and pastor Adam Clayton Powell, Jr.

And Daddy could get pretty fiery when he felt he'd been wronged. Like the time he bought a bag of onions and returned home to find one was rotten. He went back to the greengrocer, and, I suppose after an argument, turned over the entire stand of onions. Word of the incident traveled up and down our block, reaching me as Lonnie Wright and I were concocting yet another noxious mixture with the chemistry set Daddy had given me that year on my thirteenth birthday. My mortification over the onion incident is as clear to me as Lonnie, whose own father was in prison at the time, pronouncing Daddy a "badass legend!"

Highly superstitious, my father would have a fit if a broom touched his feet. "Don't sweep my feet!" he'd yell, as he snatched the broom away and spit on it. Only Johnny was bold enough to tell him that he seemed to make a point of being just in the place we'd be sweeping as we did our Saturday morning chores. He had, according to him, a "foolproof system" to find out if one of us told a lie or did something we weren't allowed to, like go to a friend's home when there was no adult present. He'd fill the deep porcelain sink in the kitchen with soapy water and we each had to, in turn, put our hands in, palms down. The one who came up with suds resting on the back of their hands was the clear culprit. I was terrified of the "soap test," but I also thought, *This is crazy.*

I loved to brag to my friends that my father could "put the pots on." With just the bare essentials, he made stews and soups, cornbread, spoonbread, gingerbread, and biscuits—no cookbooks, recipes, measuring cups or spoons. I'm sure it's precisely because we never ate canned or frozen anything that Johnny, Mollie, and I looked with longing at what was presented as typically American meals, three-things-on-a-plate (something brown, something white, something green). We couldn't have imagined anything more tantalizing than a TV dinner. Sometimes our cupboard was truly bare, and mayonnaise sandwiches would do to stave off hunger. In those days, I assumed everyone was hungry some of the time, and that they were as happy as we were the times our father came home and placed A&P shopping bags bulging with all the foods we loved on our kitchen table.

He was old-fashioned about everything. There was no instant or automatic anything in our home. He mended our clothes by hand, made rag mops from rags. We didn't have a washing machine; no one in our neighborhood did. Every Saturday morning he'd be bent over the clawfoot bathtub, scrubbing on a tin washboard with a large bar of brown laundry soap. I'd trail after him as he carried an enamel basin filled with well-wrung-out clothes and a paper bag of thick wooden clothespins up to the clotheslines on the roof, the "tar beach" where we slept on hot summer nights.

Saturday nights, he ironed our cotton dresses and pinafores with wide sashes, and the ladies at church would declare, "Oh, he ties those girls' sashes as well as any woman." In tones just above a hush, I'd often overhear neighbors say, "He does everything a woman would do for those kids." And women admired how well he straightened and braided our hair. "Sister, I want you and Mollie to look just as nice as the other girls," Daddy would tell me. I knew he meant the girls who had mothers.

Nothing was easy about not having a mother. Mrs. Wright gave me Kotex, but I was a ball of twelve-year-old awkwardness when I had to tell my father that I'd begun to menstruate. And although I'd already scoped out Woolworth on Broadway, I didn't think I'd get the words out of my mouth to ask for money to buy my first bra. It used to hurt like hell when some well-meaning person would say, "Your father is a wonderful and exceptional man to do all the things he does for you children," because it underscored the fact that we didn't have a mother.

And I didn't like to be told that I, much more than my sister and brother, looked like my father. But now I'm all right with that, and happy that I, and my children, have inherited his generous smile.

2

Seeing my mother required a long train ride. To visit her, we'd go to places far out in Brooklyn, Queens, or Long Island. Kings Park State Hospital was the name of the last institution I recall.

Johnny, Mollie, and I would stand together looking out the large window at the front of the train. That's when my tears would begin to build up. I always wondered if they wanted to cry, too, but I never asked them. And they never cried. I didn't either.

We always visited her on a Sunday, and it was the only time there was an excuse not to go to church. Our father made a lunch of fried chicken, potato salad, collard greens, biscuits—our usual Sunday dinner. It was like we were going on a special outing, a picnic. But it wasn't a picnic. When we arrived at the hospital, my father went in, took off his hat, and asked for "Mrs. Iris Hill." We were never allowed in because we were too young. So we waited, playing on the steps of the institution until the attendants finished dressing Iris Hill and my father escorted her out. Her dresses, floral prints just like any mother would wear, were always new because she only wore them for these visits, and our father always bought her more. Her lipstick was smeared. Every time. There'd be a smudge of red lipstick on her teeth. It gave her away.

Daddy introduced us, one by one: "Iris, this is Karen," he'd say. "Say hello." In a sweet voice she'd say, "Hello Karen." Sometimes she wouldn't say anything. She wouldn't even look. She'd just continue talking to herself, as I guessed she did all day. She usually laughed, too. But sometimes the sweet smile would suddenly change and she'd scowl, looking angry. Real mad.

Since we weren't permitted in the hospital, we only visited in spring and summer so we could sit outside. It seems strange, I think now, that the desolate experience of visiting my mother was always against a backdrop of blue skies and marigolds.

Now at home in Japan, when I bend down to catch the scent of the marigolds, the only flowers I have in my traditional garden of stones and bamboo, it's to remind myself. I purposely smell memory. It's not enough just to see the irregular orange and maroon petals. I must smell the flower to really be five years old again and visiting my mother at a mental institution.

I never wanted to go there. Never.

When my father told his friends at church, matronly women in hats and men who wore hats too, that we wouldn't be coming the following Sunday because "I'm going to visit my wife if the weather is fine," they'd smile down at us beneficently as if we were the luckiest children in the world. "Now, isn't that nice," they'd say, presuming our happiness at the prospect, and never imagining, I suppose, what a hateful, heartrending experience it was.

We sat on a bench on the hospital grounds to eat our lunch. We could have our favorite parts of the chicken. Johnny got the leg, Mollie the thigh, and I got the breast. Iris just put food in her mouth—she didn't seem to care what part of the chicken she had, or how she ate it. The oily chicken made a mess with the lipstick around her mouth. My father made sure she had a napkin. I never figured out how I could eat at all with a torrent of tears dammed up behind my eyes, bursting through the back of my head, and blocking my throat. But I did eat. And I never cried. Not even once.

"But how did you feel while you sat there on the bench?" asked Dr. R, the therapist, a Filipina practicing in Japan, I sought out much later.

"Feel?"

"Yes. Describe it to me. It's all right."

I'd never let myself feel anything. How could I? It wouldn't have been "all right" to sit there crying for "no reason." Would my father have understood? He'd made a nice lunch and brought us that long way to see our mother. He was doing everything he could. And I wouldn't want to upset my sister and brother. No. Those tears had to be checked. I couldn't have survived otherwise. It was much too painful. Feel? It's pretty simple: I wanted a mother. I wanted her to know me. I didn't want to be visiting her there, sitting on that bench.

While we ate, our father talked to her, as if she were a normal person. I could hear the hope in his voice as he talked to his "wife." He hoped she'd be responsive, but she wasn't. The few times I talked to her, I looked her straight in the eye thinking that was the way to get through. But the eyes that looked back didn't see me. I knew she didn't know who I was—didn't have any idea and didn't care.

I often heard my father talking about her on the telephone, saying the doctors said, "She's coming along now, she seems to be getting better." He acted like he really believed that, and I wanted to believe it too—maybe she'd be better and would come to live with us to be our mother. I was a year old, Johnny was two, and Mollie just a few months when she disappeared. My father never told me about it, but when I was about ten, I found a bunch of notices announcing her disappearance. These were index-sized cards in assorted colors in the top drawer of the same mahogany-colored bureau that held the wedding gown. I suppose the cards were passed out to people on the street.

"MISSING" it said at the top and asked if anyone knew of the whereabouts of Iris Hill, five feet, five inches tall, brown hair, brown eyes, last seen wearing... There was an extra plea at the bottom that said the missing person had three young children at home.

I don't know if my brother and sister ever saw those cards. I never asked them and I never told them. Why would we want to talk about such a thing? We didn't sit around crying and being sad about a mother we didn't have. We had friends, toys, dolls. My dolls had first, middle and last names. They had their ears pierced. They had library cards. When necessary, I could take them to the doll hospital on Broadway, a magical place where headless, limbless dolls lined worktables and were put right again. I had roller skates and ice skates, too. I had a dollhouse, and the chemistry set, and I could turn my room into a lab anytime I wanted. I took ballet lessons (Johnny and Mollie took tap) and I was a butterfly in a recital at which I wore a fluffy yellow tutu with sparkles that I bet I'd seen in my dreams.

Every year, our father took us, and a bunch of neighborhood kids, to the Ringling Bros. Circus and to Coney Island, where we could eat big clouds of pink cotton candy and green pistachio ice cream. Not all kids got to do stuff like that. Our father was respected in our community, we knew that. Everybody knew Mr. Hill, and they'd say things like, "He's doing a wonderful job. That man is mother and father to those children."

Those cards that told about the missing mother were my own secret, not to share. When no one was around, I'd take them all out—there were a lot of them. When I was in high school, I took one, just one, and put it with my things. I knew then that one day I would want to remember. It would be evidence. Proof. But the apartment burned down, destroying those dolls and diaries, Joan Baez and Miriam Makeba albums, snapshots from my Brownie camera, school class photos and yearbooks. No photos exist of me as a child. But I was a child once. That one card I'd saved, the evidence of the motherless child, was lost in the fire. Still, I know those cards answered the mystery of why there was no mother. Instead of words like "amnesia" and "hospital," they said she disappeared. She walked out the door one day and was gone.

I've forgotten a lot. And now that my whole family is gone, there is no one to check with to find out if this or that happened. Incidents notched in my life belong to a past now veil-shaded, vaguely remembered. But memory doesn't entirely fail. It is the memory that made me that lives with me. And I remember those cards were in all the colors of the rainbow.

Iris did come home for a trial run, but by that time I was eighteen and subletting an apartment downtown. When I'd visit, she'd be sitting on the sofa like a guest—a guest who laughed and talked to herself and stared into the empty space between us. It was never like having a mother—that was a hope and a dream that became a fantasy and then a forgotten idea. But I couldn't believe or accept she didn't know I was her daughter, and the minute my father left the room, I'd begin to talk to her— rather, interrogate her.

"What's my name?"

"What hospital was I born in?"

"When did you come to America?"

By this time, she'd say things like "So you're Karen," though it wasn't convincing. She even told me the name of the ship she sailed on from the West Indies. But was she right? She said I was born in Harlem Hospital, whereas my father told me I was born in Mother Cabrini Hospital and that it was Mollie who was born in Harlem Hospital. But Iris insisted and I wanted to believe her, and I was glad she was so sure. She'd given birth to me, she should know. And if she knew it would establish her as my mother, it would validate her, even if she didn't know my name.

I was born in Mother Cabrini Memorial Hospital, April 11, 1945.

· · ·

It didn't work with her being at home. She needed constant care and couldn't be left alone, and my father was already too old to look after her, so she was put in a neighborhood nursing home. I would visit her because my father told me I should. Like Mr. Rochester's wife in *Jane Eyre*, she was my secret. No friend of mine ever saw her.

Johnny visited her at the nursing home, too, but he didn't have to be told. And just like my father, he acted as if she were normal—at least it didn't seem to break his heart to talk to her or about her. He seemed to have a relationship with her, and I suppose both he and my father had a memory of her from the time before she became the woman who talked and laughed to herself and had lipstick on her teeth. They both sincerely cared about her, whereas I thought of her as a duty and I pitied her. Though I'm sure I pitied myself more.

At the nursing home, I'd sit with her, expecting nothing, sometimes talking, sometimes not. I'd always found it difficult to look at her because there was nothing to be found in her face. Even her angry looks or sudden laughter didn't reveal anything about her.

Four years later, when I returned from Europe after Nanao was born, I took her there and introduced her.

"This is your granddaughter, Nanao. Say hello."

"Hello Nanao."

Living in institutions for so many years left its mark on Iris: untreated diabetes left her partially blind, she developed tuberculosis, and she had heart disease. But she wasn't old. She was forty-seven when she died, a few months after my father. I don't know the date. I don't remember if it was Johnny or Mollie who telephoned me. I have no photograph of her. I don't remember if I called her Mother, Mama, Ma, Mom. None of those words are familiar to me. They didn't belong to her or me, either.

· · ·

I've spent my whole life observing women, mostly the mothers of my friends. Unknowingly, they presented themselves as examples for me. I admired these women and watched them closely, with their husbands, their children, and their homes. I saw what they did with food, clothes, books, emotions. They couldn't know I watched. I didn't know. I had no idea that I was picking and choosing. And unlike my girlfriends—who had no choice, and who would be, to some extent, like their mothers whether they liked it or not—I could take what I liked, what I found useful, what I would come to value.

I wasn't sure I could be a mother, that I would know what mothers do and how to imitate it. But I am a mother. I may be faking it, but my children call me Mama and they seem to mean it.

3

I didn't do well in high school. I was a poor test-taker.

My senior compositions on *Narrative of the Life of Frederick Douglass* and *Hamlet* both received A+. My spelling tests were always marked "100%"—my father saw to that—but writing and spelling weren't on the SATs. I've never forgotten how, when I went to retrieve my scores, the head of the math department laughed in my face.

Inquiring of my "guidance counselor" about colleges, I wasn't given information, but short shrift. I wouldn't have known then, in 1962, how to describe it, but I got the message loud and clear that it was assumed that I, a black girl, with less than outstanding grades, would not be seeking higher education. There was no affirmative action, and I knew nothing about scholarships. No, I wasn't strong in math, but in spite of the department head's crooked smile, I knew I wasn't stupid. My eighth-grade teacher had told me, "You're a smart girl. I know you are. Don't ever believe otherwise." I never have.

During my last year year at George Washington High School, they offered Art History for the first time—and it was as if the entire school curriculum had been illuminated. New to our school, the teacher, Mr. William Spilka, showed up sporting a thick black handlebar mustache, a beret, and sandals. This wonderful man who shared his passion for the world's great art treated us like intelligent young people who could not only grasp, but also appreciate great art. He didn't put distance between his class of kids from Washington Heights and Harlem —working-class kids of black, Jewish, Greek, Irish, and Puerto Rican backgrounds— and the world of art and culture.

From the moment he showed us slides of the Venus of Willendorf, Stonehenge, the cave paintings at Lascaux, and explained the differences between Ionic, Doric, and Corinthian columns, it was as if this knowledge became part of our daily lives. By the end of the first semester, we knew Braque's cubism reflected his admiration of African masks. I doubt there was anyone in the class who couldn't easily distinguish a Manet from a Monet, identify a Modigliani and a Matisse. We could discuss the work of Lucas Cranach the Elder and express appreciation for the etchings of Albrecht Dürer. How lucky for us that these artists were a subway-ride away at the Metropolitan or the Modern! The days we played hooky, we'd go see the medieval Unicorn Tapestries at the Cloisters, overlooking the Hudson River, just a short walk from our high school.

When Mr. Spilka told us about the Louvre, the Prado, the Rijksmuseum, it was as if he assumed we'd go there, and places further afield. One day. Those classes were pure enchantment, making the world beyond the only world I'd known less foreign, more accessible, within reach.

I'd always been aware there was a whole other world "out there," but what I didn't know then is that it had anything to do with me.

After graduating from GW, I promptly sublet an apartment in Greenwich Village on Carmine Street. I'd heard about the apartment from Rosetta Reitz, who I met when she came by the Peace Center on West Fourth Street, a place I hung out stuffing envelopes and passing out nuclear disarmament pamphlets. I babysat Rosetta's three daughters during the year, and summers I went with the family to Fire Island, a great place to be outside the city. Every day we were at the beach or the bay and might cross paths with artists and writers, like Joseph Heller, our nearest neighbor.

I'd just graduated high school the summer Joe told me *Catch-22* would become a movie, and asked if I would, as a small summer job, go through the book and type up all the dialogue. Rosetta had a portable typewriter in the house, so I spent a portion of every afternoon typing the dialogue on index cards. Joe Heller was a great guy, and I remember talking and laughing with him while he sat back in his beach chair. I didn't know then what a literary phenomenon he was, but knew he was totally cool hanging out on the beach talking with a teenage girl. He gave me his telephone number and address in the city and told me to always feel free to get in touch. Whenever I'd call him at his West End Avenue apartment, almost the first thing he'd ask me was, "What're you reading?"

We didn't have books in my home. I'd read anything I got my hands on and it didn't matter to me if it was a tattered Mickey Spillane pocketbook or the Reader's Digest. I'd go to the library up the street on St. Nicholas Avenue and pick books by their covers or titles: *Marjorie Morningstar, Exodus, A Separate Peace, Days in the Yellow Leaf.* And, naturally, I chose the books I wasn't supposed to read: *East of Eden, God's Little Acre, Peyton Place, Bonjour Tristesse, Lolita.*

I don't remember what Joe wrote after "for Karen" when he gave me a signed copy of *Catch-22*.

I still regret lending the book to a friend. I never saw it again.

Rosetta was the food writer for *The Village Voice*, and often when I'd arrive at her Washington Square South apartment, she'd have a dish she wanted to test out on me. "What do you think? Too much sherry? Not enough tarragon?" she'd ask me about stuffed mushrooms.

I'd never eaten food cooked with wine, I wouldn't have known tarragon from marjoram, and Rosetta wasted no time in developing my palate and taste for fine food. Long before I went to Europe, I'd stopped eating American "cheese" as I'd learned to appreciate Bel Paese, Brie, Bleu de Bresse, and fine dining in Rosetta's kitchen, a magical place with copper pans hanging overhead and flame-colored Le Creuset pots lining the counters in front of windows overlooking Washington Square Park.

Playing albums from her extensive music collection is how I first heard the Goldberg Variations and Vivaldi. Listening to Rosetta and her friend, the writer and jazz critic Albert Murray, talk about Bud Powell and Carmen McRae, I played them them too. I never knew furniture had names but learned from Rosetta that the black leather and walnut chair I always chose to sit in when I did my homework was an Eames. Homework finished, I'd delve into her bookshelves. Rosetta had once introduced me to Grace Paley, and her book *The Little Disturbances of Man* was just the kind of title to catch my attention. Some books Rosetta directed me to read, almost dictatorially telling me "You have to read," were *Native Son, Invisible Man,* Edith Wharton, Edith Hamilton's *Mythology, A Raisin in the Sun,* and everything Henry James and James Baldwin had in print.

Tamar Cole was the first person I told about the sublet apartment on Carmine Street, hoping she'd want to share it with me. We'd been friends since junior high school. I was one of the kids who'd come from the mostly black public schools in Washington Heights in 1957 and integrated at the mostly white Humboldt Junior High School. I first spotted Tamar in our modern dance class. Her thick black curls contrasted with blue-gray eyes, and it was entirely possible she was skinnier than I was. I don't know if I noticed she was white—her skin tone was olive, in any case—

but I did notice she was one of the best dancers in our class. We shared our love of dance along with that of reading. We went through our "Romantic period," reading Byron and reciting whole passages of *Childe Harold's Pilgrimage* out loud to each other, bringing ourselves to tears as we recited with passion and in unison, *"Roll on, thou deep and dark blue ocean—roll! Ten thousand fleets sweep over thee in vain; Man marks the earth with his ruin —his control stops with the shore."*

Tamar moved into Carmine Street with me and we two Washington Heights girls got to declare our independence. Her parents were writers, liberal, progressive, even hip—they'd easily acquiesced, giving Tamar permission to move out. I had to do some begging with my father. "Oh Daddy, please. It'll just be for the summer." In addition to all his rules and limits, I always had to report who I was with all the time. I hated it. He finally gave in, saying that once I lived on my own and had "a taste of freedom," I would never be able to live at home again. He was right.

Our schoolmate Sheri Saltzberg, hearing we'd escaped Washington Heights, asked if she could move in, too. It was a large four-bedroom railroad apartment, and we said sure. I felt I kind of owed Sheri since she'd shared her Yiddish-speaking mother's chopped liver sandwiches with me in the lunchroom all the years I was at George Washington High School.

My father's lessons on his Royal typewriter came in handy when just a month out of high school I got a job as a secretary in a small private diagnostic laboratory on East Sixty-Third Street. Typing up lab reports and telephoning test results to doctors up and down Park Avenue, I'd show up appropriately attired in Peter Pan collar blouses or cardigan sweater sets, the look for a secretary circa 1962 in an office around the corner from Madison Avenue. Back in the Village, I wore embroidered Mexican blouses bought from Piñata Party, wraparound skirts, and custom-made leather sandals with long straps that tied around my ankles.

. . .

That summer was one of the best times of my life.

I'd always longed for liberty, and now I had it. I could come and go freely. The one thing I'd always wanted to do was stay out late—and that was the one thing my father would not permit. I had to be home, at specific times. I got around this by staying with friends. If I said I was spending the night with Tamar—or with Joanna Lawrence, whose book-stuffed home was a harbor throughout my teenage years—then it was all right. He knew their parents would be there, knew that adults were "in charge." But what he didn't know was that these parents were a whole lot cooler than he was and didn't freak out if we stayed out late.

Living in Greenwich Village, I could go straight from listening to folk singers in the park all day to hanging out in Caffe Reggio where I'd order a Florentine apple tart at midnight. I satisfied my taste for Jewish food, frequenting delis where I bought pickles from barrels and expertly sliced lox and sable. I'd eat gefilte fish at Ratner's, kasha varnishkes at B&H, and matzoh ball soup at the 2nd Ave Deli.

Billy Anton came by often. He lived just a few blocks away on MacDougal Street, Little Italy, and told me where to get the best Sicilian pizza, and often brought long hero sandwiches of capocollo and peppers. It was then he introduced me to Zen Buddhism, mystifying me with the koan, "What is the sound of one hand clapping?"

Sundays, I'd take the long subway ride uptown, arriving when I knew Daddy would be back from church, frying chicken and making biscuits. Mollie was still living at home. Johnny would come by and our family of four ate at the kitchen table just big enough for four plates.

I was happy to go home. But returning to my old neighborhood, I could see, and feel, the familiar had already become strange. I knew I'd never live there again.

. . .

When I was a senior, I applied to Juilliard, auditioned, and didn't get in. Although I thought of myself as a strong dancer, I didn't know that taking up modern dance in my teens was too late to have the technique to even be considered by a school like Juilliard. Love of dance, energy, enthusiasm, and long thin legs just didn't count.

I told myself that even though I didn't get into Juilliard that year, perhaps I would the next, and I'd audition again. While still working full-time as a laboratory secretary, I took daily evening lessons at the Martha Graham School of Contemporary Dance. And I took it as a good sign that the lab and the school were both on East Sixty-Third Street.

Having learned from Graham teachers—company stars like Bertram Ross, Helen McGehee, Bob Cohan, and Ethel Winter—within a year I auditioned at the school and was awarded a scholarship. Once, in a master class, I was touched by the great lady herself when Martha Graham placed her hand on the base of my spine. I think I can still feel the spot. I know I have stood up straight ever since.

While studying at Graham's, once a week, I went further downtown to the New Dance Group, where I could learn other modern dance techniques like Humphrey-Weidman. That I hadn't studied ballet was a shortcoming, so I enrolled in a class at the Metropolitan Opera Ballet, where I was fortunate to have as my teacher the great Uruguayan ballet master, Alfredo Corvino. He was the kindest, most wonderful teacher imaginable, and I was grateful he gave me the same attention he gave the obviously more promising dancers. Soft-spoken, he was also strict and demanding. Once when Rudolf Nureyev had practiced in our studio earlier in the day, Mr. Corvino pointed out the burn marks in the wooden floor from Nureyev's fierce pirouettes and smiling slightly told us, "I want you to do that."

. . .

At the end of that year of intensive dance lessons and a rigorous dance schedule, it was clear to me I didn't have a better shot at getting into Juilliard than I'd had the year before. I'd find out later that dancers trying out for Juilliard didn't make up dances, as I'd done; they worked with professional choreographers to prepare their audition.

Taking lessons all over the city, I could see what I was up against. The bone-thin girls who subsisted on yogurt, who ignored injuries and bruises, who rarely exchanged a word in the dressing rooms were hardworking, focused, and ambitious. These dancers were single-minded in a way I could not imagine —then or now. I grasped who I was in competition with, and the simple truth is, I'd never even realized it was a competition. But it was. A fight to the death if there ever was one. I must have been born without the competitive gene. Being in competition with anyone, under any circumstances, does not appeal to me. The best way for me to lose interest and stop doing something is to think I am in competition. It was clear I didn't have the resolute, almost fanatical dedication I saw all dancers need to have to make it in the dance world, especially in New York City.

I wasn't discouraged. A wider world was waiting for me. There wasn't one thing I wanted to do, but many.

The earliest extant photo of myself. Modern dance class at George Washington High School. Photo taken by art history teacher William Spilka, 1962.

4

I got my passport and left the United States for the first time when I was nineteen. In February 1965, my one-way ticket to London was also my first flight. The thrill and excitement of taking off above the lights of a nighttime New York City has never faded.

I wasn't in London two days before I made my way to the Buddhist Society in Eccleston Square. Sitting in that somber atmosphere among white-haired British Buddhists and Theosophists, I noticed it was all quiet decorum. While they might have wondered at the presence of the young American woman who mingled with them, I felt welcomed. I adopted a demure air as I sat enrapt listening to the renowned Christmas Humphreys reading in sonorous tones from the *Tibetan Book of the Dead*. The whole while he spoke, I thought, *I can't wait to tell Billy Anton!*

I learned to use the Tube and wandered around the city day and night. I thought I'd be spending all of my time at the great museums, seeing firsthand the art treasures Mr. Spilka had told us about. After going to the British Museum and the Tate, I found the experience of being in a foreign country was more fascinating than anything I could've imagined. That I could speak and understand the language seemed an incredible stroke of good fortune.

I stayed in a rooming house just off Hampstead Heath, barely managing to keep warm as I fed shillings into the gas stove. The landlady, Jamie Blackstone, who I never saw without a cigarette clenched between her blackened teeth, told me the way to get to know London was at the pubs, and she took me to hers, a place I'm sure she patronized every day. I was drinking my first shandy in the dimly lit, smoke-filled room when she introduced me to two of her "young friends."

George Witt and his friend Tommy were close to me in age, and we struck up an immediate friendship. I was soon hanging out with them on the Heath during the day and in the pub at night. They schooled me on the things they said were important for someone new to London to know. First up, food. I'd been eating fish and chips every day because it was good and cheap and the shops could be found everywhere. The best food in London, they insisted, was Indian—and it was good, cheap, and ubiquitous. I switched immediately.

They were fascinated with all things American, crazy about R&B and soul, and wanted me to teach them to dance; they just had to learn how to do the Mashed Potatoes. I heard from George and Tommy about the upcoming Motown Revue (The Supremes! The Miracles! Little Stevie Wonder! Martha and the Vandellas! The Temptations!) and we went together to the Hammersmith Odeon, never sitting back in our seats as the three of us sang along with every song.

When I left London that spring, George hitchhiked with me as far as Dover, where I boarded the ferry to Calais in France. I wouldn't see him again for ten years, when he'd be married and living the life of an English gentleman in the Yorkshire countryside.

In those days, it was safe to hitchhike, even for a young woman alone, and after I left England, hitchhiking rides is how I traveled the length and breadth of France, Spain, Germany, and Denmark. The only place I didn't hitch was Morocco.

With an ocean separating me from the life I'd known, I felt a freedom I'd never experienced before, and I couldn't get enough of wandering. If I thought I'd found independence living in Greenwich Village, now I definitely had it. I could go anywhere, and I did. I didn't hesitate.

I suppose like many people who go abroad for the first time, I often found myself wondering why didn't this country or those people do things the way I was familiar with, the American way —which I'm sure I thought then was the right way. By the time I left Europe late that winter, I'd made many discoveries—and the one that made the most lasting impression on me was that there was so much to learn about the world, about the different people in it and their cultures, and that the way of life I was familiar with, the American way, was just one of many, many possibilities.

That first experience of living outside the United States changed me in ways I don't even know how to describe. But I do know I haven't been the same since.

Returning to New York City in November, my good friend Keith Johnson, a George Washington schoolmate, picked me up at the airport. He took me to a loft he and some friends, including Tamar, were sharing downtown on Pitt Street.

"What happened here?" I said to Keith, noticing a garbage-filled empty lot between two apartment buildings.

"What do you mean?"

"It's so dirty."

"Karen," he said, "it's always been like that."

I actually hadn't noticed before. Coming back from Copenhagen, where I felt I could have eaten off the streets, I realized I was seeing New York City for the first time. It was my first experience seeing my country, the United States of America, from a new perspective.

I was in the city a week before I let my father know I'd returned. When I did get in touch, I acted like I'd just arrived. He was now living in the housing project and there was no way I would stay there. I'd glimpsed a whole other world, one of Mediterranean food, Danish design and the European way of life. The impression it had made on me was permanent, and I knew it would forever influence my lifestyle choices.

When I'd flown out of Copenhagen, I'd said goodbye to Bent Jædig, the Danish tenor saxophonist who'd awed me when I heard him play in a jazz club in Ibiza that summer. I was twenty and thought twice about living with an older man (he was thirty), but when he asked me to come to Copenhagen, I'd agreed—not realizing he'd just been having a summer fling when I thought it was the beginning of a love story.

My father would have been shocked to know I had lived with a man. I had no intention of telling him.

I'd spent some time in Stockholm before going back to the States and was befriended by the painter and textile artist "Moki" Karlsson. When I'd visit her at her apartment in Gamla stan, Stockholm's old town, her husband, the trumpeter Don Cherry, was usually there—her daughter, Neneh Cherry, was just a baby. Moki introduced me to other artists, as well as photographers who asked me to model. The American "expats" I met through her thought I was crazy to even consider returning to America when I, a black woman, could "have it made" in Scandinavia, though the idea of capitalizing on my skin color held no appeal for me.

Now back in the States, I managed to get some modeling jobs. One of my first assignments was posing with Abbey Lincoln for a spread for *Look* magazine. After appearing in the *New York Times Magazine* fashion section, the very first time they used color photographs, I was introduced by the photographer Gösta Peterson to a top modeling agency. Gösta was Swedish and might have thought I had a shot at a modeling career. He was surprised when I told him the agency had said, "We already have a black model."

The modeling work I did paid well enough for me to start looking for an apartment. Some of the jazz musicians I'd met in Copenhagen I could call friends, and I was soon connected to the free jazz scene in NYC. At the time, it included Albert Ayler, Archie Shepp, Pharoah Sanders, Marion Brown, and Giuseppi Logan. Giuseppe told me he'd be moving out of his apartment on Bleecker Street, and when I went to see it, Keith went with me. The two-story building off the Bowery had just three apartments. Giuseppe lived there with his wife and child in a studio apartment in which everything could be seen when you opened the door. And at a glance, I saw a piano and numerous musical instruments. I think I recall a set of drums. I distinctly remember a particularly large overstuffed chair. It only took me a few minutes to say no thanks.

I guess it was a good thing Keith was there because he convinced me it could be made livable, and even nice, pointing out the bricked-up fireplace, which, he said, he would expose. There was just one window, but it looked out on a backyard that actually had a tree. The $35/month rent helped make it attractive.

Enter Don.

He literally blew into my life when Keith ushered him into my Bleecker Street apartment during a big New York City snowstorm. Keith often ate dinner with me, and that evening as the three of us sat in front of the fireplace with bowls of my lentil soup and pumpernickel bread, Don pronounced, "Why would we stay here when we could be on the beach in San Juan?"

Before the night was over, I'd agreed to go to Puerto Rico

with him. The next day. Our seven-day stay was the beginning of an on-again-off-again seven-year relationship. Tall, blond, and blue-eyed, Don Kallman was Brooks Brothers handsome. A systems analyst and programmer, he was working with the UNIVAC 9000 series at a time most people didn't know what a computer was. Computer manuals the size of Manhattan telephone books were soon taking up precious space in the Bleecker Street apartment we began to share.

We might have only had in common the fact that neither one of us had been raised by two parents. He'd been left at an early age to be brought up by his grandfather. But Don's young years, growing up in the wealthy Chicago suburb of Kenilworth, bore no resemblance to mine. His father's father, who'd immigrated from Sweden, was the creator of Toni, the popular at-home hair permanent for 1950s white women. He'd made what must have been a fortune at the time, and, demonstrating none of the frugality of his Swedish heritage, he indulged Don, giving him his first Porsche while he was still in high school. Don promptly wrecked it.

Admitted early to Yale, Don wasn't there long before he was recruited by IBM and from there headhunted by a defense contractor, which is what brought him to New York City. On our first real date, he took me to the gospel show at the Apollo. We both loved the Staples Singers, and Don had often heard them live in Chicago. When they came to New York, he said we couldn't miss them. I could have loved him just for being as crazy about Roebuck and Mavis as I was.

Living with Don, I learned to live with the unexpected. Bleecker Street and the Bowery at the time was mostly warehouses; at night the only people on the street were winos. Don befriended these men other people called "Bowery bums," and often they'd be waiting for him in the doorway of our building for a handout. They were harmless, even friendly, but I dreaded the thought I might one day return to the apartment and find Don entertaining them.

Don didn't see or accept boundaries, did not recognize limits. None had ever been set for him, and at twenty-six, he'd never set any for himself. Regular work hours meant nothing to him, and he'd show up at his office when it suited him. I can remember answering the phone and lying to his employer, as I'd been instructed, that he wasn't there. It was difficult to believe they paid him, but they did continue to pay him, a lot. Forget lentil soup. Even on weeknights, he'd insist we go to Max's Kansas City for a lobster dinner. And champagne. He always had money and was always running out of it. When he did, he'd think nothing of writing a bad check. "I'll sign" was Don's way of covering bills in hotels, restaurants, and Abercrombie & Fitch, at the time one of the most expensive stores on Madison Avenue. The day came, unsurprisingly, when he was fired. Don didn't blink.

When he proposed we go to San Francisco, I thought it was a great idea. I had traveled all over Europe but the only states I'd been to were New Jersey and Connecticut. Don bought a car, a Triumph convertible, making the drive cross-country an even more exciting prospect. We stopped in Chicago long enough to catch Howlin' Wolf and the Ike & Tina Turner Revue on the same set. Driving through Don's Kenilworth enclave, I was flabbergasted seeing the houses that made up his "neighborhood."

"Look at *that* house!" I exclaimed at one house that seemed to top all the others. He slowed down just long enough to say, "That's where I grew up."

Arriving in San Francisco at the height of the hippie revolution, it was party time as far as Don was concerned. He was content to crash in different pads, hang out day and night, and never miss a love-in. He'd traded in his Brooks Brothers suits for bell-bottom pants, and he now wore a Tibetan beaded necklace. It was 1967, the Summer of Love. The Grateful Dead, Jefferson Airplane, and Janis Joplin provided the soundtrack to incense and marijuana smoke-filled rooms, where people wandered around in tie-dyed and vintage clothes, and all talk was peppered with "groovy." The hippie scene bore little resemblance to my Bleecker Street life, and none to my life in Europe.

I found an apartment for us in the Japantown area and in quick order a job to pay for it. My laboratory secretary experience helped me land a job at the University of California, San Francisco Medical Center. While I was showing up every day from nine to five at the hospital in Parnassus Heights and taking a course in medical terminology during the evenings, Don was hanging out in Golden Gate Park during the day and the Fillmore at night. We weren't just living parallel lives; our lives increasingly had nothing to do with each other.

Almost predictably, he crashed the Triumph. The tow truck driver seemed more upset than Don, who only said something like, "Yeah, it was a cool car."

His penchant for burning the candle at both ends and in the middle found full expression in the "do your thing" atmosphere of Haight-Ashbury. By now, I knew his predilection for doing everything over the top, and for not being reliable, though it was not yet clear to me he would not be tamed, no matter how much homemade lentil soup I made.

When Don was around, it seemed the party never ended as champagne flowed, and clocks and watches were regarded as merely objects with no intrinsic meaning. He handed out money, and literally gave away the shirt on his back. Everyone loved him. So did I. He swore he loved me, but I don't think he had any idea of what a mature expression of that love would be. It could vanish in a day or a week of not just getting stoned, but staying stoned.

He went back to New York before me. I gave up the Pine Street apartment in Japantown when my old friend Billy Anton, then living in San Francisco, said I could have a room in the large house he rented with his wife Sharon. Their son John was a cute-as-can-be two-year-old with thick dark brown curls. They were as typical a young American family as could be expected during that "flower child" summer.

Sharon didn't share Billy's interests, and he was glad I'd go to yoga class with him and follow him to the Zen Center in Japantown for meditation. He was then adhering to a strictly macrobiotic diet, and the only time he went off it was when he was fasting—and the time he took me for my first unappreciated taste of sushi. Twice we'd gone to Tassajara, the Zen retreat down the coast in Big Sur. I wasn't interested in the heavy meditation schedule, but I loved the natural beauty of the area and the hot springs. During my stays there, I worked in the kitchen, where I learned how to prepare vegetarian food, and especially how to make Tibetan barley bread.

Billy gave me a copy of the *Bhagavad Gita*.

I gave him the *I Ching*.

In handwriting uncharacteristically timid, I wrote on the flyleaf:

> *December, 1967*
> *Billy –*
> *To you, with deep respect and admiration,*
>
> *Your friend*
> *Karen*

When Don begged me to join him in New York, I thought I might be able to get him to change, not just by eating health foods, but maybe I could get him to meditate. I was under the illusion that I could change him. It would be years before I found out you don't change other people. Then, I was convinced—or rather, I convinced myself—that a new environment would be the thing to change him. He'd never been to Europe, and I thought getting away from his familiar environment would be a good thing. I told him I'd come back to New York if he agreed to go to Europe with me.

After two months in the city, in February 1968, we left the States. Arriving in London, Don got in touch with friends he'd met at the Monterey Pop Festival, the Steve Miller band, who were then in London recording. A great bunch of guys, they invited us to stay with them at the house they were renting in Chelsea ("There's plenty of room!"). We ended up sharing a bedroom with Boz Scaggs.

Returning to the house one afternoon after visiting my old landlady Jamie in Hampstead, I was greeted by some unfamiliar faces, dressed in even less familiar fashion: suits. It was Scotland Yard. Turns out one of the band members had been sent a package from the States containing marijuana. Just being in the house meant we were all implicated. I didn't like having the contents of my pocketbook emptied on the large dining-room table and inspected as we were "interviewed," but it was all so civil you would've thought we were having tea in that well-appointed dining room.

We flew from London to Tangier and went from there to Casablanca. As in San Francisco, we were soon living parallel lives. While I spent my days in the bazaar buying spices and eating couscous and the traditional bean soup *bissara*, Don, having made friends with hustlers who hung around the cafes, was smoking hashish. It was cheap and could be had as easily as a glass of the sweet mint tea always offered.

It was clear we were at the end of the road as a couple. This running around defined our life together. Never anywhere long enough to get settled. Certainly never long enough to call anyplace home. It suited Don fine. He wanted no part of home life. We had a brief and last shot at domesticity in Torremolinos, on Spain's Costa del Sol where we rented a small cottage covered in bougainvillea just a short walk from the beach for $25 a month. And we weren't in Torremolinos a month before I realized I was pregnant. I also had the immediate realization this was something I was going to do on my own.

At last, I accepted Don was not going to change. He was lost, and I knew that I would have to extricate myself or I would be lost, too.

5

It was one thing not to have plans, but not planning for having a baby was not something I thought of as smart. My whole world was about to change, and I had to tell myself this was something I could do. I knew my father, who, even when he was not around, always loomed large in my life, would not take it well that I was pregnant, not married, and was in no way acting a like a "responsible adult." I was glad I could tell him I did have a job and a place to live.

In September 1968, I arrived in Denmark four months pregnant and went directly to Odense on the island of Fyn, where it was arranged I'd take on the management of the kitchen and introduce a healthy diet to the residents at Hesbjerg Højskole. The Danish folk high school system of education is geared for adult learning, and the students at Hesbjerg ranged in age from eighteen to forty. I was twenty-three and was sure I'd fit in with the forty students and faculty living at Hesbjerg Slot, a nineteenth-century castle.

The castle had about sixty rooms, stretched out on long corridors and four high-ceilinged floors. Large towering white ceramic stoves stood in the corners of the spacious main rooms on the ground floor. These stoves were for practical use, to heat the great rooms, but they were also an imposing and impressive interior feature. The castle was a veritable warren of rooms, some very small and some quite large. The large room I was given on the ground floor was drafty, as I'd find out in the middle of winter.

Once settled at the school, I registered with the local commune, a regional body overseeing all matters related to social welfare. As a registered mother-to-be, I was given all the clothes the baby would need for the first six months, plus diapers, a crib, and a baby carriage. In Denmark, this is what all pregnant women could expect. I also received a coupon for a daily liter of milk, because, as one of the younger students, overly emphatic in his English, told me, it was "illegal" for pregnant women in Denmark to be malnourished or unhealthy. I wasn't unhealthy, but I'd been following a strict vegetarian diet and I was anemic. I hadn't given much thought to ensuring I got enough protein and, as it turns out, iron. With what I came to find out was the typical efficiency of the Danish medical system, they sent a nurse to Hesbjerg Slot to give me a series of iron injections. Hesbjerg was a place so far out in the countryside that its address could only be given as *per* Holmstrup—meaning near the village of Holmstrup. This didn't deter the nurse, who showed up at my door until blood tests showed my iron was at an acceptable level.

When my labor pains started, I was at a party dancing.

No. I was throwin' down to "Jumpin' Jack Flash."

"What do you want, a boy or girl?" the midwife said as she rubbed my back. I found her warm Danish-inflected English comforting, and in the throes of my first labor and childbirth, I definitely needed a heavy dose of comfort.

"Oh, I already know it's a boy."

I had a boy's name picked out. In the overnight bag I'd

brought to the hospital, I had the infant set I'd knitted: a light-blue baby gown, hat, and booties.

"Really. How do you know that?"

"Everyone told me."

They'd said the shape of my stomach clearly indicated it.

"Is that a fact? Well, if it's a girl, can I have her?"

I appreciated her humor. I needed the situation to lighten up. I could not believe, and barely handle, what was happening to my body. I thought her rubbing my back was keeping my spine from snapping. I was exhausted. It didn't help that I'd been out dancing until after midnight. I'd fall asleep the three to four minutes between the active stage of contractions, and then be woken with the body jolt of late-stage contractions, and seriously reminded of what I was doing, what was going on.

After twenty hours of labor, I held a baby girl in my arms—and no, no one could have her. From the instant I held her, I became another part of myself, someone I didn't know. A mother. From that moment, I knew I would protect her with my life, I would give my life for her. That's what the word *mother* means.

Three days after her birth at the Odense Amts og Bys Sygehus, the main hospital in Odense, a social worker came to my bedside to tell me I would be charged for my delivery and five-day stay in a room shared with another first-time mother. The total cost: $28. The social worker actually apologized, explaining I hadn't been living there and registered with the commune long enough for it to be free. I paid the $28 in full the day I left the hospital. The 10 kroner notes I laid out had a picture of Hans Christian Andersen and a stork's nest on one side, a scene with windmills on the other. How fitting for a country that was so much like fairy-tale land.

Exactly a week later, the seven days it took mail from New York to reach Denmark, a letter from my father arrived. John

Henry Hill would never use an aerogram, and the creamy white envelope, strong, fine penmanship, and commemorative stamp easily identified the missive as his. The letter included a list of possible names, all of which started with J or were variations on a feminine version of John. He also included a warning: "Be careful you don't start spreading out," which made me laugh. I was five seven and my weight before pregnancy 110 pounds. I was practically see-through.

Presciently, he wrote, "Karen, you must now begin to cultivate patience."

How does he know that? Of course, he knew me, and knew the last thing I could be called was patient. I was always ready to move on to the next thing, even when the outlines of that next thing weren't clearly drawn. Never making plans, my basic approach to life was, *I'll figure it out when I get there.*

For the first month after my daughter was born, a nurse visited me once a week to weigh her and see if everything was going smoothly. She'd later come once a month, always exclaiming, "Oh, look how big she's getting!" What could she be talking about? She was still so tiny, so delicate, each leg no bigger than a chicken's. I didn't think I'd break her, but it was scary just to hold something—someone—so small, so precious. The nurses especially wanted to make sure there were no problems with breastfeeding. My milk was sufficient, but good god, I didn't know anything about engorged and impacted breasts, sore and cracked nipples. What about those pictures of mothers looking lovingly at their babies as they nursed? Was it all a lie? I was in terrible pain and tried to delay right up until the last minute before I'd breastfeed. I'd been told to nurse her every four hours, and I stuck to that. If she was supposed to nurse at 3:00 and it was 2:59, I waited.

I'd been surprised they let me out of the hospital without checking if I knew what I was doing. Desperate for information,

I got my hands on a British book on childcare that was published in the 1940s. Even though it was as thick as a bible, I must have read it twenty times, combing the pages looking for instructions on how to take care of a baby. The book's black cover signaled its stern tone, and when, for example, it dictated that the baby should "never" sleep in your bed, I was sure never to do that.

The nurses and social workers were helpful, but they wouldn't be around forever. There were no other mothers at Hesbjerg, so I was really going to have to rely on my wits—and I couldn't help but think that might not be so good for a baby whose mother did not have a mother herself. I had more confidence to be a race car driver than I did to be a mother, and I didn't know how to drive. What may have come naturally to other new mothers—maternal instinct—I wasn't sure I possessed at all. I could feel my breasts filling with milk when she cried, but I was almost scared I'd be scolded (by whom?) if I fed her before the scheduled time. And although it was obvious I could soothe her by just holding her, should I be holding her when she's *supposed to be sleeping*?!

It would be no exaggeration to say that I thought I'd found the Holy Grail when I found a tattered copy of Doctor Spock's *The Common Sense Book of Baby and Child Care.* The last thing I was using was common sense, and the book's famous first line, "Trust yourself. You know more than you think you do," was my salvation. At last, I could breathe. I could relax. I was not going to kill my baby.

Common sense in Denmark then, and it's still common, is to put babies for their naps outside, even in winter. I was pretty shocked when I first heard this, but not having any better ideas how to get my baby to take an extended nap, I thought I'd give it a try. And given that every Danish child I saw appeared to be billboard advertisements for health and robustness, I bundled up my baby, and tucked her deep into her carriage with its hood;

she slept deeply in the cold air in the cold Danish winter. I often left her sleeping in the carriage outside the kitchen windows so I could hear her when she woke, but that wasn't necessary. She was the only baby around, and her birth at the castle was as welcome as the arrival of a princess. When she'd wake from her nap, I could hear students running down the stairs from top-floor rooms, trying to be the first to bring her in.

When I first went to Denmark, in 1965, a single mother could receive aid without any stigma attached. Childcare services, employment guidance and training, and government subsidized housing were the basic assistance provided. Of course, there was free health care for everyone. Single mothers didn't live with their children at standards below what the rest of society found acceptable—they were treated with consideration, not censure. That awareness may have influenced my own thinking that I could raise a baby on my own, though I could not have known I would have a baby in Denmark.

My best friend Kirsten was a single mother. She had a lovely second-floor apartment that looked out on a park in Christian-shavn, one of Copenhagen's nicest neighborhoods. Her daughter, Pia, a classic Scandinavian beauty with cream-colored skin and rosy cheeks, white-blond hair and blue eyes, was the very picture of health. Kirsten could afford to eat and dress well, and when she dropped Pia off at her nursery school before going to work, she had no concern that the care was poor or the facility substandard.

I've often thought the support of nurses and social workers, the society I was living in, as well as that of the Hesbjerg community, is what made my first-time-mother experience as good as it could be. I had no worries or concerns, and all my energy and focus were on being a good mother to my baby. I was on my own with my little girl, and although I didn't have all the pieces in place, step by step, I saw I would be able to take care of her. Gradually, I gained the confidence to nurture her, and I didn't think there was anyone who could be a better mother to her than me.

And although I wasn't with her father—Don and I had said goodbye on a beach in Torremolinos—I could picture a day I would have a family.

The Danish authorities were patient, but when May came around, they contacted me to tell me I must give a name to my baby. Admittedly, I was taking my time—she'd been born in February.

I thought about naming her after Arwen Evenstar in *The Lord of the Rings*. I also liked Arwen Hesbjerg, but I realized that no one who wasn't Danish would be able to pronounce it, and she would forever have to suffer her second name mangled as non-Danish speakers produced a hard-consonant *b*, *j*, and *g*. *Hesbjerg* properly pronounced sounds like "whisper."

In the interim, I called her lots of different names, while everyone at Hesbjerg school lovingly called her "Skat." It means treasure. A baby without a name may have been indicative of my whole situation. I had no plans that could be called long-term and didn't know if I'd be staying in Denmark or some other country in Europe, or returning to the United States. I did know that I wanted to be in a place I could call home.

6

The headmaster of Hesbjerg Højskole, Jørgen Laursen Vig, a peace activist, librarian, multilingual theologian, and lifelong bachelor, personified the word *eccentric*.

Headmaster Vig could most often be found in his rooms, just to the left of the foyer, once you passed through the intricately carved wooden doors at the entrance to the castle. Thick dark drapes were always drawn against sunlight—he was barely visible among the floor-to-ceiling books. It was difficult to tell where he might have slept.

When he first saw me, I could tell he was doubtful I'd be able to take on the job of cook by myself. Clearly, he was comparing me to Helga, the cook who'd given her notice the same day she put her packed bags in front of her door. A head taller than me, Helga may have been twice my weight and was clearly the largest person at the school. When I first saw her heft the heavy pots, I too doubted I'd be able to take over her job, but in a short time I was lifting great pots of *solbær* soup, everyone's favorite. I made it all the time, though I never developed a taste for this hot, sweet berry soup. I was slowly weaning the Hesbjerg residents from potatoes, but until I did, I had to heft large boiling pots of potatoes, too. Helga stayed on two days, just long enough to show me the ropes in the kitchen. Then she was gone, having refused a ride to Holmstrup station, she carried her two valises down the lane leading away from the castle.

Headmaster Vig was always last to come into the dining room. Something of an ascetic, he was largely indifferent to food, never noticing or caring that a dish served hot had gotten cold. But he told me himself how pleased he was that I'd introduced some traditional Danish dishes like buckwheat and barley gruel. I think the only time I saw him excited, seemingly beside himself with joy, was when he realized I'd learned how to pickle herring. One of the students had helped me translate the recipe from an old Danish cookbook. The strong fumes of boiling vinegar were overpowering, and I had to leave the kitchen windows wide open no matter how cold it was, but the finished product was a welcome delight for everyone.

I threw myself into creating a healthful diet for the students and faculty, who'd been living exclusively on the traditional Danish diet of meat and potatoes, usually served with "brown sauce," a floury gravy to which brown food coloring was added. At that time in Denmark, a salad was practically exotic, and no one could imagine a meal could be eaten, and enjoyed, with only vegetables. I planned to change that.

I baked most of the school's bread, called *franskbrød*, denoting its French origins. And once a week I made the trip into Odense to buy *rugbrød*, rye bread. These loaves, heavy rectangular blocks the color of dark chocolate, were baked in wood-fired ovens, exactly as it had been since the time Hans Christian Andersen lived on that street. I'd pass his childhood home as I hauled sacks of rye bread to the end of the cobblestone street where a student would pick me up. It seemed a lot of trouble to go to for bread, but everyone at the school loved it, and so did I.

· · ·

The arrangement at Hesbjerg required that everyone contribute four hours of work a day to the school in return for room and board. As the cook, I think I was the only one receiving a salary, which I surely earned—I was easily working twelve-hour days. In addition to preparing three meals a day plus two high teas, I ordered foodstuffs and supplies and dealt daily with the delivery of provisions from greengrocers and fishmongers. And I'd take delivery of large wheels and wedges of the smelliest cheeses imaginable. I worked from morning until evening. During my breaks, I boiled diapers and baby clothes in huge laundry vats, as all Danes did then. Throughout the night, I was up with the baby. In the middle of the night, in the middle of the Danish winter in a cold castle, I'd wake up, get up, and nurse while sitting in a straight-backed chair.

My kitchen assistants, such as they were, were all students. And although they were earnest, and got a kick out of calling me Karen Kok, a popular Danish food brand at the time, I couldn't count on them. They might be studying, or hiking, just when I needed them. Perhaps they'd left to go home for a weekend visit. I'd made it through fall, winter, and spring. Now as summer approached, totally exhausted and ready to quit, I did quit.

I didn't want to leave Denmark just then, so when one of the students told me her aunt living on a farm in the south, on the island of Langeland, would welcome help, I wrote her to ask about the arrangement. I liked that Lene responded right away. In a handwritten three-page letter, she described the farm, told me what I'd be expected to do, and said that I, and my baby, would be welcome. I wasn't looking for a long-term situation and thought this might be the best place to be for the summer.

Going to Headmaster Vig's rooms, I found him, as always, buried in books. When I told him I planned to leave, he replied, "Yes. I think you've had enough. You look more tired than when you came here," almost one year earlier. After leaving that summer, I didn't see Headmaster Vig again until, thirty-five years later, I took Nanao on a journey to her place of birth. By then, he had a full white beard, and Hesbjerg Højskole had been turned into a Russian Orthodox convent. He died just months after our visit.

Before I left Hesbjerg for Langeland, my friend Kim Lawrence, Joanna's brother, came to visit. He'd pursued Zen Buddhism right up to its door and had just come back from Japan. As I was still in name-choosing mode, he suggested Nanao, after his Japanese friend, the poet Nanao Sakaki.

I loved the sound, and after repeating it several times, I decided that would be her name. It's pronounced Na (like *ma*) Nao (like *Mao*).

"It might only be a man's name," Kim said.

"It doesn't matter. I'll probably never be in Japan."

Nanao later chose kanji characters for her name that denote it as feminine.

Kim invited me to Saanen, in Switzerland, where he was going to hear the talks of Krishnamurti. I'd read Krishnamurti and would've welcomed the chance to listen to him in person, but I'd replied to Lene telling her she could expect me in Langeland at the end of June.

After hitchhiking and taking a train and two ferries, I arrived on Langeland to find a storybook landscape of cherry trees and half-timbered thatched-roof houses that looked like the dwellings of hobbits. My hosts, Lene and Bent Jensen, had three years earlier left Copenhagen and their professions—he as a policeman, she as a schoolteacher—to raise their six children in the countryside. The failing strawberry farm they'd bought and planned to revitalize would become their main source of income.

Soon I was helping weed the strawberry fields, which I did alongside six university students who were spending their summer holidays on the island. I did some of the cooking, but it was Lene who baked, and preserved fruits and vegetables. She also taught an exercise class in Lohals, the port where we bought plaice straight from the fisherman. We always cooked the fish the same day we bought it since there was no refrigerator at the farm —all perishable food was kept in a cool storehouse.

Their property bordered the Baltic Sea, and most afternoons we'd take a break to swim. I soon felt like a fool sitting around in a wet bathing suit and joined the family swimming nude. After swimming we'd pick hazelnuts, eating them green. We ate our fill of wild blackberries that grew thickly in bushes on the edge of the strawberry fields and still had plenty to eat with fresh cream or to make tarts with. Their four boys and a girl were active throughout the day, swimming, boating, fishing, and tending the chickens. The youngest girl, Gitte, had been born a month before Nanao. The bigger kids all did handicrafts. I'd just learned to knit, having been taught by a student at Hesbjerg, and was happy when the second son, Jan, helped me knit my first pair of socks.

Evenings, Lene oversaw the children's homework and still found time to knit or read a book. I did a small fraction of what she did, but most days I felt I was just managing to catch my breath between the chores, breastfeeding, and washing diapers. Lene radiated beauty, strength, and contentment. Seeing her I thought, *So it's possible to have children and a baby, work hard, have personal interests, and be healthy, energetic, even happy.* I was both awed and inspired by her example. It's not possible to exaggerate the influence she had on me.

One afternoon, while helping Lene make blackberry tarts, her son Steen came running in with a just-delivered letter for me. It was a notice from the immigration authorities telling me my visa had expired, that I was no longer in Denmark legally and must leave. That was all right with me. The summer would soon be over, and although I loved living in Denmark, I did not want to spend another winter there.

A friend of Lene's, a journalist, hearing about my plight,

wrote an article about me, saying that I was being thrown out of the country and "forced to go back to Harlem" with my baby daughter, who was born in Denmark. The story was published in a newspaper, accompanied with a photograph of me with Nanao in a baby carrier on my back. I cut out the article and sent it to my father, since I didn't have a camera and knew he'd be happy to see any photo of his first baby granddaughter. I made no mention of what the article said—I knew my father couldn't read Danish.

Then came the call. "Karen! What is happening to you over there?! Come home with that baby!" Telephoning me at goodness knows what expense, my father was worried I was being "thrown out of the country." I had been foolish to underestimate John Henry Hill. He'd taken the article to the Danish Consulate General in New York, where the good consular officials were more than willing to translate it for him.

I'd leave Denmark, but I had no intention of returning to the United States anytime soon. Everything about European life suited me. I had no bright prospects in the United States, nothing that would draw me back. I knew my father would welcome me, but he was living in a Harlem project and I didn't plan to live there. I certainly would not bring up my daughter there. I had no desire to live on a farm, but I wanted to raise her in an environment like the one Lene raised her children. I told myself anyplace I took Nanao would be safe, clean, and healthy. I didn't yet know where that place was, and I didn't know when my father would get to see his granddaughter. And by the time he called me, Danish Immigration had changed its mind. So many people who'd read the article besieged and beseeched the authorities, they contacted me again, essentially saying, "Never mind. You can stay."

It was 1969, and immigration to Denmark in large numbers was still decades away. It was a time when even government bureaucracy was simple and straightforward. After telling me to leave, they might have thought it wouldn't matter much to add one more person "from Harlem" to the country's population, which then totaled just four million.

When I'd first visited four years earlier, I knew only one black person who lived in Copenhagen. At least I thought he was black. The musician John Tchicai and I met at the Jazzhus Montmartre, a mecca for jazz musicians. At Montmartre I'd also met Dexter Gordon, Kenny Drew, Jackie McLean, Freddie Hubbard, Donald Byrd, Lee Konitz, Ben Webster, and Roswell Rudd, to name a few of the big names in jazz who played there.

Seeing John play the first time, his huge hands making his alto sax look like a toy, I assumed he was just one of the many black American musicians who'd found a haven in Scandinavia. But this son of a Danish mother and Congolese father who introduced me to New Jazz was thoroughly and culturally a Dane. He also introduced me to *hygge* and taught me how to pronounce it. Well over six feet tall, gentle and soft-spoken with a thick and unmistakable Danish accent and appreciation for the Danish aesthetic, John embodied hygge, this Danish concept of comfort-contentment-coziness.

There was one other black person I knew: my friend Carol. A black Latina who'd grown up in New York and California. That year, she'd traveled with me from Formentera in Spain to Copenhagen. She later married the bassist Bo Stief, whom she met at Jazzhus Montmartre. Carol Stief still lives in Copenhagen. When I visit, we reminisce and, naturally, wonder what it would have been like if I, too, had chosen to stay in Denmark—"the happiest country on Earth."

The last strawberries had long since been picked when fall came and I helped Bent stack bundles of straw to rethatch the farmhouse roof. I'd never done any labor that could be described as heavy and was surprised at my own strength in hefting the large sheaves that required you first balance them on your thigh to lift them.

It was September. I was waking up in the dark, and it would be dark again by four p.m. I wanted to leave before winter, but it wasn't just the weather that impelled me. Living with Lene and her family, in a home, only highlighted how much I wanted the same. It may have only been an illusion, but I actually felt I was getting closer to fulfilling that desire.

Lene had become like a big sister, one I admired. She admired me, too, but I baffled her. She'd more than once asked me if I hadn't been "afraid" to come to Denmark on my own. I didn't know what it was I should be afraid of. "But you are a woman by yourself. What if things didn't work out?" Lene had never been outside Scandinavia and said she couldn't imagine going to live in a foreign country, even within Scandinavia. That was an awakening for me. I realized then that situations others might approach with apprehension, I embraced without reservation.

Although it was originally agreed I'd stay just for the summer, Lene assured me I didn't have to leave. I knew she was concerned about me. Still, she would often say, "You'll be all right."

I thought so, too.

With Switzerland as my destination, I started my hitchhike through Germany from the northern port city of Kiel.

As I stood with my thumb out on the Autobahn just outside of Lübeck, a police car pulled up. The policeman who got out was pretty shocked to see my backpack contained a baby. Baby carriers were unusual at the time, and I'd had to search everywhere before having one sent from England.

"Whose baby is that?"

"Why mine, of course," I said, and promptly produced my passport. In those days they didn't issue separate passports for babies—the photograph showed Nanao sitting on my lap.

"It is much too dangerous for you to be standing here. I will take you to the rest stop," he said, as he opened the door of the patrol car, a Porsche.

It wasn't the first time I'd hitchhiked on the Autobahn, and I knew cars traveled at scary speeds. The policeman, young and friendly, was trying to be helpful and seemed genuinely worried. When we reached the rest stop, he cautioned again, "Please be careful. The cars go very fast. It is better for you to get a ride here." Seeming to forget his policeman's role for a minute, he peeked at Nanao in the carrier and said, "That's a cute baby."

Before crossing the border from Germany into Switzerland, I was picked up by four young Germans traveling in a van. Just before letting me out, the young man at the wheel said, "How are you fixed for money?" (And yes, he spoke English in the vernacular.) I don't know what I said, but I remember his exact reply: "Let me just reach into the old cosmic pocket. . . ." And then he handed me some deutsche mark.

Traveling in the precarious manner I did, you might not know what to expect, but I'd come to expect kindness. People were generally kind. They were generous. They were helpful. I had every reason to believe I would have good experiences because that's exactly what I was having.

7

I knew I needed more than a change of venue. It was clear my wandering days were coming to an end. Although I had chosen to live an unconventional life, I had not at any time consciously forsworn a conventional one—it was not anathema to me, I had just not found it. It clearly had its attractions, and not least because it would've given me the satisfaction of providing a stable home for my daughter. But I still wasn't ready to leave Europe altogether. Every new place had its charms. Rather than apprehension of the unknown, I was comfortable in ambiguous situations, always fascinated going to a place I had not been before. I could be sure I'd learn something new. I would have some experience I had not expected.

I didn't expect I'd find more than goats and cowbells in Saanen, but I wasn't there long before I was charmed by Switzerland's clear-blue-sky sunny days, which were such a welcome change from the seemingly never-ending gray and damp of Denmark. The Krishnamurti talks were over before I arrived, and Kim stayed just long enough to help me find a chalet to rent. A short distance outside the town, the windows of the small chalet opened on a landscape that was straight out of *The Sound of Music.* At night, I kept the windows open and slept under white down quilts in crisp Alpine air.

When winter was full on, every morning I'd put Nanao in a sled and trudge uphill in the snow to Frau Mösching where I could get fresh goat's milk, yogurt, apples, and homemade cheese. Frau Mösching didn't have children and practically ran to lift Nanao from the sled when I knocked on the door of her gingerbread house. There were pretty hand-painted floral designs on every piece of the wooden furniture, cabinet, chair and table, wall and doorframe. Warm and cozy, this was the kind of house where you'd expect to see Hansel and Gretel.

My small chalet was comfortable and more than sufficient for my needs, but it looked like I was about to have a serious change of domicile when I was considered as a caretaker for the Gstaad home of Elizabeth Taylor and Richard Burton.

One sparkling Swiss afternoon, I went to their chalet to meet them. The butler who showed me in kindly said I might like to wait in the garden so my little girl could play outside on such a beautiful day. While sitting on the grass with Nanao, who was just starting to walk and tottered about in her Danish red wooden clogs, I recall the moment the clear light of the Swiss sun hit Elizabeth's diamond. It had only recently been purchased at auction, and widely reported. Even I, who couldn't have been living a life more austere, had heard of its famed magnificence.

So this is what they meant when they said it was "dazzling."

I'm sure I saw the diamond before I saw her, as she stepped on the veranda, and taking in the view with a sweep of her arm, said in a voice I recognized, "Isn't it glorious!"

They invited me in, and I spent an entire afternoon entertained as these two legends of cinema, theater, and life itself regaled me with tales of their glamorous world. As they regularly refilled their glasses, it was like a performance, with Elizabeth, standing at the fireplace mantel dressed in her signature caftan, holding forth. And as easy as water flowing, she'd step away and refresh her drink, and then Richard would command center stage, with that rich baritone voice filling the room, making magic even out of the mundane.

They were warm and friendly, and I had the sense they were enjoying being in the company of someone who was in no way glamorous. In fact, Elizabeth said at one point, "We're seldom around normal people." She fawned over Nanao and carried her up to her daughter Liza's bedroom, returning with a stuffed animal she said Nanao could keep.

"I'd like to show you something special," Richard said, and took me to his library. There, he told me he'd received the greatest gift of his life when Elizabeth, learning he had collected editions of the Everyman's Library as a boy, presented him with the complete collection. The entire library was in an array of subtle shades from pink to blue, and the lilac, soft suede bound book he held out to me was a pleasure just to touch. In that brief moment, I saw the Welsh coal miner's son, appearing almost humble as he gently held the book.

It was an enchanted afternoon that extended into early evening. My life didn't include encounters with people I saw on movie screens or in magazines. Now here I was in the home of Elizabeth Taylor and Richard Burton. I found them normal, too.

I never got to live in their house.

I was soon to learn Richard's brother had had a terrible accident that left him paralyzed below the neck. They were putting the chalet at his disposal for his care and convalescence.

About a week after I met them, Elizabeth sent a note saying she was sorry they couldn't ask me to be caretaker, but she hoped the $100 she included with the note would be helpful.

She ended her note saying, "Give that darling baby a kiss."

Undoubtedly it would have been great to live in the splendor of their chalet, but I was fine. With the amount she'd given me, I could rent my chalet for another month, cover my living expenses, and buy Nanao organic baby food. And I had money saved from Hesbjerg and from working on the strawberry farm. Living as simply as I did, I was never concerned I'd be destitute.

I spent the winter in Saanen, and by the spring of 1970, I knew my European express was grinding to a halt.

At the end of May, Tamar came to visit, bringing her daughter Kristina. Since high school, our paths had seemed to run almost parallel, diverging when I took off for Europe in 1965. Now, she lived in Vermont, and we had in common that we'd both given birth to daughters six months apart.

While Kristina and Nanao sat splashing in a washtub in the garden of the chalet, Tamar and I caught up. She told me about her life in Vermont, and it sounded not only wonderful, but so much like the kind of life I hoped to put together. It was a rough life given the fact her husband Richard was literally building their house around them, but I could only think: *At least you have a home.* Later that afternoon, as we walked to Frau Mösching's to get apples, Tamar said, "Come to Vermont. You'll love it there."

Vermont did seem like a good idea. I was twenty-four years old and didn't have a better plan. I'd never been to the Green Mountain State, but it was easy to conjure up postcard visions of profusely colored autumn days and brilliant red maple trees. I could already taste the rich dark maple syrup and smell the woodsmoke-scented air.

At a minimum, Vermont offered the prospect of raising Nanao in the wholesome environment I envisioned. And so I decided, I'd go back to America. I was tired of moving around. I'd had my fill of the wandering life, and from the moment Nanao was born, I'd denied myself the thing I wanted most: a home. It was more than just the normal instinct to nest. I was ready to unpack. I needed a place I could stay.

No, I wasn't destitute, but deciding to go back to America

and being able to afford it were two very different things. My little savings did not come close to the cost of an airplane ticket. I called my father, who called my brother Johnny, who'd recently left the Air Force. He told him to send me the money, which he did right away.

8

I was going to have to put a life together in this new place, Vermont.

First I needed to find somewhere to live and get a job. I hardly knew which priority was the more pressing. But I'd arrived at the start of the Vermont winter and it was soon evident that dealing with extreme cold would be my first big challenge. I'd spent the previous two winters in Denmark and Switzerland and had more than a passing familiarity with cold, but this was different. That first winter in Vermont of thirty-degrees-below-zero temperatures was you'd-better-have-your-act-together weather, and I didn't.

It wasn't just that you needed a warm home. You needed a house that didn't lose heat. Woodstoves had to be fed and your wood had better be cut and stacked, or cords ordered and delivered well before the snowbound roads were impassable. That a unit of cut wood was called a *cord* was news to me, but by the end of that first winter, it was simply part of my vernacular.

I thought the sweaters I'd knitted with lanolin-rich Icelandic wool, worn under my winter coat from Switzerland, would be sufficient. They weren't. But point number one of How to Keep Warm in Freezing Weather was having good boots. Your boots didn't only have to be warm and waterproof, they needed to be insulated snow stompers that allowed no moisture to seep in. This was a serious matter as there was simply no way to keep your body warm without solid boots. Once your feet got cold or wet, there was no longer any possibility of getting warm, a fact I could confirm as I huddled in front of friends' woodstoves trying to get the blood flowing into my rock-hard feet.

I toughed it out that first winter in one drafty cabin after another. Hardwick, Cabot, Calais, Woodbury, and Northfield were all places I stayed, rent-free, through people I easily became acquainted with in Vermont's everybody's-a-friend community. But a cabin that was built as a summer getaway, or had not been properly maintained when the weather was good, was little more than crude shelter once winter set in. I got Nanao the warmest bright-reddest snowsuit money could buy, but my clothes and nonwaterproof boots just managed to keep me from freezing.

And Vermont wasn't looking like the best place for me to live without a car. But this was just a side issue because I didn't know how to drive. Growing up in Manhattan, it never occurred to me to learn to drive. In Europe my main mode of transport had been hitchhiking and riding second-class on trains. But not being able to drive in Vermont was out of the question. Teenagers drove and had cars. I could not function like a fully competent adult without one.

Plainfield, Vermont, where I would live, was home of the progressive and very liberal (students walking around campus naked in warm weather) Goddard College.

With a population of just under a thousand, Plainfield was made up of "locals" and those young people who had created a culture called counter. They were committed, heart and soul, to growing their own food, chopping their own wood. Using snow-shoes to walk the long lanes to their properties and stoking woodstoves around the clock defined the essence of their "back to the land" lifestyles.

Sure, they were called hippies, but they didn't think of it as a pejorative. Longhaired and energetic in overalls and homemade plaid flannel shirts, they were in Vermont to homestead, taking old farmhouses and untended fields and turning them into viable properties. In the process, they could learn from The Locals how to plant and sow, pick and harvest.

And these back-to-the-earth folks were enthusiastic consumers of The Locals' farm-fresh produce. Everyone was familiar with McIntosh, Golden Delicious, and Granny Smith. But autumn in Vermont meant picking or buying by the bushel such apple varieties as Newtown Pippin, Quinte Gala, Idared and Paulared, Jonagold, and Jersey Mac. The Vermont cornucopia presented endless opportunities for the newcomers to seriously deliberate over abundant squash, confidently asserting buttercup was sweeter than butternut, offering recipes for the best way to roast acorn squash—and just forget it, because you didn't know how good squash could taste until you'd eaten a Hubbard.

Growing up, I'd never seen a squash in our house. I'd never eaten Swiss chard. We ate lots of corn on the cob, my childhood favorite, but city girl that I was, I never knew corn could be so sweet until I ate Vermont corn that went straight from the stalk to the roadside stand. I'd been raised on my father's cooking, which was Southern, though we never gave it a name—it was just food. Okra, fried or in gumbo, and baked sweet potatoes were the vegetables my father regularly put on the table. He cooked turnip, mustard, and collard greens in a big black iron pot I want to call a cauldron.

But lest I sound too provincial, I had just returned from two years in Europe, where these New England food culture aficionados might have found shopping in a market a challenge as they tried to identify such common vegetables as celeriac, mâche, and sorrel.

. . .

I rented a house from a man who, it'd been rumored, had participated in burning down the cabins of hippies.

He sure looked an awful lot like "Joe," I thought, from that scary movie Johnny took me to see almost as soon as I'd stepped off my Pan Am flight from Paris. In the movie, hippies were hunted—and now here I was practically in hippie headquarters. But I needn't have worried about being shot by hippie haters. By the time I settled in Plainfield, it appeared a truce had been brokered between The Locals and the peace-seeking hippies. That made sense. After all, The Locals could sell or lease land as well as rent houses to them. The "Joe" who rented to me had a thick red neck and a rifle on a rack in his pickup. He lowered my rent by $20 a month, put in a new stove and refrigerator, and regularly checked to see if I needed anything. I think he was concerned because I was a single mother. He was a kind man.

My rented house sat on a small lot between the homes of the poet Louise Glück and novelist Jack Pulaski. Louise would go on to win a Pulitzer Prize. I would recognize many of the characters in Jack's first novel. Louise moved in after I did. I didn't know her at all and only saw her in passing. People whispered to me who she was, and I recall an aura around her that said, "I am a poet. I am not to be disturbed." I'm pretty sure she didn't have children, which would ensure we would not move in the same circles.

Jack, on the other hand, had three daughters. Friendly and exuberant, a knock on Jack's front door was answered with "Welcome! Come in!" Middle daughter Rachel and Nanao were the same age, and the two of them ran back and forth between our two houses like they were one, reminding me of how Gloria and I did the same thing on 159th Street. Jack's vivacious wife Margie's life-embracing style matched his own. A Puerto Rican beauty who'd gone to Manhattan's hip and prestigious High

School of Music & Art, she was the kind of friend you talk to at the kitchen table while you fold laundry.

Once stepping into the open door of Jack's study, I admired a small rust-red bookcase. It was narrow and had just three shelves, papered in a Florentine paisley print. Hearing Jack's heavy steps on the wooden stairs to my house not an hour after I returned home, I opened the door to see him with the now-emptied bookcase, insisting I have it. I always counted myself lucky to have the big-hearted Jack Pulaski as my next-door neighbor.

The bookcase was precious to me and it was one of the few items I didn't sell or give away when I left Vermont. Tamar has it in her Montpelier home, and she's been saying for forty years and more she's holding it for me until I move back.

I almost want to say Goddard College was to Plainfield what General Motors was to Detroit, but that would be an exaggeration. But it wouldn't be stretching any facts to say that a large segment of the local population worked there in administration, maintenance, and cafeteria services. I thought of the college as my best chance for employment. The little money I had was going to run out. I could've asked Johnny to help me, but I was determined I would make it on my own.

Many former faculty and alumni who were originally from out of state had stayed in the area. I'd run into them and current faculty at the general store—a place with creaking wooden floorboards and an old-style cash register that made a loud *ding!* every time the aproned proprietress, Bea, rang up a purchase. I'd also cross paths with these Goddard folk at the Plainfield Coop, one of the first food cooperatives in the country, while bagging millet, bulgur, and brown rice.

Like many colleges at the time, Goddard had established a Third World Studies program. While it was assumed everyone had read Langston Hughes and Richard Wright, Ralph Ellison and James Baldwin, this curriculum highlighted those writers of the diaspora (a word I had to look up): Frantz Fanon, Aimé Césaire, Ousmane Sembène.

The atmosphere at Goddard was hardly academic, often seeming more like a summer camp than a college. Classes were sometimes held outside on the open green, and students and faculty, not always distinguishable, could be found in easy conversation, everywhere and all the time. Goddard's bulletin board postings of lectures, readings, and discussion groups made it an inviting place. I considered the campus library, open to everyone in the community, an extension of my living room. I was starved for intellectual stimulation. The last time I had access to a library was in Langeland, and I think I read every novel they had in English.

At the Goddard library, I'd often meet students from the Third World Studies program. Easily identifiable, they wore thick Afros under black berets, elaborate cornrows and braids, and the dashiki was practically a uniform. They were surely the first in their families to attend college, coming from such "high crime and distressed" areas as Dorchester, Roxbury, and Jamaica Plain near Boston, and the bucolic Vermont lifestyle was a first-time experience for them, too. From these students, I learned the fledgling program was struggling to keep records and answer telephone queries of prospective students and anxious parents. Thinking it could be a job for me, I introduced myself to the director, a highly educated scholar, then completing his doctorate. During our brief interview, it was clear he was flummoxed by the administrative side of running the program. He didn't seem to know he needed someone to read, and answer, the many memos that crossed his desk, the letters that lay in a great pile.

"You think you can do this?" he asked me.

"Yes," I answered, and I had no doubt.

· · ·

Returning to America late in the summer of 1971, I had the clear sense the USA was a country I needed to get to know again.

The America I'd left in 1968 had been one of civil rights and anti-war demonstrations. Don and I had only been gone a few weeks when I learned, while on a London bus, that Martin Luther King had been assassinated. We'd just arrived in Casablanca when I saw on the front page of an international newspaper that Robert F. Kennedy had been slain.

The students in the Third World Studies program were helpful in the project of reintroducing me to the U.S. and opening a window on American culture. Listening to their music tuned me in to what was happening. Against a national and worldwide backdrop of hijackings, kidnappings, anti-war protests, demonstrations, and radical movements, the Temptations' "Ball of Confusion (That's What the World Is Today)" seemed to sum things up. The daily carnage in Southeast Asia was reflected in "War."

But it was Marvin Gaye's *What's Going On* that could be heard throughout the Third World dorm like an anthem, that set the tone—for the time, the era, the zeitgeist. That album was nothing less than visionary, and it was Marvin's genius that had created an album that served as the perfect soundtrack to the Vietnam War—a war that cast a bloody shadow over everyone and everything, every day.

I still regularly listen, and dance to, *What's Going On*, but I find it hard to look at the cover of the album because it's heartbreaking—even though Marvin never looked more handsome than he does on that cover.

He also looks a lot like my brother Johnny. And like Marvin, Johnny was shot and killed.

That wouldn't happen for years yet. Ten years. By that time, I'd be married, a mother twice again, and living in Japan.

9

Don had stayed in Spain, and when he eventually returned to the U.S., he followed me to Vermont. I didn't mind that he'd come to Vermont, but I knew too well his penchant of messing things up, and I didn't want him too close to me, or Nanao. He'd visit my Plainfield apartment, dote on her and shower her with presents, but I never fooled myself in to thinking he could be a father. Unreliable, he could not take responsibility for himself, certainly not for a family. But he did soon land a well-paying job, and also soon, lost it.

I knew Paul, the director of an independent school, who'd hired Don for a position that was never spelled out. Paul had simply said, "I want to work with someone so brilliant." And he was genuinely downcast when he told me later, "Don is brilliant. He is also self-destructive." His drinking was out of control, and after a short stint, Paul did not want him or his "vibe" around the students or the school.

Fortunately, Don was together enough, and sober enough, to teach me to drive. Sitting next to me, telling me to "pick a gear, any gear" as I released the clutch and rolled down a hill on a back road outside of Plainfield, he was a taskmaster until I got my license.

I had a good salary from Goddard, and wanted a good car, one that started in below-zero temperatures, a major concern for every Vermonter. Don advised I buy a BMW, a car few people would've been able to identify then. The BMW could not only be relied on to start, but that year had been selected as the safest car on the road. When I got a tip from a dealer in White River Junction, a Vermont town on the border with New Hampshire, that a retiring Dartmouth professor was selling a BMW 2002 he'd scarcely taken out of his town, I drove down there and bought it on the spot. Although he'd advised me to buy it, saying "the BMW is a solid car," ever impractical, Don added, "You should really get a Porsche. A *Carrera*."

My first summer vacation from Goddard, I drove cross-country to visit my friend Jackie in Albuquerque. In the summer of 1966, Jackie, an artist, and I had worked in a New York state camp as co-counselors. We became tight friends, relying on each other to get through what was a tough time. I'd taken the job knowing I'd be working with underprivileged children, but these kids weren't just disadvantaged, but damaged. Often Jackie and I didn't sleep because we'd be up to comfort a hurt child, or calm a hysterical child. I am still haunted by the tragedy of eight-year-old Anita, who'd been hideously burned by being tied to a radiator in a Bronx apartment. Anita's face was almost expressionless, the only emotion she showed was fear.

Speeding through Colorado and Wyoming on the way back east from New Mexico, the rare times there was another BMW on the road, we'd flash headlights. While driving the long empty stretches of highway, somewhere before the Dakota Badlands, I did one of the most dangerous things I've ever done in my life. I picked up a hitchhiker.

I didn't think of it as dangerous at the time—I thought I was honoring the Code of Hitchhikers: Always pick up people. And it felt good that after all the years of getting rides hitchhiking through Europe, I could return the favor. I didn't think, *I'm a woman alone, and this isn't safe.* I wasn't worried that I had a stranger in my car and that Nanao was napping in the backseat.

As we chatted, the young man I'd picked up told me that he'd recently been released from prison. Then I thought about those things. During those empty expanses where there was not a house in sight, I gripped the steering wheel. I think I'm a good judge of character, but that's not something to do from the side of the road. Instinct and intuition would not have served me.

Stopping the car at a lookout point, we both got out, ostensibly to see the view. But I needed to take a breath. I needed to connect with humanity. I don't remember if he told me what he'd been imprisoned for—and I would remember if he'd said murder—but nothing about this young man appeared threatening. After we got back in the car I willed myself to relax, and extend to this ex-convict all the generosity of good intention I could muster. I must have driven on for another hour before he asked me to let him out. His clear blue eyes were the same color as the wide western sky, his handshake firm as he took my hand and thanked me.

I'd had the BMW about a year when I lent it to Don and he crashed it. He was fine, had suffered no injuries. As for the car, the passenger side was completely bashed in, and that was just the damage that could be seen.

George Boardman's gas station, the go-to place in Plainfield where George regularly and reliably resuscitated vehicles, couldn't handle a BMW. It had to be towed to White River Junction where the mechanic told me it had hit something so hard that the chassis was twisted. They'd get the parts, it'd take time, they'd fix it, but he had to be honest: the car would never be the same again. And it wasn't.

My hero Aldous Huxley who'd talked about feeling "clean" after losing everything in a fire, may have also said, "Everything is yours as long as you regard nothing as your property." I tried to adopt this perspective, tried to cultivate a disdain for possessions. Although fixing the car was an expensive ordeal, it was, after all, just a car. But somehow my BMW wasn't just my wheels. That car represented independence, solvency, stability, and the fact that I had, quite seriously, gotten my act together.

I told myself, *Do not be attached to material things*, an attitude I'd picked up from my many books on Zen Buddhism. Maybe it had been in *Zen Flesh, Zen Bones*.

Many of the people I knew in Vermont lived in houses they'd built themselves. But it was Tamar and Richard's house, seemingly in a state of constant construction with its exposed aluminum-foil-like insulation almost an interior design feature, that was a home.

By the time I showed up in Vermont, Tamar Cole, a city girl as much as I was, had become a Vermont homemaker. With a cast-iron pot, often filled with lentil soup, simmering on the woodstove, the house smelled of fresh-baked bread and most definitely apple pie. She'd learned to sew around the time I learned to knit and made all of Kristina's clothes and Richard's plaid flannel shirts. Richard Lear was a self-taught architect and architectural designer extraordinaire. I loved looking at the carefully drawn houses, discrete works of art, that were always on his drafting board. Richard designed houses anyone would dream of having, and people lined up to have him design their dream homes.

But at that time, I didn't even fantasize about having a house. Something I assumed was out of reach, the thought of owning a house never entered my mind. In the world I'd grown up in, people rented apartments. No one bought an apartment, and no one owned a house. I couldn't have said what a down payment on a house would've been. I had no idea what, say, a three-bedroom house in Vermont cost. I didn't know what a mortgage was. My horizons were so limited, I could only think of owning a house as something other people did.

In my Vermont world, everyone was a carpenter, cabinet-maker, weaver, potter, musician, writer, artist. Naturally, we agreed on most things—all the vitally important stuff like brown rice, wooden toys, no sugar and no polyester. Political talk was unnecessary—we were all on the same side. When George McGovern campaigned for the presidential primary, Plainfield was the only town in staunchly Republican Vermont where he won. In that environment, consensus came easily, and as Dan Glick, a friend who wasn't there summed it up, we were all "varying degrees of hip."

But there were some real differences. Many of the people who made up my community, living their simple lives off the land, embracing a lifestyle without conveniences, were people who'd walked away from comfortable, often suburban, lives. Some came with trust funds. I knew a few who had substantial inheritances. Land in Vermont was cheap, and acres covering a mountain or meadow, along with a farmhouse, could be bought for a song. But you couldn't sing that song without money. I was doing fine, but owning more than a car was not something I contemplated.

I was satisfied I could provide Nanao with the kind of life I wanted for her. Her first nursery school, which looked like a dollhouse, was a parent cooperative. When she later went to a Montessori preschool, the fees were entirely manageable. Along with my deep-maroon BMW, I had developed my own Vermont-chic style consisting of long skirts, my hand-knit sweaters, and colorful woolen socks, and everything worn with Dunham boots. They were *the* boots to have, and I knew I'd arrived when I could finally afford a pair. They did the job in snow or mud, and I was grateful I had them those times I stomped through the deeply muddy chicken- and dog-filled yard of Worthy and Thelma Griggs.

"Thelma! Kar'n's here. Get'er a jar of them eggs." Worthy dropped the *e* in my name like it had never been there.

Thelma put the egg money in a coffee can on a ledge over the stove before pouring us boiling coffee into chipped mugs. She'd given me her recipe for pickled eggs, but I preferred to buy them directly from her. I liked to visit with her and Worthy, and just briefly, for just the time that passes on a late Saturday morning, I'd get a whiff of the *real* simple and impoverished Vermont life. Thelma grew and canned their food, and Worthy shot all the meat, mostly deer. Between them, they might have had enough teeth for one mouth.

They had grown-up children and very young ones, too, all sharing a run-down trailer far down the road that ran by the river. Debris they had piled up in the yard had a date with destiny, according to Worthy, and he'd announce his intentions to me as if I were a property inspector. "I'm gonna take that board and fix the side of the chicken coop," he'd say. Or, "Kar'n, you see those tires there? Next time you see 'em, they'll be part of the fence I fixin' to build in back."

I had no thoughts of marriage and was surprised, and flattered, when a man I dated, a research fellow from Uganda, asked me to marry him.

"You're not like any woman I've ever known. You're a true free spirit. You do what you want. I want you to be my wife," was his proposal.

He'd often told me he admired that I'd traveled and lived on my own, abroad, and was impressed that I was "educated though not schooled." I'd never thought about the difference.

"I will be able to give you a comfortable life," he said, as though it was his highest self-recommendation. "I will become an ambassador and we will be able to live in many places." Indeed, he did later become an ambassador in the Ugandan diplomatic corps. What he liked most about me, that I was independent, I was sure would be the first thing he'd try to change. But more than anything, the death knell of the relationship and any chance of marriage were his ideas about women and the role they should play in relation to men.

"It is a wife's duty to follow her husband." We'd just walked out of the Goddard library when he told me that. I thought he was joking—and made sure I wasn't walking behind him. His paternalism was practically medieval. Once when I asked how he'd respond to a wife who wanted to travel on her own, he said, "She would have to get my permission. And I would never give it."

In saying no to his proposal, I'm sure I avoided what would've been one of the biggest mistakes of my life. I wasn't looking for a man who could give me "a comfortable life." That kind of relationship held no attraction for me. I was just twenty-five years old, but I knew my own strength, and by that time I was confident I could create the life I wanted.

Any man I chose to spend my life with would be a partner.

After four years in Vermont, I'd established what I'd longed for: a place I could call home, a place I felt at home.

Having a home spelled the end of living out of suitcases, moving on a moment's notice, packing up and sending boxes. And losing things. Before I went to Europe in 1968, I'd packed a trunk of treasures, truly my favorite things: an early edition of Romain Rolland's *Jean-Christophe*. A book of Robert Burns poems, covered in the tartan of his clan. The biography and large picture book of the great Russian ballerina Galina Ulanova had been a gift my friends pitched in and bought for my eighteenth birthday. I was sad to lose the portfolio of photographs taken by Gregers Nielsen from the time I modeled for him in Copenhagen, at Delta Photos, a celebrated photographers' collective. I'm glad I no longer remember all the things I put in that trunk. The loss of it always reminded me of the fire that obliterated my childhood.

My home in Plainfield, a comfortable remodeled duplex apartment, had originally been part of a larger house. I was happy when it had the well-lived-in and welcoming aroma of hot bean soups and baked bread. I hung pots, made by my potter friends, of trailing Swedish ivy in every lace-curtained window. I'd planted the ivy from cuttings, but I played no part in tending the garden that led to my entrance, which was scented in season with honeysuckle and lushly blossoming lilac bushes.

I could furnish my home with real antiques—bureaus, desks, and rocking chairs—bought at yard and barn sales. I knew I'd scored when I bought a small sofa—a loveseat—and two chairs. In excellent condition, this furniture had never sat in any yard or barn. When I went to see the set at the home of the seller, a former editor of a Vermont wildlife magazine, it was still in the parlor. The authentic Persian fabric of the upholstery stood out against the rich dark mahogany wood.

As a Goddard employee, I could audit classes, and I helped myself to an anthropology course taught by a Ghanaian professor who had spent most of her life in Mali. Often after class we'd walk over to the cafeteria and I'd listen, as an afternoon passed, to her stories of places I hadn't yet dreamed I'd visit.

Tall, full-figured, perhaps forty, Nana spoke an English I'd never heard before—careful, shaded, rich, each word enunciated, every phrase colored. I loved to hear her articulate her view on any matter—she was so clear. She'd been politically active in Mali, and once told me in serious tones that it was important to think critically: "Never let yourself get swept away in the passions of the time nor the positions of others."

One day, she presented me with a gift she held out in both

hands, saying, "I'd like you to have this. It's traveled far, as I think you will one day." Intricately woven with white thread, the dark maroon Malian cloth is still a cherished possession, one that has covered walls and beds in my home for forty years.

At Goddard, I could take modern dance classes, and those early years in Vermont were the first time I'd resumed dancing since I'd quit the Martha Graham school. Five years had elapsed, but I'd studied the Martha Graham technique seriously enough for it to be part of my physical memory, no different than walking.

When Nora Guthrie came to Goddard as a guest teacher, I told her that I was no longer a dancer, but that I was eager to take her class. All energy and no nonsense, Nora fixed her eyes on me and said, "What do you mean you're not a dancer? You dance. You're a dancer."

Woody's daughter and an Arlo Guthrie lookalike, Nora was thoroughly original and had developed her own technique and choreographed amazing dance routines. Her classes were intense and absorbing, body and mind, flowing freely. While in the dance studio, nothing seemed to exist outside of those mirror-covered walls, as we stretched, leaped, danced. I credit Nora with renewing my love of dance. She made it clear I didn't have to compete as a dancer, and I didn't have to give it up because I no longer wanted to be a professional or performer.

I could dance because I loved it. I'll always feel that way.

Luckily for me, Nanao was an easy first child. She could be happy in unfamiliar surroundings, would sleep anywhere, and didn't require security blankets or favorite stuffed animals. At two years old, she'd already heard five languages and didn't speak any of them. The friendly pediatrician who'd sat next to us on the Pan Am flight to New York told me not to expect her to speak anytime soon because it wouldn't be clear to her what language to choose: English, Danish, French, German, or Swiss German.

Now, naturally, she spoke English. She easily entertained herself drawing, and her talent, while a mystery to me, might have been natural for a little girl who had been in no hurry to talk. I was delighted to have a girl and couldn't stop myself from buying her a new dress with every paycheck. I played house with my little doll, had her ears pierced, and didn't tire of dressing her up. Although it took me a while to manage her hair (I couldn't manage my own), I'd braid it with ribbons and tried to learn to make cornrows.

Her playdates were usually outside, but when inside, I set up paint and easels, drawing pads, wooden blocks, and handmade rag dolls. Kids playing at my house were likely to hear *Free to Be . . . You and Me* on the record player. Gender neutrality, a theme of that album, played well in our Plainfield neighborhood, where we parents knew we were raising a generation of free-thinking, creative girls and boys.

Somewhere among the young students, back-to-the-earthers, The Locals, and the open access to all Goddard College had to offer, I had found my place. Vermont was working for me. I had everything I needed for a comfortable life, a good life. A home. I felt sure I'd succeeded in making a home when I could invite Nanao's playgroup friends for her third birthday party. Still much too health-conscious to think of having a typical birthday cake with icing, I made my first cake, a pineapple upside-down cake. The batter-splattered page in my fifty-year-old copy of *The Joy of Cooking* still stands as evidence to my efforts.

Nanao was sick once, with bronchitis. She had a high fever and the doctor told me she had to stay home. He admonished me as one might admonish a child when I told him I had to work. "Look. She's a sick little girl. You will have to stay home with her. If you don't, I will have to put her in the hospital." That hit me hard. She wasn't someone that I could tend to when it was convenient. Looking after her couldn't depend on a job or anything else. She was under my care and was my responsibility. I would always need to put her first.

The Vietnam War raged on television, but I never saw it.

I didn't have a television and didn't know anyone who did. *The Burlington Free Press* was where we went for news. The *Whole Earth Catalog* was where we went for information, whether it was "How to save 20–90% on everything you buy" or to learn about Cuisenaire rods so we could teach our children a hands-on approach to the basic concepts of mathematics. For spiritual guidance and sustenance, I'm sure there was not a parent among us who hadn't read, indeed steeped themselves in, Carlos Castaneda's trilogy: *The Teachings of Don Juan: A Yaqui Way of Knowledge, A Separate Reality,* and *Journey to Ixtlan.*

With the beginning of Amtrak, weekend trips to Montreal became a regular getaway, adding a little continental distraction to my rustic life in the Green Mountain State. With Tamar, Richard, and a few friends, we were a merry band on the train. Tamar brought a portable chess set and taught me how to play. Arriving ready to explore, we appreciated the architecture, found charming hotels and great restaurants, and enjoyed the distinct difference of a place so close by.

I spent four years in Vermont, as measured by the winters I endured.

Although I remember it as endurance, and I say now that I could never again live in a cold climate, then I wasn't particularly discouraged by the cold, the snow, or the ice.

10

During my last spring in Vermont, and while still in my snow-stomping boots, I visited my father at his apartment on Amsterdam Avenue. I brought Nanao with me and Daddy wouldn't let her little four-year-old snow-booted feet touch the ground as he carried her everywhere and showed her off to his neighbors. Mollie had given him two grandsons by then, but Nanao was John Henry Hill, Sr.'s first granddaughter, and every resident of the Manhattanville Houses had to meet her.

The first morning of my visit, I woke up from a vivid dream in which my friend Billy Anton was prominent. The only thing I remembered upon awakening was that he was with a woman I couldn't identify, and they were surrounded by a lot of children.

I haven't seen Billy Anton for a long time.

I wanted to get in touch with him right away. I wasn't sure where he was living, so I telephoned his mother.

"You won't believe it," Felicia said. "He just left a few minutes ago to take the bus back to Boston."

The last time I'd seen him was in Boston, three years earlier, when I stopped to visit him on my way to Vermont. I wrote Billy a letter as soon as I got home. He answered my letter with a telephone call saying, "Come on down! We'll have a great time!"

One of the best things about my life in Vermont was that although I was a single mother, I never felt I was struggling alone with my child. I had the support of any number of friends. I could ask them to look after Nanao, and they could rely on me to look after their kids. Our children regularly played together and stayed at each other's houses—it might be a pickup after school and then a weekday dinner. My visit to see Billy would be a weekend sleepover. I left Nanao with Tamar and Richard, and her best friend Kristina, and skipped off to Boston.

It was spring.

Billy and I met so long ago neither one of us remembers where, but it was probably at a party. In New York City when we were growing up in the early sixties, few weekends went by without a party.

He was in his last year at Stuyvesant High—I was in the eleventh grade at George Washington. Our schools were at the opposite ends of Manhattan, but no matter, we regularly rode uptown and downtown on the subway, late into the night, in groups and pairs and alone. Our friends were at other high schools, such as Manhattan's Music & Art and Performing Arts. Some of the girls, like Joanna Lawrence, and Billy's first girlfriend, the strikingly beautiful Alma Moy, went to Hunter College High School. Friends like Stokely Carmichael came from Bronx Science—I'd see him at parties, and knew him as a good dancer before the world knew him as a civil rights activist.

I'm pretty sure the party where Billy and I met was in Brooklyn, which was about as far afield as we went. Our band of friends would stay out late, late enough to watch the sunrise from the Staten Island ferry. We'd then go to the back door of Italian bakeries in Greenwich Village to buy bread while it was still hot, which was as cool as we knew how to be.

And the Village, the coolest place in New York City, the place we all visited, was where Billy Anton lived—where it was entirely possible his family was the only Jewish family in that all-Italian neighborhood. I hung out with Billy and Kim, Joanna's brother, who may have been the friend who introduced us, watching them play chess in cafes, and when it was too late to do anything else, we'd walk around Washington Square Park laughing out loud while Billy entertained us with monologues much like rap in which monkeys swore and put people down.

When Billy came over to my Carmine Street apartment, he often brought books. At the time I was devouring Aldous Huxley's novels—*Crome Yellow, After Many a Summer, Eyeless in Gaza, Time Must Have a Stop, Point Counter Point, Ape and Essence*—but what Billy and I read together and talked late into the night about were Huxley's *The Doors of Perception* and *The Perennial Philosophy*.

It was then Billy introduced me to Zen Buddhism, and it wasn't long after he gave me a copy of Alan Watts's *The Way of Zen* that he told me he was getting married.

I tried to talk him out of it.

I had met his future wife, Sharon, and I liked her. They'd met in college, and when I went to visit Billy at his school in Binghamton in the middle of a blizzard, the three of us hung out together. Billy later brought her to Carmine Street and she impressed us all with her deep knowledge of film—and because Billy called her a "cinemaphile."

Still. Something told me they were not a couple. But I was eighteen. I hardly knew who was a couple and who wasn't.

Sure, I loved Billy—we were friends. We were great friends, and I can't think of anyone, among my friends at the time, who I more enjoyed spending time with. We could talk for hours and laugh a lot longer. He'd acquainted me with a world I didn't know at all: the films of Kurosawa, natural foods, the philosophy of Bertrand Russell. Although I had a passing familiarity with Latin music, Billy *knew* it, and Jimmy Sabater singing "To Be with You" with the Joe Cuba Sextet was our favorite. It's a romantic love song, for sure, but I never thought of him as a boyfriend, and he didn't think of me as a girlfriend either. We were friends.

I went to the wedding, drank too much, and cried.

When I met up with Billy in Boston, it had been almost five years since we'd last been together in San Francisco. I was happy to reconnect with my old friend. We'd kept in touch, and when I'd written asking for his advice when I took over the management of the kitchen at Hesbjerg school, he'd answered right away, writing out a long list of staples for the pantry, and ideas to get the students off their typical Danish diet.

Now divorced, he was living in an apartment on Newberry Street where a half-empty living room matched the mostly empty refrigerator. He was working as a chef in one of Boston's first natural foods restaurants. Paid in cash, he threw his salary in the drawer where he kept his socks. Sharing memories, talking and laughing as we drank Metaxa, I explained where in Denmark Odense was, and he didn't bother to explain why he'd relaxed his strict macrobiotic diet. Our talk and laughter that late spring afternoon was that of friends long separated who'd found each other again.

While I stood by a fireplace that had never had a fire in it, Billy sat in a large chair by the window.

"Come and sit on my lap."

That wasn't subtle.

The next day I asked him to marry me.

We were sitting on a bench by the Charles River. He'd taken me to breakfast at the Ritz-Carlton, and later while he was at work, I'd spent the afternoon in the lilac-scented park, reading while someone played a flute in the background. Billy joined me in the park just before sunset. As I said, it was spring, and maybe everything conspired to make me ask the man who had been my friend for twelve years to marry me. But I don't really think it had to anything to do with the season.

Billy Anton was the man I should marry. It was so clear, so obvious, I only wondered why I hadn't seen it before. Never mind. Now I knew he was the one. I loved him dearly. Always had.

I sat next to him there by the Charles River and said as plainly as I could, "Will you marry me?"

He said, "No."

He told me he never planned to marry again. I'd later learn that his breakup and divorce from Sharon had left him not trusting marriage. She'd left him, he hadn't seen it coming, and the subsequent and unwilling separation from his son John had been devastating. No, he said, he wouldn't be marrying me or anyone else.

I knew I'd found true love, because his answer didn't matter. I went back to Vermont, to my child, my work, my life. I experienced more contentment than I'd ever known. I didn't need anything. I didn't want anything.

I had found love and there was nothing I needed to do about it.

When Billy got in touch with me later in the spring and asked if I would come with him to work as his assistant chef in a summer camp, I said, "Sure."

I quit my job at Goddard College and followed him to a summer camp in upstate New York where the pay was nominal, the accommodations basic, and the cabins had that same unmistakable smell of damp woolen blankets as every summer camp I've ever known. Our small cabin's only amenities were a shower and toilet. There was a child-sized bed for Nanao, and we each had a metal locker to keep our things.

The camp was for poor city kids and the director, a friend of Billy's, wanted to introduce them to natural healthy food.

Although Billy had given up following the macrobiotic diet so strictly, he was still into healthy eating, and was eager to prepare and serve the children wholesome food that he hoped would have a positive and long-lasting impact on their lives. These kids, ill-nourished on fast food, would get their first experience of brown rice, seaweed, and miso soup. They'd be back in the city before they got a taste of sugar.

I'd learned a lot about macrobiotics and vegetarian cooking from Billy and I didn't doubt I could be a useful assistant, and I welcomed the chance to "work with the master" and learn directly from him the Japanese cutting techniques he'd told me about. Although the large razor-sharp Japanese knives were at first intimidating, I could soon slice mounds of carrots and onions as thin or thick as Billy instructed.

The camp, staffed with talented artists, musicians, and crafts-people, made it an environment rich with creativity and play. My sister Mollie came to visit, bringing her three young sons. And Billy's son John, then about eight years old, spent part of his summer vacation with us. Nanao loved the camp. She could join in the arts and craft activities, swim every day, and be outdoors with the other kids by a campfire at night singing, and listening while the counselors told stories under the stars.

Billy has said that he felt Nanao was his daughter from the start. I don't think Nanao felt the same way. She'd never had to share me with anyone, and now there was someone else in my life. She was four years old and I didn't think I needed to explain anything to her. I trusted it would work out, somehow, organically. It helped that he was willing to read her favorite book, *Blueberries for Sal*, as many times as she liked, and was always available for a cuddle. I can still see the smile on her face the day he took her to the general goods store in the town near the camp and let her pick out new barrettes and a big red dump truck. I am sure that sealed his place in her heart.

I'd been independent so long, I, too, had to adjust and make room to have another person, a man, in my life. I may have asked him to marry me, but I'm not at all sure I was prepared to have an intimate relationship. Before we went to the camp, Billy would sometimes call me from Boston. I'd ask him what was he calling *about*? I never expected to hear "I miss you" or "I just want to hear your voice."

Over that summer, we three were soon a family. Billy became Papa, and we have never used the term "step-." When the summer was over, Billy said he would leave Boston and come to live with me in Vermont.

We've never lived apart since.

11

Billy and I were now a couple, and we wanted our parents to meet.

When summer camp ended, since we were already in New York state, it seemed the perfect time for a visit. We made dinner reservations at a restaurant that would be convenient for our folks, but unfortunately on the evening we planned to go, Billy's father wasn't feeling well.

Billy had grown up regularly eating out with his family. Harold Anton was a painter and, according to him, "the father of abstract expressionists." Whenever he sold a painting, he'd tell Felicia to bring Billy and his older brother Anatole to meet him at the Minetta Tavern. There they could have their fill of spaghetti marinara, meatballs, and Billy's favorite, eggplant parmigiana.

I'd never in my life eaten in a restaurant with my father—unless you count the Automat, where my father had taken Johnny, Mollie, and me a few times when we were young and thought getting macaroni and cheese in return for putting a nickel in a slot was the biggest treat imaginable. I happily anticipated our dinner with the parents and was disappointed not to have this opportunity, not just for them to meet, but for the adult experience of dining out with my father.

Daddy said, "Oh, that's fine. We will do it another time."

Too bad, I thought. It would soon be winter in Vermont and I didn't know when I'd make the six-hour drive to the city.

The camp director had given us the use of his apartment uptown. With dinner plans canceled and not knowing the neighborhood, we stayed in, had a simple meal, and went to bed early. When the telephone rang after midnight, the last voice I expected to hear was my brother Johnny. Barely awake, I could only just comprehend his words when he said, "Karen, you've got to come now. Daddy is in the hospital. He was hurt in his apartment."

Billy goes from deep sleep to wide awake in seconds, and now he sat bolt upright in bed with questioning eyes. I couldn't tell him anything because I didn't know anything. "Hurt" didn't sound like he'd had a fall or some other home accident. But I didn't want to conjure up anything, any situation or circumstance in which my father could be hurt.

"That was Johnny. He said my father is in the hospital. Something happened."

After Billy reassured me he'd stay with Nanao, I was dressed and downstairs hailing a taxi in minutes. I don't know if that taxi ride was half an hour or an hour. I tried hard to keep my thoughts quiet, create a blank space in my brain. But I couldn't make that work. Swathed in a cloak of dread, I had to be in my own head, thinking not one good thought. I knew I could not expect anything good on the other end of my speeding through a New York City night to my father's hospital bedside.

"Who do you want to see?" a nurse in the intensive care unit asked as she wrote on a pad in front of her.

If she'd looked at me, she would have known that was my father in the bed surrounded by two nurses, a doctor, and a policeman. Didn't I look like my Daddy? Maybe I was invisible. I felt invisible. I didn't exist in the past or the future, and the last place I wanted to be was the present. No one took notice of me as I stood by his bed and asked no one in particular, "Why is he shaking?" His entire body trembled beneath the thin sheet that covered him. "He's in shock," a hospital voice said.

"There was just a Mrs. Dowling here," a policeman said, "the victim's daughter. She went down to the cafeteria."

"They're both the patient's daughters," said another voice that still had compassion in it.

"We need to talk to you," the voice speaking for the New York City Police Department said to Mollie when she came back in the room. "Did your father have an ice pick in the house, ma'am?"

I sat by his bedside. I knew the life was leaving him. I sat in silent petition that he not suffer too much. That I not suffer. That I be relieved of the pain that bore down on me and stole my breath. I wasn't holding my breath, but it didn't flow, staying in my throat and stopping there until I remembered to breathe out.

I'd never experienced tragedy before. I didn't know the paradox of how it shows up with distinct, sharp, ugly lines, deep colors and loud sounds, and then switches into lines that are blurred, vague, gray, and all sound comes through muffled.

Daddy didn't know we were there, but desperate to comfort him, I went to the hospital library and borrowed a Bible and just started reading from the first page I opened: *And the children of Israel spake unto Moses, saying, Behold, we die, we perish, we all perish. And now, O Lord my God, thou has made thy servant king instead of David my father: and I am but a little child: I know not how to go out or come in. And Jehoshaphat reigned over Judah . . .*

It didn't make sense.

I turned from page to page looking for something meaningful or familiar. My tears and agony kept me from turning to the New Testament. I would've found the Beatitudes, which I loved and could recite by heart. We'd been raised in the church of

Christian Science and had to read the Bible every Saturday night in preparation for Sunday school. We were teenagers when my father told us, "I have taken you this far. If you want to stop or continue to go to church, it is up to you."

I never went to church again.

It had been something we had to do, and I knew I wasn't going to miss sitting through interminable Sunday mornings. I'd always wondered why my father hadn't been a Catholic so I could have at least enjoyed the grandeur of mass. Or a Baptist, where "the spirit" entered people who sweated and shouted and sang songs from their souls. I'd sometimes go with Gloria Wright to her church where we could join the excitement and do the "gospel stomp." At the Fourteenth Church of Christ, Scientist, they read a lot and no one ever got excited.

It was about three in the morning when Mollie asked me to go with her to Daddy's apartment to pick up some papers while Johnny stayed at the hospital.

Arriving at the apartment in the housing project where he'd moved after the fire, we stood before the door marked 12C. The steel door, with a miniature peephole, seemed impervious. Nothing distinguished that door from 12A or 12B. Or 14G. A "random robbery," the detective had told us. Why would anyone come here instead of 6K?

I'll always be sorry I saw the telephone. There wasn't a lot of blood. If the phone had been black, the blood wouldn't have been noticeable. Daddy had a beige phone because Mollie said it would "brighten the place up a bit."

An errand to retrieve a Medicare card turned into the dark realization that I'd entered a crime scene. My own Daddy had been attacked in his apartment and had tried to get help. That knowledge was now mine. No happy moment, no distraction, no distance would ever separate me from that reality.

Spotting the Christian Science hymnal, I grabbed it. Later at the hospital, I saw Daddy had written on the inside cover in his "fine hand," *Remember whose child you are. Be not afraid.*

That night, I slipped into a sleep that was like a protective coma.

Johnny woke me to say Daddy had died early that morning.

The five days before the funeral were strange. Time sped up as it slowed down. Morning afternoon night were indistinguishable. I tried my best to do whatever was required, but I was useless. I'd been back in the States three years, those years spent in Vermont, where a snowstorm was the worst thing anyone could imagine. I relied on Johnny and Mollie. They talked with the police, the detectives, made the funeral arrangements.

I suffocated in the dark funeral parlor, in the cool air perfumed with the oppressive smell of lilies and roses. I couldn't take my eyes off Daddy. His dark brown skin was an unearthly gray. Makeup covered the wounds on his face. Removed from all around me, I could not be exempt from this moment in my life and I sat there bound in anguish, my blank eyes full with tears.

Mollie and Johnny had asked my father's friend, Mr. Taylor the barber, to give the eulogy. Written in pencil, he read it from a piece of paper taken from a loose-leaf notebook. His voice warm and reassuring, it was the same voice that had told me, "Don't worry, Karen. I'm gonna make it nice," that time I cut my hair and had begun to think I'd made a mistake. "You're going to look beautiful," he'd said, "just like that woman—what did you say her name was?"

"Miriam Makeba," I'd answered feebly, as I glanced at myself in the barber shop mirror. Skinny with glasses, I knew nothing was going to make me look like her, unless Mr. Taylor was also a magician.

"Yes. Miriam Makeba. She is a beautiful woman. And I'm going to make you look just like her."

Now Mr. Taylor read slowly as if that made it easier to hear:

"Mr. John Henry Hill was born to Mr. and Mrs. Louis Hill of Yazoo City, Mississippi, on August 19, 1893, the youngest of their eight children. In 1917, he graduated from Hampton Institute in Virginia. A productive member of the community from the very beginning to the very end, he was instrumental in forming the Community League of 159th Street. Always at the forefront of every cause, he will be remembered by many as the first person at their door in a moment of need. Although he did suffer in his last moments, he bore it with fortitude. As we sit here at his funeral, we know John Hill is with his creator, he is in the best of hands, and we need not worry about him. Let us now be concerned about his bereaved loved ones and support them through this time of mourning.

"Let us now join in a solemn moment of prayer for the soul of our departed brother.

"Resolved, that inasmuch as Almighty God has removed from our midst our beloved friend and neighbor, Mr. John Hill, we do bow our heads in grief and submission to His divine will. We question not that which He has done. We bid him a fond and loving farewell, praying that he will rest eternally in the bosom of Abraham. May he ever live where Saints Immortal Reign."

Someone played the piano and sang the Christian Science hymn "Shepherd, Show Me How to Go." It was my favorite. The only one I remembered. And along with that memory was the many Sundays Mollie and I stood next to each other, both singing loud, proud in our starched and ironed matching dresses. Someone was sure to say, "My, you girls look so lovely," and then, turning to Daddy, "Mr. Hill, you are mother and father to those children."

Daddy was my only parent, and the effect of his loss tore away a large part of myself. For a while, I couldn't see that there was a reason to do anything. Daddy wouldn't be there to appreciate it. Praise me. Give me advice. Disapprove. I'd never again hear the refrain I'd grown up with, "What will become of you, I do not know."

It's a long time ago now, but the experience, the shock, of my whole world turning into a nightmare has never left me. My father was eighty. He was in good health, but I had known I should be prepared to lose him one day. I just never expected it to be so soon, so suddenly. So horrifically.

I was glad he'd met Billy. He told me, "He's a fine man," giving his stamp of approval. He'd added, "You're finally starting to get some sense."

After the funeral, Billy, Nanao, and I returned to Vermont, numb with grief and shock. I didn't tell Nanao what had happened to her "Nana," as Mollie's boys called my father, but had to tell her "Nana died." Billy took care of Nanao, and for the first time in her young life and the first time in mine, I knew what it was to share the responsibility of looking after her. I could not have produced a meal, and now I didn't have to, and was not concerned I was neglecting my child. I could close my eyes. I could turn my back. Traumatized, truly, it didn't seem a good portent for Billy and me to start our life together. I didn't know where I could go with my pain.

I buried it.

One cold, blue-sky day, I walked up the street in the town of Plainfield and went to Ben the Barber. In that little Vermont town, it would have been a wonder if he'd ever had his hands on hair like mine. Never mind. He wouldn't be doing much handling of my hair. I asked him to shave my head.

Ben was old, and I recall his liver-spotted hands were shaky. But he didn't nick me. He didn't blink, and never asked me why I might want to shave my head. That evening at dinner, I kept a scarf on my newly shaven head, and after we'd finished our lentil soup, I took the scarf off. Billy never said a word.

Even now, I'm not sure why I did it. I think I might have felt I had to give up something, if only symbolically.

I had to atone for my father's death.

When I'd walked away from my job in the Third World Studies program three months earlier, I didn't think I'd be looking for work at Goddard again. Now, I would've been happy to have any job to distract me, and when, hearing of my loss, the college offered me a position in the Student Affairs office, I jumped at it. I couldn't bear to be alone at all, and practically followed Billy around the house. I either slept like the dead or woke up in the middle of the night with inexplicable dreams. Nightmares in which I was chased, or worse, were now regular.

The job gave me the opportunity to interact with students and administrators daily. I got to invite, and host, people like the great drummer Elvin Jones and Patti LaBelle and the Bluebelles. I was happy Sonia Sanchez accepted our invitation and I was there when she fired up students, faculty, and the Plainfield community with her impassioned poetry reading. I felt these artists lived at the very center of life, and just being in their company was soul enhancing. They were engaged, stimulating, and inspiring; around them I could feel hopeful.

No one offered Billy a job. As in many rural communities, opportunities for employment in Plainfield were limited, and we found out just how limited when he tried to get work. His BA in philosophy didn't open any doors, and you can be sure the fact that he had a university degree at all was never mentioned when he took a job as a short-order cook in a local diner. He made a go of it, showing up at 4:00 a.m. to flip pancakes and eggs over easy for deer hunters. That didn't last long. Years later, he'd tell me how hard it had been for him not to be able to earn a living, not to be a provider for his family.

The invitation to go to Japan came at just the right moment.

Billy had been a part, indeed an integral member, of the

macrobiotic community in Boston, and when he learned that a sensei (master) was inviting three foreigners to live in Japan on a one-year scholarship to study yoga, martial arts, and traditional Eastern healing methods at his dojo (training center), it seemed an opportunity he shouldn't pass up.

But he wasn't ready to jump. He'd never been out of the United States, and was hesitant, doubtful about every aspect of this potential adventure. Knowing of his long-standing interest in Japan, I thought this offer came not just at the right time, but to the right person, and I urged him to accept it. I wasn't eager to get away, but I could see having real physical distance from my recent tragedy could be a good thing. Maybe I, and our nascent relationship, would have a chance to start anew.

Years later when we met at her concert in Japan and became friends, I'd be able to tell Roberta Flack that "Killing Me Softly with His Song" was our soundtrack as Billy and I spent many nights lying in bed talking about how we could make it work. We thought about taking Nanao out of school, although she was only in preschool. She had friends who were like siblings, and we had friends, too. I had to ask myself, *Are you really ready to pick up and leave?* Even though I'd been there for three years, it seemed I'd only just gotten myself firmly settled in Vermont.

But I was ready for it, and when Billy said, finally, "Let's go to Japan," I pretty much answered, "Sure."

Before Vermont, and with the exception of the short time I lived in San Francisco, I'd never lived anywhere in the United States other than New York City. Health and environment conscious, crime free, neighborly, Vermont was a good place to live. I thought of it as a place that embodied the ideals of the hippie revolution without the accompanying dysfunction. Most important for me, Vermont represented stability, staying put, the end of being transient.

If Billy hadn't received the invitation to Japan, I could still be in Vermont. I'd arrived there with a suitcase and a longing for a home. I'd succeeded in creating a home, becoming part of a community, and building a life that was comfortable and stable, for my daughter and me. In the process I learned something I didn't know about myself.

I could make a home anywhere.

With Billy a few months before we left the States, 1974.

12

B illy contacted the dojo and they told him his apprenticeship would begin when he arrived, and the date of arrival didn't matter. That was our cue to go to Japan the slow way, overland. We didn't have any idea how long an overland journey to Japan would take, but one year would have been a good guess.

For all of Billy being hesitant about our upcoming journey, leaving the United States was easy. Leaving his son John was hard. Sharon, now remarried, had full custody. Still, Billy could see him freely, and the reason he'd chosen to live in Boston was its proximity to where they lived in Northampton. I knew from the time I'd stayed with them in San Francisco that Billy had been hands on in raising John. He was especially serious about what he ate and fed him according to the concepts of the macrobiotic diet. A puree of fine whole grains formulated for babies was John's main food, and I recall the two-year-old John in his high chair gobbling it up with gusto.

Billy was my first friend to become a parent. Babies were something of an alien species to me at the time, but I found John just impossibly cute. He'd inherited Sharon's dark curly hair, and both of their long eyelashes and green-gray eyes. I was glad he could come stay with us in Vermont before we left. I put myself in the background, but since I knew he played chess I thought that might be a good way for us to interact. I also knew he was good, but I figured, *He's ten years old, how good can he be?* Turns out, very good. He checkmated me so fast I had no idea what'd happened.

Nanao said goodbye to her friends, and I don't recall any tears. She appeared as game as we were for the adventure ahead. I remember thinking then that kids will go along with whatever their parents put before them. As long as they feel safe, they're fine. And their sense of security is likely not to be found in blankets and the same bed every night, but dependable adults who will look after them and protect them with their lives.

In July 1974, we flew from New York to Brussels, and went straight from there to Holland to buy a cheap car at the informal and flourishing "used-car market" in front of the American Embassy in Amsterdam. We were among the many hopefuls looking over cars, hoping we'd be lucky and find something good, at a bargain. We were lucky. The 1962 Volkswagen Beetle we bought for $200 served us well.

But the car had a lot of rust. In heavy rain, the floor of the passenger's side would flood. On the driver's side, we could see the road passing beneath, which left us to wonder if the bottom of the rusty old Bug wouldn't drop out from under us. This became the theme and source of innumerable jokes and much laughter as we traveled east.

We went first to Langeland. Five years had passed since I'd been at the strawberry farm and I was happy to embrace Lene and Bent, introduce Billy, and reintroduce the now four-year-old Nanao. And the children, Bjørne, Jan, Steen, Ulf, Jette and Gitte, were as happy to see me as I them.

Billy and I both helped weeding the long rows of strawberries, not as a job, but just to pitch in. After we'd been at the farm about three weeks, Billy, Lene, and her twelve-year-old son Ulf went on a camping trip to Sweden and Norway. She told me that for a long time she'd wanted to visit a brother living in the north of Sweden, and though it took some urging, I told her this would be a good opportunity to go. I could not step into her shoes, but I could cover for her the two weeks they'd be away.

When Billy and Lene returned, it was with stories of the majestic beauty of the Norwegian fjords and the forests where they camped. Billy was especially impressed that you could camp anywhere in Norway, and it was considered an obligation that the owners of the land provide travelers with, at a minimum, wood to make a fire. Sometimes the sheds also had blankets and basic provisions.

Saying goodbye to them, I was glad to see Lene glowing, looking happy and refreshed. She told me many times how grateful she was she could take the time to get away. I was grateful, too. I received an important lesson in seeing how time away, even a short time, from daily life and responsibilities could be rejuvenating.

Backtracking, we drove southwest to Belgium.

Billy's friend Ed Balke, with whom he'd worked at natural foods restaurants in Boston, had opened a Japanese-style restaurant in Antwerp. They'd studied traditional Japanese cooking together, and Ed was both envious and intrigued that Billy was now going to Japan and would get to study at the source. When we arrived, the restaurant was in its early days and we were glad we could pitch in to help. Nanao helped, too, setting up the tables and laying out chopsticks and condiments like *gomashio* (ground sesame seeds and salt) and shoyu (soy sauce). After three weeks, our help was no longer needed. We've been back several times in the intervening years, happy to find Izumi has become the place in Antwerp for excellent Japanese cuisine and sushi.

. . .

Except for a couple of camping trips to Maine when we lived in Vermont, this was the first time Billy and I were traveling together. I quickly learned we had different traveling styles. I like to wander. A good day when I'm traveling is getting lost.

But every day in London, Billy would say, "Today we're going to the Houses of Parliament," or St. Paul's Cathedral, or Madame Tussauds house of wax. I'd just go along, only thankful after the fact that I'd seen places I hadn't before. On this trip, I would've been happy just visiting old haunts and looking up old friends, the few I still knew in Hampstead. George Witt and I had kept in touch, as every now and then he'd dash off an almost illegible postcard. It was he who told me my landlady Jamie had died of lung cancer a few years before.

Going to Stonehenge seemed like a great idea when Billy, who studied the maps carefully, said it would be an easy drive from there to Lancashire where George now lived. We would continue on to neighboring West Yorkshire so I could visit the home of my favorite Brontë, Charlotte, before going to Wales. I hadn't thought Wales would be on our itinerary, but how glad I was to see what must be the most charming country on Earth. Picture book pretty, it looked like a landscape painting. And the best thing about that beautiful landscape was it had nothing to do with me. I thoroughly embraced being a traveler again. A wanderer, with all the freedom that word denotes. Each day new, there was nothing I had to do, nothing that had to be done. I could just be there, beguiled by the beauty. Like Lene, I started feeling refreshed.

Reaching Scotland, Nanao was excited seeing the thick herds of deer that ran in the hills alongside our car in the evenings. In the dusk they appeared as shadows, though we could hear the heavy stamping of their hooves. We pitched our tent anyplace that wasn't too rocky, and though cold, huddled closely together we managed to stay warm enough to sleep.

. . .

We weren't looking for jobs, but anytime we could work, either for money or in exchange for room and board—and it didn't matter to us which—we did. Upon returning to London after Scotland, Billy took a temporary job as the head cook in a popular vegetarian restaurant. This provided us with a small income for the remaining time we'd be staying in England. As soon as the weather warmed a little, we bid our British friends goodbye and headed south. Crossing the Channel from Dover to the continent in a hovercraft was the most miserable trip of my existence. The entire way I had to talk myself out of vomiting.

The only bright moment was seeing a rainbow against the backdrop of a dark gray sky—it was so vivid you felt like you could touch it.

We'd been in Europe about five months when we arrived in Paris, and stayed with our old friend Kim. The three of us hadn't been together since we'd last hung out in Greenwich Village. Now, the place he called home was his tiny apartment on the Boulevard de Port-Royal. Kim's Paris living room was a fascinating salon where an international group of friends gathered and talked over repasts of cheese, bread, hot millet, nuts and dried fruit, and dishes cooked with herbs picked from the garden of his friend Zoe's home in Provence.

By this time, Billy and I realized we'd have to have if not a plan, at least an outline of how we would get to Japan. Just flying to Japan from Europe would have been simple enough, but it also seemed a great pity as we would miss so much. We thought about taking the Orient Express and then the Trans-Siberian Railway. Although the cost then was not as expensive as it's become, it would still cost a lot more than if we drove ourselves. And so it was decided: we'd go overland in our VW. Like Kim, most of the friends who gathered in the Paris apartment had already made the journey to the Far East that we were about to embark on. From this well-traveled group, we gathered valuable information and advice on routes to take, and situations to avoid.

"Never drink the water unless you know the source," Douglas from Canada told us.

"Stay together. Don't turn your backs on your belongings, and don't let your passport out of your sight. Ever." That warning came from Kurt, from Switzerland, who said he'd gotten into "unbelievable and unimaginable trouble" when his passport was taken from him in India.

"Here's the address of friends in Tehran. I used to study with the son," Zoe said. It would be the only address we'd have outside of Europe, until we reached India. Paco, from Brazil, told us about a young couple who lived in the south of France who might need help on their farm. It was still cold in Europe, so it seemed like a good idea to be stationary for the winter and start our journey east in the spring. After spending New Year's Eve in Paris, we drove south to the tiny village of Flassans-sur-Issole.

Locating the farm, we found they needed quite a bit more than help. The woman of the house was expecting her second child within the month. She told me she'd had two miscarriages and that her doctor had put her on complete bed rest. She certainly could not do any farmwork. Her musician husband was on tour, and their two-year-old son, a normal active toddler, was just this side of neglected.

We were given a small stone house on the property, and although it took some doing to heat it, it was better shelter than our two-man tent. Mice ran about the house freely. As long as we kept the bread and cheese well covered, the mice didn't bother us much. The work we did on the farm was the work for which the term "backbreaking" was coined. We helped lay a tile floor, busted deeply embedded rock with pickaxes, and mixed wheelbarrows of cement to build a stone wall. A big part of our labor was choosing the right size rocks to mulch the farm's many olive trees. Nanao helped out by feeding the donkey, chickens, and a goat. And she was a playmate for the toddler—his mother clearly couldn't keep up with him.

During those winter months, it was often warm enough to sit in the sun and have a picnic lunch. The mistral, the wind blowing in from the Mediterranean, filled the air with the sweet mingled scents of thyme, lavender, and mimosa.

The best times of all were Saturdays, when we had a day off and joined everyone in town at the large open market. Flowers and herbs were abundant, and villagers could buy tools, pots, clothes, a live chicken, or a cleaned and quartered one. We bought artichokes by the kilo, and delicious concoctions of olives prepared by kohl-eyed Tunisian women, and couscous, that North African staple that became a staple for us, too.

After doing our basic shopping for the week, Billy and I bought treats for our Saturday afternoon lunch: Roquefort and goat cheese, figs and almonds and pears, all to be eaten with a salad, good olive oil, and fresh loaves of bread. We brought bottles to be filled with good cheap red wine from local vineyards. A pot of crème fraîche was a special treat to put on top of pumpkin pie I'd baked for dessert.

Their baby boy was born, winter was over, and we prepared to leave.

The day before starting out, we got a telephone call from Kim telling us there was a man living not far from where we were who was not well and who was desperately looking for a macrobiotic cook. At this point, we were ready to get on with our trip. Although we didn't have a specific date we needed to be in Japan, we did want our progress toward Japan to be steady. I could see how a side trip here, a detour there, could end up extending our time on the road. But since we could easily pass this man's house on our way out of France, we headed further south thinking we could help him, even if for a short time.

Yves was a successful businessman who owned a great deal of real estate in the area near the famous resort of Saint-Tropez. His large house sat high on a hill overlooking the Mediterranean. About seven years earlier he had, quite suddenly, completely lost the ability to move his legs. When we met him, his condition had improved a little, and he could walk with the aid of crutches.

Looking out over an expertly tended garden, seated on chairs covered with prints of lavender sprigs, he told us one day he was fine, and the next he woke up to find he couldn't walk. Having the necessary resources, he sought out the best medical specialists, orthopedic surgeons, and neurologists. The only thing they agreed on was his ailment was a total mystery and they had no idea how to cure him.

Willing to try anything, he went to Boston to see Michio Kushi, the principal teacher of macrobiotics in the States. Michio Kushi, with whom Billy had studied, was the person who'd told him about the dojo in Japan, the place we were headed. Michio put Yves on a strict diet, and recommended shiatsu massage and acupuncture. When he returned to his home in France, he was still on crutches, but he felt better both physically and mentally than he'd felt in a long time. He committed to following Michio's instructions to the letter. He gave up his typically French diet of meat, butter, cheese, white bread, pastries, and wine. He ate whole grains and vegetables, little or no fruit, and absolutely no sugar. Feeling as good as he did, he hoped to convert his family to his new way of eating. But his wife refused to cook this new food and his children balked. Finally, believing he'd lost his mind, she took the children and left.

We liked Yves immediately and were touched by his sincerity and enthusiasm. Like someone who'd been given a new lease on life, he exuded gratitude. The day we arrived was his birthday and he was busily, and with quite a lot of difficulty, preparing a dinner for six friends he'd invited for the evening. He was eager to introduce these friends to natural food, but we could hardly believe he'd taken on such a big task.

Once again, it seemed we'd arrived at a good moment. Given a room that looked out on the pool, we put our bags in it and left them unpacked. With Nanao trailing behind us, we immediately returned to the kitchen to help. After an afternoon of cutting, cooking, and baking, ten of us sat down at a table laden with a festive variety of healthy food. I remember braised fennel was the main dish, simmered leeks with white miso one of the sides – and that Yves said the carrot salad was dessert, because it had raisins.

We stayed with Yves two weeks, until a young man from Paris answered his advertisement for a natural foods cook. Luc, a medical student, was taking time off from his studies to learn about the effects of foods on health. He didn't have any experience as a cook, but was earnest in his desire to learn. Over several days, Billy worked with him in the kitchen, teaching him the basics of the macrobiotic diet and preparation of natural foods. By the time we left, we were confident he could cook for our new friend.

On a lovely Côte d'Azur day, a few days before we left, Nanao sat on my lap holding Bearie while we sat by the pool. Now missing her two front teeth, she gave Yves big smiles as he took photos.

"I feel like I have a family again," he said. "Thank you."

Yes, we'd been a family. Yves's warmth and generosity had made his large empty house a home. I felt bad leaving him, knowing that aside from his physical affliction, he was lonely. Luc would be with him for a while, but not permanently. The last embrace I gave Yves carried the hope he would have family, and love, in his life again.

. . .

Piling into our trusty, rusty VW, we hit the road again.

Billy prided himself on not wasting even an inch of packable space, and by this time the Volkswagen was packed full. We had our original one bag each, which included hot- and cold-weather clothing, two sleeping bags that could zip together and easily accommodate the three of us, and our small lightweight "two-man" (plus one child) tent. Since Amsterdam we'd collected, bought, been given, or found: blankets, a tarpaulin, cookware, dishes, a camping stove, and maps. Along with spare parts and tools for the car, what kept us rolling was the indispensable manual *How to Keep Your Volkswagen Alive: A Manual of Step-by-Step Procedures for the Compleat Idiot*.

Also keeping us mobile was our large store of nonperishable food: brown rice, couscous, beans, chickpeas, lentils, noodles, herb teas, and such Japanese preserved staples as *umeboshi*, miso, *takuan*, and the seaweeds wakame and nori. We intended to do as much of our own cooking as possible to save money, but also to avoid (the unavoidable) dysentery that afflicts most Westerners who travel to the East.

Nanao was entirely portable. She had the back of the car to herself, and, still small enough to stretch out on the backseat of a VW Bug, she napped as comfortably as she would've in a bed. When not looking out the window, she could entertain herself with things friends had given her on the way: a hand puppet, modeling clay, books, drawing pads and crayons, and even a small watercolor paint set. She had Bearie and her "little box of things." I didn't always know what was in that box, but I know at one time or another it contained dead flowers, beads, broken barrettes, and rocks and pebbles she had picked up on the way. Our friend Barbara Lebensfeld (the jewelry designer "Biba Schutz") who worked at the summer camp with us, had made her a doll especially for travel. The doll had clothes to put on and take off, a necklace and bracelet, hair that could be styled, and was designed to fold easily and be stuffed in corners. Nanao was set. It seemed she was hardly aware we were no longer in our cozy home in Plainfield, Vermont.

We drove through Monaco and into northern Italy in a day. It was the first time in Italy for all of us, and once over the border, Billy and I babbled gleefully to each other in make-believe Italian —though Billy could remember some from his childhood, a time when some Greenwich Village shopkeepers spoke Italian as their first and only language.

After driving all day, we arrived in Genoa toward nightfall, and looked for a suitable place to camp. Finding nothing better, we set up our tent on a stretch of beach. The air was cold and damp, and no sooner had we crawled into our sleeping bags than it began to rain. It rained hard throughout the night, but we managed to stay dry enough to sleep. In the morning when Nanao woke up and said, "Oh! It's raining!" I had to smile. If we didn't know before, Billy and I knew then she'd be all right on the rest of this trip.

The rain continued, and by the time we were on the outskirts of Bologna, the bottom of the front of the car on the passenger's side was full of water. As soon as the rain let up, we pulled over to the side of the road to bail out the water, though I'm not sure *bail* is the right word since we used a little cup to do it. All the stuff packed under the seats was already soaked. The whole episode could be classified as a drag. But when you're living in such a precarious manner, nothing is assured or guaranteed, and mishaps are not so much expected as accepted. You roll with the punches—and if you can't, you can't take a trip like this.

We spent just one day in Venice, walking around from morning until evening feasting our eyes on that extraordinarily beautiful place. We also feasted our eyes on the restaurants, having agreed that in Venice we would abandon our Spartan meal plan and treat ourselves to a real Italian meal. Tired and very hungry, by late afternoon we were ready to sit down and dig into some delectable Italian dishes—our imaginations amplifying the ample meal we knew we'd have.

We looked with an investigative eye at many restaurants. Because they all seemed much the same, we chose a moderately priced one in a small piazza next to a Venetian stationery store. It was soon obvious we'd chosen the wrong restaurant. The portions were exceptionally small, the spaghetti wasn't al dente but almost uncooked, and I'd swear the sauces came out of a bottle, or a can. The waiter hovered over us, not to be solicitous, but to snatch the Parmesan cheese and olive oil as soon as we'd used them. Admittedly, we were trying to stretch our meal.

Billy and I didn't go back to Italy for twenty years. When we did, we ate our way from Como to Sicily. By then, aside from being able to afford it, we knew where to go and how to order.

We crossed the border into Yugoslavia late at night and prepared to camp in any suitable spot as we'd done everywhere.

"You cannot stop along the road. Nowhere. It's forbidden." The border guard was gruff, but not unfriendly. "Only can stay in camping place."

"Can you tell us where there is a camping place?"

"All closed this time of year."

He directed us to a government-run hotel, sketching a crude map as he said, "You follow this paper."

Yugoslavia was the first Eastern European country we'd been in—and the difference was felt, immediately. It was a poorer, grayer place. Filling up our car, we got a taste of what was to come—no way to make sense of signs, not able to count. To communicate we spoke a jumble of English with a little French, Italian, and German thrown in. I haven't the slightest idea why we thought this could work.

After that first night at the "hotel," practically a barracks, we found out that Yugoslavian families lodged travelers for short periods. So we spent one night in a small house with a woman and her three children. The eldest daughter had vacated her room for us, and remade the beds with thick quilts covered in beautiful hand-embroidered linen. After so many nights of bedding down in sleeping bags, this little touch made our modest room seem as luxurious as any fine hotel.

Moving on, we stayed a few days in a little town by the Adriatic Sea with a very large woman whose head almost touched the low ceiling of her cottage. Every morning she invited us to share her slivovitz for breakfast. Billy tried it, and she seemed to think it odd that I couldn't down a shot of this strong liquor first thing in the morning. Through pantomime she told me I was too thin and that she could fatten me up with slivovitz and potatoes.

Driving along the Adriatic coast, we saw few cars and many people walking long distances. Means of transportation long since forgotten, obsolete, or seldom used in the places we'd come from were now commonplace, and we shared the road with carts, wagons, horses, oxen, and heavily laden donkeys. Leaving the seaside, we drove through high and perilously narrow mountain roads that had no guardrails but an unnerving number of floral shrines. Climbing higher, at nighttime we looked down on small, scarcely lit villages.

Late one afternoon, we stopped in a mountain village where I, nonchalantly, entered a store to buy vegetables. Surprised by the number of people hanging around inside, it was clear the store was also the village café and gathering spot. In that place I could only be a stranger, and all eyes unabashedly turned on me. I wasn't obtuse. The situation was utterly incongruous.

By the time we reached the city of Skopje, capital of Macedonia in southeastern Yugoslavia, the subtle change from West to East had become more apparent. We couldn't read anything, which was the most obvious indication we were encountering unfamiliar cultures. We couldn't have known then that the country of Yugoslavia would cease to exist. About fifteen years after we were there it broke up into the states we know today as

Macedonia, Croatia, Bosnia and Herzegovina, Montenegro, and still others.

Our overland journey revealed the fascinating change as cultures flow into one another. We could see that there is no sharp line that separates one country from another the way we view it on a map. Rather, the change is gradual.

Traveling overland, we saw the West literally blend into the East.

We drove straight through Bulgaria, stopping only one night and one day in Sofia—long enough to have two bad experiences.

Just after checking out of our hotel (Bulgaria too had very strict rules about camping), I realized I'd left the car key, which I kept in a small purse I'd bought in Wales, in the room. Going back to retrieve it, I thought luck was with me when I saw a chambermaid already in the room.

I went to the table where I'd left my purse and was surprised it wasn't there. I asked her for it thinking she'd already dusted the table, but she appeared to not know what I was looking for. No doubt she didn't speak English and didn't understand my words, but I felt certain she knew what I was talking about, and that I didn't need to resort to my made-up English-French-German gibberish. I tried to explain I didn't care about the money (there was only a little) but that I needed the car key—we only had one; our "car dealer" in Amsterdam didn't provide a spare. When this failed, I went back downstairs, first to explain to Billy what was taking me so long, and then to enlist the help of the desk manager, who spoke English.

He returned with me to the room and after a few words with the chambermaid told me she hadn't seen my purse. At this point I began to doubt myself, and fully aware that it was my own carelessness that had gotten me in the predicament, I wanted to drop the matter and walk away. But the untold problems we would have if the key was indeed lost were easily and instantly imagined. And the picture of the woven wool dark turquoise and magenta purse I'd left on the glass-top bedside table was crystal clear. Without saying much else, I believe it was also crystal clear I could not leave without my car key.

The manager then suggested we look around the room for it, which I straight away felt was a game since the three of us had checked the sparsely furnished room several times. But if the game would produce my purse, I didn't mind playing. Both the manager and the chambermaid went to "search" in the bathroom, and no sooner had they gone in than they came out, with the purse. I apologized for the trouble I'd caused, thanked them both, and left.

Relieved, I was also reminded how vulnerable you can feel sometimes when traveling. I'd come to expect kindness, but one could not always expect honesty. I relied on my innate sense of trust and lack of suspicion to help create good relations, even with strangers. You need a certain amount of trust to be on the open road, to move about freely and feel comfortable in unfamiliar situations with unknown people. I knew this from traveling alone. It was especially acute traveling with a child.

Our dried-food supply was holding up and we were still doing most of our cooking. Whether we camped or stayed in a hotel, our routine was to prepare food every night. Whoever woke up first would light the stove under our little pressure cooker, and by the time we were washed, packed, and ready to move on, our lunch for the day would be cooked. We varied our basic diet of brown rice and beans with couscous and chickpeas, vegetable soup and bread. When time was short, we'd eat pasta with olive oil, or soba (buckwheat noodles) with shoyu, sesame seed oil, and nori. We bought fresh vegetables and fruit as we went along.

After leaving the hotel, we went to a department store in the center of Sofia to look for items we needed, most importantly camping gas. This was our lifeblood—the only way we could cook. The department store was huge, but its mostly empty display cases and dusty shelves had nothing we wanted. There were few shoppers and the dour-faced saleswomen looked like they didn't remember the last time they'd made a sale. They didn't have camping gas, so after a little browsing around, we left. Driving out of the parking lot, I became confused as to which was the exit and which the entrance. I was soon put straight.

A taxi driver, coming in the opposite direction, stopped, rolled down his window, yelled some words, made an ugly face, and spat at me. My window was up—though I'd thought to roll it down the better to hear what I was sure would be helpful directions when he'd pulled up alongside our car. He sped off. Billy, who had continued his daily habit of jogging while we traveled, sometimes running alongside the car while I drove slowly, jumped out of the car and chased the taxi. Neither he nor I had any idea of what he intended to do.

Goodbye, Bulgaria.

Our first night in Turkey was spent in an inexpensive but fairly nice hotel not far from the Bulgarian border.

Tired and completely ready to sleep, we couldn't because of the boisterous party going on downstairs. It kept us up but it also excited us. Attracted by the exotically beautiful music, we left our room to listen and see what we could from the lobby. We were told it was a wedding party. When they saw us peeking in and invited us to join in the festivities, we were thrilled. The large room with low-hanging chandeliers was positively jubilant with men and women dressed in their finest. I wonder if anyone would have noticed us, but for the fact that we were in no way dressed for the occasion.

From that night on, the fact that we had left behind the Western world became increasingly and fascinatingly obvious. However, being a woman, I was made extremely uncomfortable by the hungry-eyed stares of men. I'd been to Morocco, twice, so seeing women covered and veiled was not new. But what I experienced in Turkey soon felt oppressive.

I wasn't concerned about Nanao, as most people just appeared astonished to see a foreign child. As for myself, I lowered my eyes, shortened my stride, and stayed close to Billy's side. Although I dressed with conscientious modesty, compared to the all-covered dress of Turkish women, I felt as if I were in a miniskirt. Any surface of skin showing seemed to call out for attention. Although it was warm, I took to wearing a long skirt, and I wore a shawl to cover my neck and chest—it sometimes covered my head, too. I wore socks with my sandals so as not to draw attention to my naked toes. But even with all this, men looked at me with eyes that appeared to have X-ray vision. I gradually assumed the lowest of profiles, receded into the background, and left it to Billy to do most of our shopping and all the talking.

This was too bad, because I liked the daily interplay of shopping and bartering. There were never prices on anything and the sellers, whether in shops or markets, would tell you anything they thought you'd pay. A relatively simple act like buying a kilo of oranges—and the Turkish oranges were the best I've eaten, before or since—was always a three-ring circus of offer, refusal, and final acceptance.

After spending the day at the Hagia Sophia, the cathedral that became a mosque and was now a museum, early evening found us sitting in the blue-white light of a fluorescent-lit café, directly under the stern gaze of Atatürk. These retouched and tinted photos of the founder of modern Turkey, dressed in a tuxedo, could be seen always and everywhere.

"Looks pretty scary, doesn't he?" we heard a man behind us say.

We turned around to see a European (we could easily tell) couple with a little girl.

"Hi. I'm Martin," he said, offering his hand. "This is my wife Fiona and daughter Milja." The little girl wasted no time jumping up from the table and grabbing Nanao's hand.

We joined them at their table and, while sipping strong Turkish coffee, learned they were Dutch, and that Martin made regular trips to the Near East to buy clothes and jewelry for his shop in Utrecht. He was obviously knowledgeable and experienced about the trip we were taking, and his freely offered advice and information were gratefully accepted.

"Look. Whatever you do, do not drive the whole way to the Eastern border."

Since this was exactly what we were about to do, we listened carefully.

"There's a ship you can board here in Istanbul that crosses the Black Sea to Trabzon in eastern Turkey. Take that and you'll avoid endless kilometers of bad roads and worse drivers."

We changed our plans and travel route on the spot.

We were happy for the company of another family and enjoyed talking with them. Nanao and Milja were the same age and instant playmates, seemingly oblivious to the fact they didn't speak the same language. As we four talked leisurely, they skipped about at the entrance of the café. Both clearly seasoned traveling children, they knew not to leave their parents' sight, even for a minute.

And so we crossed the Black Sea on a ferry, to avoid the perils and literal pitfalls of the road.

On the ferry, it was possible to rent a berth or stay in your car. Since the weather was fine, we decided to stay out on the deck during the day and sleep in our car for the three-night journey. The first night Nanao slept on the backseat as usual while Billy and I spent half of a tortuous night contorted in various positions in the front. Unable to sleep, he took his sleeping bag and slept on the deck alongside the car while I managed to sleep a few more uncomfortable hours across the two front seats. The morning after that first night, he decided to implement a plan he'd had since we'd bought the car: convert our little VW Bug into a big VW bus. He took out the front seats. Although the car was roomier for the time we were on the ferry, it was not more comfortable to sleep in, and a whole lot less comfortable to sit in.

People—men—wandered all over the boat aimlessly and continuously and they gathered in groups to watch us as we ate, washed, talked. I got tired of the many eyes that watched my every move, and took to sitting in the car, hiding behind curtains of towels I'd hung to ward off the ever-peering eyes, but no one was deterred. It wasn't apparent if the unconcealed interest was because of my being a woman, a black woman, or a foreigner, but the three of us being there at all was clearly a curiosity and captivating.

On the third night, Billy stayed up late and climbed in a perch directly above the car, unseen by the unseemly characters who peeped in the car to look at Nanao and me as we slept. When Billy startled one unwanted visitor by dropping from his lookout place, the man, realizing Billy was guarding us, quickly apologized and slid into the night.

The ferry made one port stop and everyone disembarked. We got off to buy food, and separating from Billy just briefly while I looked in shops and stalls, a small crowd began to follow me. I can't say I'd become used to this kind of attention, but it was definitely not the first time. Hitchhiking alone on that first trip to Europe in 1965, following my trusted Hallwag map, I'd ended up in some out-of-the-way places. In Spain I was like the Pied Piper as children gaily followed me to the outskirts of small villages while town folks called out, "*Hola! Morena!*"

Now in Turkey, I was aware that my presence causing a small commotion wasn't unusual, but in this market I was at a loss as to what to do. I came to the end of the market and had no choice but to turn around and go through the gauntlet again. Halfway back, a dark-skinned man came up to me and said something. It was the strangest thing, because I felt I recognized him. I wanted to tell him I was sure we had met before, maybe at a party. No doubt I was having a traveler's hallucination. I don't know if he was a person of authority or what, but he spoke to the crowd following me, and they listened and dispersed. I was grateful he'd come to my aid, but, flustered, I couldn't remember how to say "thank you" in Turkish.

We disembarked in Trabzon, and following Martin's detailed instructions, we hit the road for Erzurum. He'd told us we'd be going out of our way, but warned the most obvious and direct route was hazardous, with many dangerous drawbacks, and the smartest thing to do was to go around it. Martin also told us that on the more direct road we'd risk a tire blowout as well as a broken windshield, caused by children who threw rocks at passing cars for the fun of it. As we drove along the prescribed route, we became convinced we took the wrong road. There were no children throwing rocks, there was nobody doing anything. The road was desolate.

But the potholes were big and innumerable, and the general disrepair of the road forced us to drive at a snail's pace. When we finally reached Erzurum, the distance of 150 kilometers (93 miles) had taken us eight hours and cost us the loss of two hubcaps. Later, meeting up with Martin as planned, we told him we must have taken the wrong road. After asking us some questions and checking a few details, he assured us we'd taken the "good" road.

Reaching Iran, we drove on endless bad roads and through pitch-black tunnels into blinding sun.

Passing through one stretch of dry open land, we were startled by a wake of vultures that reluctantly swooped away from an animal carcass as we approached. We could hear their huge wings flapping as they flew directly over our car. Further on, stopping to have our lunch, we were surprised, most pleasantly this time, by a formation of Iranian women and young girls winding their way down a path from an abode unseen in the hills above. From where we sat, we could see their richly embroidered clothes and hear the light tinkle of the silver jewelry that adorned them. It was a beautiful sight, a picture straight out of *National Geographic*, but we wouldn't have photographed them. Even if we'd had a camera.

That first night in Iran, we stayed in a cheap hotel and found out just how cheap when we were surprised to learn we were sharing a room with about six other people—again, people being men. All I remember about the place was that there was one dirty sink in the corner of the room and one shared toilet in the hall, and that Billy couldn't wait for us to get out of there.

As soon as we got into Tabriz in the Azerbaijan region of western Iran, Billy left Nanao and me in the car and went to buy bread, and yogurt, which had also become a mainstay of our road diet. No sooner had he left than four children noticed us sitting in the car, where we'd stayed, sweltering, simply to avoid being stared at. The kids came over, pointed, gaped, laughed, while Nanao and I sat there in a futile attempt to ignore them. The first group were soon joined by other youngsters—were they all getting out of school, I wondered, and would there soon be hundreds? The car was soon surrounded with children pressing their faces to the windows on all sides. For a moment I thought to get out and look for Billy, but I had no idea where he might have gone. When I tried to speak to the children, they mimicked me as soon as I opened my mouth. A small eternity passed and both Nanao and I had begun to cry as they started pushing the car.

"Mama, why won't they go away?"

Feeling like an animal that couldn't protect her young, I answered feebly, "I don't know. Papa will be back soon."

And I could hear him before I could see him, yelling, "Get outta here! Get outta here!" This wasn't a particularly bad experience; nothing happened to us, and there wasn't even any damage to the car. But it was unsettling and and I felt somewhat distraught.

From the time we'd left Europe, we met few women, and fewer children, on the road. We sometimes saw dark people, but I don't recall ever seeing an African or African-American. Although I never did,·or wore, anything that could draw attention to myself, I was always noticed. And while the attention we received wasn't particularly negative, what started to grate was the fact that we were never, and never could be, anonymous. We could never be just another face in the crowd. Never just another family at the market.

And I never thought, never anticipated, what that might be like in Japan where 99.9% of the population did not look like me.

We drove for long hours without stopping. We'd heard tale after discouraging tale of incidents of harassment, robbery, molestation. We had long since abandoned our instant-camping ideas of sleeping by the side of the road wherever the ground was flat. We were carefree, but not careless. Often our calculations of when we'd arrive somewhere were completely off. Often it was because roads were closed or impassable, or a necessary detour was unmarked. There was never an expectation there might be road crews to redirect us.

And so we arrived in Tehran late at night completely exhausted. Every hotel where Billy inquired claimed to be full. Giving up, we went to what was obviously an expensive and completely-out-of-our-budget hotel.

"I'd like a room for three for the night," Billy said.

In the spacious lobby, a large man with "Manager" printed

on a lapel tag greeted us at the reception desk. With a British accent oiling his speech, he said, "I'm sorry, sir. We have not any room for this evening."

"What's going on here?" Billy demanded. "All I want is a room for my family! Are you telling me there isn't a room in the entire city?!" It seemed Billy had lost, or discarded, the ability to distinguish between yelling at some ragamuffins on the street and this man dressed for his position.

With no explanation for the original refusal, the manager said, "Very well," and we were ushered to a room overlooking all of Tehran.

I have no idea why we weren't given a room in the first place and I don't think we could have asked for or expected an explanation. Perhaps the simple fact of a foreign couple with a young child appearing at that hour of the night was just out of the ordinary.

By the time we entered our room, it was already two in the morning, too late to take full advantage of the luxury of our accommodations. We'd slept in our clothes more times than I care to remember. There were many days we hadn't been able to wash more than our faces. Now we were ecstatic over our hot water ablutions. Nanao fell asleep in seconds.

Billy opened a bottle of champagne he'd picked up in France when we went through Reims and said, "We need to celebrate."

The following day, we checked into an establishment for which the word *hotel* was but a euphemism. A place frequented by foreigners headed east or back west, where Iranian hustlers wandered in and out day and night, offering to change money, sell drugs, buy the jeans off your body, or show you around the city.

Posted around the hotel were signs warning guests to keep a close watch on their things, most especially passports and money. The largest sign, written in red and nailed to the door, stated, "Management will not take the responsibility for the loss or theft of any of your possessions." There were no safes, and your locked room was not considered a secure place—the man at the desk told us that to our faces.

Having heard from Martin what a prize item a pair of American jeans were, when we washed Billy's only pair and hung them in the courtyard, we took turns watching them dry. Apparently, someone was watching us watch the jeans, because in what must have been the few seconds neither of us had our eyes on the prize, they were stolen. Billy raced around asking questions and carrying out a general investigation, but it was clear from the start the pilfered jeans would never be recovered.

Tehran was a modern city—and in that statement is the good (we easily found camping gas) and the bad: the traffic was horrendous, the air polluted, and the car horn as integral a part of driving as the steering wheel. Many women wore Western dress, their dark hair flowing, while still others were enveloped in the black chador. We moved around the city freely, under the gaze of the Shah. The visage of Shah Reza Pahlavi could be found on the money and stamps, and there were photographs everywhere of him, his empress, and their children, dressed in finery and a splendor of sashes, ribbons, jewels, and crowns.

As Tehran would be the largest city we'd be in for a while, we focused on doing necessary things like getting inoculations before going further east, and it still remained for us to visit the embassies of Afghanistan and Pakistan for visas. We needed a few tools for the car—Billy tuned it up and adjusted something or other almost every day—as well as spare parts.

We'd kept the address of the Iranian family Zoe had given us in Paris, and found their home easily. After leaving France, we didn't have the name of anyone who could be called a friend, and this potential meeting, friends of a friend, was a pleasant prospect. I've never minded being a stranger in a strange place, but it's always great to know someone, a native or resident. Now in the Near East, meeting this family would be our first personal meeting with Iranians.

After inquiring in the building, we were disappointed to find no one knew them. A woman on the first floor told us, "Ask at that large house across the street. They are an old family. They know everyone." On the opposite side of the street we saw an open gate that enclosed a large house and we stepped into the garden. A gray-haired, distinguished-looking gentleman, dressed in a suit, stood up from the table where he was sitting alone and greeted us pleasantly, almost as though he were expecting us.

"That family has moved. But I cannot say where," he said. "But please. You have traveled far. I invite you to have a cup of tea with me." Pulling out a chair for me, he sat down again at the table that had a chessboard set up. Discovering a mutual enthusiasm for chess, our host and Billy were soon deep in a game.

After an ancient-looking servant brought tea, Nanao and I wandered around the garden, completely absorbed by the sweet-smelling flowers, statuary, and fountains. In this place, we were instantly transported from the commotion and grime of Tehran, and the road we seemed to never leave.

In what was a lovely afternoon interlude, Billy and I almost forgot why we had come to that part of the city. This man's graciousness and generosity practically wiped out the stolen-jeans incident. When an equally elderly gentleman, a friend he'd been expecting, arrived, we thanked our host for his kindness and left.

The following day, we checked out of our hotel in Tehran, making sure we'd taken everything—we knew we would never again see anything we'd left behind. By this time, the few clothes we had were so worn out, it was hard to imagine anyone would want them. But one of the lessons learned through traveling is about those others who have even less than you do. Things we attached no particular value to were indeed valuable, and could be sold.

Driving directly to the border crossing to Afghanistan, we arrived at dawn. The checkpoint was still closed and Billy locked Nanao and me in the car and got a couple of hours' sleep lying on the ground alongside the car.

We were happy to have an early start, and could not believe our ears when we were told we wouldn't be permitted to leave Iran because of what seemed like a ridiculous technicality: we were required to pay for exit visas. This was the first time we'd heard of such a thing, and we weren't certain we weren't being hustled, though these guys looked official.

"But we don't have enough rials," Billy told them.

"Then you must go to a bank."

"Where is the nearest bank?"

"Today is a holiday. All banks are closed."

There was nowhere for this conversation to go. We had driven over a thousand kilometers from Tehran to the border. If we had to stay in Iran, where would we stay? We were probably not allowed to camp. If we tried to get accommodations, we wouldn't be able to pay for it without Iranian rials. Billy's expression said, *We're in a fix.*

We had to drive back to the nearest town, and the next several hours were spent at the local police station trying to straighten out our predicament. And getting out of this fix also called for us to go to the home of the local judge. This big hairy man interrupted the massage he was getting when we were ushered into his home. He patiently and affably explained the problem to us as he signed some papers. One more trip to the police station, where we paid the money, all the *rials* we had left. Since we didn't have enough, part of the payment was made with a heavy wool winter coat Lene had given me in Denmark.

While filling out the forms, I saw it was my birthday. But for this incident, the day would have passed unnoticed. I only recall thinking that on my twentieth birthday I had crossed the border between France and Spain. Now on my thirtieth, I was crossing the border between Iran and Afghanistan. Although I didn't attach any significance to it at the time, I guess there was a pattern.

After going through customs, we drove into Herat in western Afghanistan.

"Karen, maybe this is all a mistake," I heard Billy say. He wasn't looking at me, but at the street.

"What do you mean?"

"What do I mean? Look around!"

Our car was one of only a few on the street. Riders on horseback galloped by us with robes flying, kicking up dust from the unpaved road.

"We could just end our trip here and fly straight to Japan." He was serious.

We had enough money and could've bought tickets, hopped on a plane, and been in Japan in a matter of hours—not the months that were still before us.

"It'll be all right," I said. It was unthinkable to me that we would now throw in the towel and throw away the chance to see Afghanistan and experience its culture firsthand. "This is a fascinating place. I've read things haven't changed much in Herat since the fourteenth century." Surely our first impressions of the city seemed to bear this out. There wasn't a woman to be seen anywhere. All we saw were moving figures draped in all-enveloping coverings. The faded-blue burqa, as we would soon learn it was called, provided just a net for women to see out. No one could see in.

"This is an adventure. Let's get into it," I said.

It was clear Billy experienced this whole "adventure" differently. He was our protector. A little twentieth-century perspective would've suited him fine. Women and girls who wore clothes, not shrouds, whose faces could be seen, would have been welcome.

But I wasn't ready to give up the road just yet. Afghanistan presented itself as a country lost in time. It was intriguing, and I didn't yet want the world of discovery through travel to be over. Jetting out of there would've been like putting on a blindfold to look through a kaleidoscope.

We went to a place on the edge of town that Martin had told us about, where we could camp on the grounds of a hotel—and in fact, there were more people staying on the grounds than in the hotel. Unpacking our things to prepare some food and still adhering to my low-profile policy, I told Billy the shopping I needed him to do. I wanted to try the Afghan bread that I'd heard was so good and baked the same way for centuries.

"And be sure and get the small sweet carrots, and I want large onions. And try to find some of those oranges like we had in Turkey," I said, adding about how much per kilo I thought they should cost.

Looking tired and harassed, Billy showed up three hours later with a few scraggly vegetables and a couple of dried-up oranges and a warning to me to not be too particular.

"This is not like shopping at a market in the south of France. In case you didn't notice."

Camped just next to us was a group of students and teachers from the American School in Kabul who'd come to Herat on an excursion. They invited Nanao and me to go along with them on their daily visits to historical sites and to see craftsmen, glass-blowers, and weavers at work.

This was great because Billy had practical matters to attend to, mainly trying to find out how to sell our car. We weren't plan-ning to take it out of Afghanistan, and didn't have the necessary documents to take it into Pakistan. I wouldn't have been comfortable going around Herat on my own. As in Turkey and Iran, I attracted attention wherever I went. Several times I'd been literally encircled by the local folk when I ventured forth. They appeared as curious and interested in looking at me as I was looking at mosques.

Sitting outside our tent one afternoon, braiding Nanao's hair, a group of five Afghani women, three carrying babies, approached me.

They immediately lifted their veils.

In no time we were in one of those animated conversations that people without a shared language somehow contrive. *Where did I come from? How old was I? How old was my little girl? How many children did I have?* I was surprised the three women carrying babies were only sixteen and seventeen because they looked a good deal older. They all smiled broadly. Some had teeth, some didn't.

And then, in a flash, they all dropped their veils.

With what appeared to be a sixth sense, they'd spotted an Afghani man coming our way. After he'd passed, we continued to "talk" for a short time more. I had questions, things I wondered about but couldn't ask. I knew the rate of literacy was shockingly low in Afghanistan, especially among women. Could they read? Did they want to? Had they been to school? They seemed awfully young to have children. Did they have a choice?

I didn't know if the veil was mandatory, but when I saw how fast the women dropped their veils when the man approached, I did want to know if they did it out of extreme modesty, security, or fear. More practically, was it their culture or religion that imposed the wearing of what literally amounted to cloth bags? This garment obviously hampered movement, obscured vision, impaired hearing, and must have been extremely unpleasant to have covering your mouth.

After they left, I never felt quite so bad about the many

women who stared at me point-blank behind the shields of their veils. Rather, I thought how stifling, in daily life and psychologically, those veils must be. It pained me to think they were compelled to wear them.

We spent one week in Herat and then drove toward Kabul.

All along the way, we could see the nomads' huge black tents camped in the open spaces under a glaring sun, and often there wasn't a tree in sight. We saw shepherds guiding flocks of sheep, and often those shepherds were children who looked as young as Nanao. Although we were basically living out of a car, compared to these people who lived in the open, we almost seemed privileged. How relative everything is. Nanao didn't have a home, but she also didn't have a job.

In Kabul, we again camped on the grounds of a hotel. It seemed to be the popular form of accommodation for that time of year, and camped along with us were travelers from Switzerland, England, France, Germany, Australia, the United States, and Canada, to name the few I remember. We were coming up on the one-year mark of being on the road, and in that time we'd never met even one person from Japan. What would in a few years become the ubiquitous sight of tour-guided camerawielding Japanese was then nonexistent. As a fact and at the time, it was relatively rare for Japanese to travel abroad as they had neither the means nor the permission—the government strictly limited how much money a Japanese person could take out of the country.

From the time we left Europe, we never saw anyone else traveling as far as we were in a VW Bug. Everyone we met on the road was in Volkswagen buses, campers, and Land Rovers— vehicles outfitted with cooking facilities and comfortable sleeping arrangements. Our rolling home was compact and minimally accommodating, but totally functional. Our fellow travelers were impressed that in our small car we had all the essentials. The most essential item of all, water, we kept in a collapsible one-gallon container that we refilled at every sanitary opportunity—embassies, restaurants, and reputable hotels.

We were careful, never ever drinking tap water, and continued to cook our own food. We did eat some local food, especially fresh yogurt, and the bread that was so good and cheap and could be bought straight from the oven, but we rarely touched food sold in the open markets. Still, while in Kabul, all three of us began to have minor symptoms of what we assumed was amoebic dysentery. I'd experienced it in Morocco, and although it had been ten years earlier, I could still remember the nausea and vomiting, the intestinal cramps that made you weak and kept you on the toilet.

A helpful nurse at the American School, where we went often to replenish our water supply (the school had dug its own well), told us that no matter how careful we were, we were still bound to get dysentery to some degree because the bacteria was in the very air. We only had a mild touch of it, whereas many travelers we met were skeleton-thin and in almost constant pain from debilitating diarrhetic cramps.

A week into our stay, two of the American students we'd met in Herat, a brother and sister, invited us to come for dinner at their home in Kabul. Their father was an officer at the embassy, and the family had lived in Kabul for several years.

Entering their house was the biggest surprise we had in Afghanistan. The house was furnished as if it were any house in the U.S. As an embassy family, it was completely feasible they could inhabit an environment as comfortable and as familiar as the one they'd left in America. The meal, cooked and served by Afghan servants, was even more of a surprise, and impossible to forget: hamburgers, French fries, salad, and soda. All of their food was bought at the embassy commissary—which is why they could have salad. For fear of dysentery, we never ate raw or uncooked vegetables and couldn't remember the last time we'd eaten salad. I love salad but didn't miss it. It's amazing how fast you can adjust, and accept, things as they are.

It was the first time I'd visited the home of Westerners, "expats" as they called themselves, living in the East. I'd had no idea it was possible, or desirable, to live in the style you had lived, so far from home. Naturally it was nice to be in a clean house, one with hot water and a flushing toilet. Those comforts aside, it occurred to me they might be missing out on not adopting more of the culture and customs of the country they were living in. I couldn't imagine wanting to have a hamburger and soda over a traditional dish and tea.

While Billy attended to our affairs, I got a little brave, and decided I'd wander around the city on my own. It was warm in Kabul, so I opted to abandon my all-skin-covered look. This meant only that I wore a skirt that came below my knees and not to my ankles, short sleeves instead of long, no socks, and no shawl. I went to the market wearing the blue-and-green dress Jackie had custom-made for me in Santa Fe. After I returned, I vowed to myself I would never pull such a stunt again. It was unbearable. I was stared at so hard I felt I'd lost my humanity.

On that very same day, we went to a traditional Afghan restaurant we'd been told was the finest in the city and had a delicious meal—the best part of which was a type of spinach ravioli. In the middle of our dinner, an Afghan man came over to our table. Asking a customer at the table to our right to speak for him, we were told he was the owner.

"He says you do not have to pay for your meal. He says you are the first black person to come in his restaurant and he feels honored."

"*Tashakor*," I said, repeating what I'd learned from the American kids about how to say thank you.

Kindness and generosity. Hospitality and welcome. All these

years later, I can still say these are the highlights of my experience of travel and encountering new cultures.

We were enjoying Kabul but knew we should be moving on—the car was holding us back. Our trusty car, our home on wheels, was a headache for us now, and Billy was getting nowhere trying to sell it. Then Ira appeared.

"Hey, my man. I hear you have a car to sell."

The man towering over us as we crawled out of our tent one morning was padded around the middle like a pasha. Still on our hands and knees, we looked up at him, which added to his impressive size.

"Yeah," Billy said, nodding toward our car.

"I'm buying," Ira said as he introduced himself. An American, he told us he wanted a car for his return trip to his home in Greece.

Billy had been spending the better part of every day in and out of various agencies, bureaus, and administrative offices trying to figure out how to sell the car. They all said something different but the essential message was the same: you could not sell a car in Afghanistan. And you could not abandon a car there, a thought that had crossed Billy's mind. A stamp, with the image of a car, was imprinted in his passport. Without the proper documentation as to the car's disposal, it was impossible to leave the country without the car itself. He was told that even if the car broke down, he would have to drag it out of the country. But we wouldn't have been able to drag it into Pakistan, our next stop, without the required *Carnet de Passages en Douane*.

Ira told Billy he'd go with him to the government office and they'd ask again. Billy, anxious to deal with our car situation, was dressed in seconds and left with Ira. When he returned later that afternoon, he told me what had transpired.

Ira could speak Dari and knew the Muslim handshakes and greetings and when to pass money under the table and when not. While listening to the bureaucrat who repeated to Billy what he'd already told him about not being able to sell the car, Ira picked up on the key word "sell" and asked if the car could be "given" away. Of course, the car could be given away, the official said.

In the end, it was a simple transaction as, officially, no money changed hands. No under-the-table money was required, and having given Ira the car, the stamp could be removed from Billy's passport. They left the office, Billy gave Ira the car and Ira gave him the money. Sold.

13

With our original one bag apiece, we were off again, and without the dubious protection of the car. For the first time since we'd landed in Belgium, we would be traveling on public transportation. And public transportation did not seem it would be a happy prospect after we crossed the Khyber Pass, seated over the wheel in a rickety old crowded bus.

Once in Pakistan, we lurched through the night from Peshawar to Lahore in another ancient bus that was brought to a halt several times by armed guards who boarded and searched the entire bus. Ira had told us they'd be looking for contraband—cigarettes and alcohol, but mainly guns.

Evidently because of the confined nature of their lives, women and young girls would not be found on long bus journeys. It was an unsettling fact for Billy as Nanao and I were the only females to be seen, and I'm sure he thought he couldn't take his eyes off us. When the bus made a rest stop in the middle of the night, I saw hundreds of men, only men, milling about in the dim fluorescent light of the "refreshment" area.

Billy got out to go to the toilet and in seconds he was back. Without boarding the bus, he came over to my open window and said, "Don't leave the bus, Karen."

He said it like a command, but he was begging me.

"We want to get out for a minute," I said.

"Look. I know you've been around and you've seen a lot, but this is a whole other thing."

Nanao and I held our bladders while Billy spent the rest of the night awake and watchful. Arriving in Lahore, we stepped off the bus and into a taxi to take us to the border with India. As extravagant as it may sound, this far east the cost wasn't much different from the three of us traveling by bus.

The Golden Temple in Amritsar was just over the border, in the Punjab state of northern India. Revered by Sikhs, this peaceful place was like a refuge, where they welcomed and served a free meal to everyone who visited. Although we ate it all the time, we were happy to be among the pilgrims enjoying a bowl of lentils and bread in that beautiful temple.

Aside from not always being able to estimate how long it would take us to get from one place to the other, the fact that we didn't have any travelers' guides meant wherever we went represented the unknown. We wouldn't know where to find accommodations or food until we found them. I don't think we made a telephone call the entire time we were on the road. We would have only the most general idea of what weather to expect. And so it was that we made the great mistake of arriving in India during the hottest season—insuring we were incapacitated by the heat.

But in India it was all right for me to go to the market on my own. Traveling just a short distance from the house where we stayed in New Delhi, I went to the market a lot. I'd walk there, very slowly, in a conscious effort to not become overheated. Although I was determined to walk back, I only made it back on my own feet once. Completely overcome by the heat, I'd ride back from the market in an open three-wheeled contraption called a "poor man's taxi."

We were fortunate to have friends living in India and their

home was cool, not with air-conditioning, but with large electric ceiling fans. But we could count on the power in New Delhi failing, every afternoon, and I failed right along with it—and lay unmoving on a cotton muslin divan until the fans started their whirring again. Still, it was too hot to even read as turning the pages of a book required too much energy. I closely watched and marveled at the launderer, Ram, who came to the house daily. I noticed he never drank anything cold and would not even eat the cold watermelon given to him but left it to sit until it had warmed up a bit. Never appearing to even notice the heat, let alone be bothered by it, he went about his work, washing by hand all the clothes for the family of four, and hanging them out under a blistering sun—they'd be dry in minutes. He'd then do the ironing.

Our friends, an American couple with two children, had membership in a swimming pool at a large hotel, and most afternoons we'd go there to cool off. We'd go by taxi and we made several trips before I figured out that even without air-conditioning, it was cooler to keep the windows up. If I opened the windows in an attempt to get the cool breeze you're accustomed to expect, my face was practically seared by the hot dry air that rushed in.

While we were in London, we'd seen the Louis Malle film *Phantom India* in a special showing, starting at midnight and ending at six in the morning. A true epic, it could have been twice as long and I could have watched it without blinking a sleepy eye. The documentary delved deeply into many aspects of Indian society. I recall the most memorable being the caste system. The images were vivid, awakening all the senses; it made you feel you could even *smell* the film. Although those images were still fresh in my mind, my dreams of seeing India evaporated in the heat.

I declined an invitation to visit the Taj Mahal, a place I'd fantasized about ever since my father told me about it. "What's alabaster?" I'd asked Daddy, as he assumed his storytelling voice, fascinating me with the tale of the Mughal emperor's marble monument and reflecting pools built to memorialize his beloved.

Now, a proposed bus ride to this fabled place sounded like torture.

I picked up the *Times of India* one morning to read the war in Vietnam was over. I cried. For joy. For the long years of suffering of the Vietnamese people. For a land defiled.

I cried for all the times my friends and I marched and protested against that war that was never declared. I hadn't watched the war on TV, but I did show up to demonstrate against it, at a time I didn't even know where Vietnam was, could not have located it on a map. In Paris in 1968, when I met a Vietnamese person for the first time in my life, I felt so deeply ashamed, I actually apologized for my country. Now, and at last, the war was over, and I cried for all the young soldiers, like my cousin Perry, who had lost their lives.

We flew north to Nepal where the refreshing Himalayan air welcomed us like a cool sheet. Riding around Katmandu on rented bicycles visiting temples and shrines, Nanao was excited we got a glimpse of the stunningly beautiful little girl in heavy makeup, colorfully dressed and bejeweled, who, we were told, the Nepalese believed was the "Living Goddess."

We hadn't had any traveling companions since Martin and his family, and we were happy to meet Murray, an Australian veterinarian who was also traveling to Thailand next. We took the same flight to Bangkok, stayed one night in the same hotel, and checked out together the following morning because there were so many American soldiers staying there. Drunk, they manhandled Thai "women of the night" and jumped out of third-story windows into the swimming pool. It was disturbing, but I have to think they were celebrating the war's end in their way.

Although we still practiced caution, we now ate everything. Along with our diminishing concerns for food safety, we had a growing desire to partake of the food on offer, even when it wasn't particularly tantalizing. It was always something new. In the colorful Bangkok markets, Billy tried everything in every stall, and Nanao tried it right along with him. Sometimes reluctant myself, surrounded by foods skewered and grilled, jellied and pickled, I wasn't sure what those two were putting in their mouths. The markets were almost overwhelming with the rich smell of spice, fresh and dried fish, and exotic tropical fruits we'd never seen or heard of before. It was all so cheap, and the sweet sun-ripened pineapple, cut and cored in a few swift strokes, was the cheapest and most delicious of all.

The world was not getting smaller with the more we saw, but larger. There was seemingly no end to discovering new places. Southeast Asia remained to be explored and Laos, Cambodia, and Burma were all nearby. But now I could say I was ready to leave the road. I felt we had done and seen enough. Such mundane acts like being able to wash our clothes regularly or sleeping in the same place every night had become appealing, but I had to stretch my imagination to conjure such a thing.

We were now just a few weeks away from our destination, Japan.

We would have one last excursion, to the north of Thailand. With Murray, we made a plan to go to Chiang Mai and from there, farther up the Mekong River to see the hill tribes. The four of us boarded a small bus and, arriving in Chiang Mai the following morning, we made arrangements for the "Jungle Tour."

In a group of ten that included two couples from Sweden and Switzerland and a young man from New Zealand, led by a Thai guide, we traveled by bus, van, and then boat upriver. The first place we stopped had the look and feel of being uninhabited. We got off the little boat—a kind of canoe with an outboard motor— and walked several kilometers into a small village. We rested a while at the hut of the head of the village, were joined by another guide, one of the villagers, then walked farther into the "jungle"—easily passable, it was not particularly lush terrain, and nothing like the thick overgrowth I'd expected to go by that name.

At the next village, the entire population came out to greet us. Apparently, our guide administered first aid to whoever was in need when he made trips there. The villagers brought out a little boy who'd been bitten by a dog. His infected leg was swollen and he limped badly. All of the villagers watched as our guide applied basic first aid. I was sure that boy needed to see a doctor, and probably needed a rabies shot, too.

I didn't know how far we'd walked, but it was evening by the time we arrived at the next village, and I was happy to hear we would be staying there for the night. Our accommodation, a simple structure built on stilts with a roof made of reeds, was the hut of the village chief. We were served a meal of hot gruel that appeared to have pieces of a gourd-like vegetable in it. It was pale green and white, bland and tasteless. After removing an insect that looked like it'd died recently in my bowl, I ate the gruel.

Finished with our meal, we were entertained by some of the villagers who danced and played instruments. Our guide told us these people were animists and seldom bathed because "they fear offending the water spirit." They were certainly dirty, but there was nothing offensive about them. Indeed, their manner was mild and friendly, and their hospitality lit with big smiles. The hospitality included the offer of opium—presented to us after the meal with the casualness you might be offered coffee.

Murray's exclamation—"Hold on there, mate! How're we going to trek for hours through a steamy jungle after smoking opium?!"—served as a "no, thanks" for all of us.

That night it rained. But "rained" doesn't quite describe the suddenness of the downpour, the large droplets crashing on the roof, that woke me from a deep sleep. I lay awake listening, and astonished I was dry and that not one drop of water had penetrated what I'd thought was pretty flimsy shelter. In the morning, we were told it was a monsoon.

We walked on and on, trekking up hill and down, passing waters steaming from the ground of natural hot springs. Billy carried the few necessary items for the three of us in a small backpack. Although I carried nothing more than my own weight, with the heat, the going was arduous. I mostly walked in the back of the line with our guide. He carried a backpack with all the provisions and first aid for our group, and although he was quick to show us a brook or spring safe to drink from, he never drank himself—and never sweated.

Nanao skipped along, never complaining about the heat, the distance we were walking, or the strange food we were given to eat. Walking by my side, she only stopped to exclaim at a flower or brightly colored butterfly.

Climbing a steep hill, we reached the Akha hill tribe. They were *really* right out of *National Geographic*, was my thought at the time. Never, other than in that venerable magazine, had I, until that very moment, ever encountered people for whom the word *primitive* was the apt description. The women wore a short costume of embroidered and woven cloth, leggings, and a tall elaborate headdress laden with beads and trinkets. They smoked long pipes they kept clenched in brown teeth. Most of the children were naked.

They showed us to a small straw hut where we could rest in shaded comfort. I swear everyone from the village came into that hut. Unabashed in a way I'd never seen before, they stared, laughed, murmured, and openly showed their wonderment at us. They busied themselves touching my hair and skin, practically breathing down my neck as they did. Some of the women grabbed my hair, examining it as if they were thinking of some practical use for it. Their curiosity was so genuine and uninhibited, I only wished I could speak their language and explain where I'd come from and why.

During this last trek was one of the few times Billy and I regretted not having a camera. Murray promised to send us the negatives of the photos he'd taken once he was home in Queensland, and he did.

Our journey almost over, the guide told us we'd walked about fifty kilometers, or thirty miles, in four days. Before ending our trek, as we came to the border with Burma, we stopped at several more communities.

The last group we visited were the Karen hill tribe.

Many people are curious to know, and many people have asked, "How did you manage to afford to travel so far and for such an extended time?"

We'd saved money for our trip, but we were not sitting on a pile of cash. Frugal doesn't sufficiently describe how we lived on the road for one year. I could count the times we stayed in a hotel. I remember every time we ate in a restaurant. Now down to our last cash, we bought the cheapest ticket we could find, and that cheap ticket took us from Bangkok to Hong Kong, then Seoul, before finally landing in Tokyo.

On the trek, I'd made the great mistake of borrowing Murray's copy of *Alive*. This harrowing tale of the survivors of a crash in the Andes ensured I'd be freaked out for all the takeoffs and landings. It was unnerving, as I could not get previously unfamiliar words like *fuselage* out of my head.

Our time on the road was at an end. We were again about to

go to a new and unknown place. Japan would not be a travel adventure, and if not a home, at least a place we knew we'd be staying for at least a year.

I had no idea what I would find, what I could expect. No doubt the words I lived by, *I'll deal with it when I get there*, helped me take this last, and, although I didn't know it then, final step to Japan.

14

Arriving at Haneda Airport in Tokyo, Billy changed our money, the fifty dollars we had left. Although crowded at midday, the silence in the airport enveloped me. It was the silence of not understanding any spoken word. The silence of not being able to read.

He had the directions to the dojo and got us to the train. I don't know how he confirmed it, but he said, "This is the one we take."

If we'd looked out of the right side of the train, we would've seen Mt. Fuji. If it had been a clear day. I don't remember the weather. But we didn't know to look anyway.

We had been on the road an entire year. And by that time, we'd developed senses that told us when we were safe, when it was okay to close our eyes, when it was all right to sleep. There was no sense that could tell us if the water was safe to drink, and that stayed a concern of mine for quite a while. But now, exhausted and vaguely aware we didn't have to keep our eyes on our dirty backpacks and our child, Billy and I fell in and out of sleep as the train sped us past Mt. Fuji.

. . .

"Call me Noda," a small man in a blue training suit said.

Mousy, he looked even more mouse-like as he surveyed us with what seemed to be suspicion. And maybe he was suspicious. We were originally supposed to have arrived at the dojo a full year earlier. Billy had written he'd be accompanied by his wife and daughter, but this man Noda didn't appear to expect us. He clearly didn't expect me.

"Sensei is not here," he said, and then, "Come here. I will show you where to put your things."

He led us up a wide freestanding staircase that seemed conspicuously misplaced, taking up vital space at one end of an office that was small and cluttered. There were maybe six or seven men in the office, all dressed in the same blue outfit Noda wore. A few lifted their heads briefly to acknowledge us, but mainly those heads remained bent, and intent. It wasn't a warm welcome, but I didn't take it personally. It looked like they were compelled to do whatever it was they were doing at those desks.

We could hear thuds and feel the ceiling shake with the weight of people running on the floor above us. After a particularly loud thud, Noda volunteered information. *"Kyoukataiso.* Heavy training class." I looked at him and wondered if he could participate in anything called "heavy training." A thud like the one we'd just heard would break him in half. He was as slight as Nanao, and in a few years she'd be as tall.

We were led down a narrow corridor that had nothing to do with the wide stairwell we'd climbed to get there. "The second-floor dojo," Noda said as we surveyed a large room covered with tatami mats.

"Ito-san," he said, addressing a very thin and pale person whose gender was not immediately apparent, "show them where to sleep." And then to Billy, "You come here." That was a surprise, that Billy and I would be separated. We'd had no idea what the living arrangement would be, but it'd never occurred to us that we wouldn't be living together. Judging from the clothes hanging around the room, we were in a women's communal sleeping room. Ito was a woman. She ventured a "Hello."

"Oh, you speak English?" I was excited.

Ito smiled.

We were pointed to two futons in the corner of the room, and Nanao, who hadn't said one word since we'd arrived at the dojo, said, "Mama, is this where we're going to sleep?" She only wanted to know so she could unpack her little blue knapsack. She wanted to put Bearie to bed, stack up her drawing pads and crayons, and take out her little box of things. That we were in a new country in a new place in a room that would soon be full of strangers (Noda had told us the *kyoukataiso* class was almost over) didn't bother her. She ran back and forth over the tatami exclaiming, "Mama, you've got to feel this!" and indeed walking barefoot across the tatami was as pleasant a sensation as my feet could ever want.

Although I didn't know anything about the inner workings of the dojo, it was obviously clean and safe. At the time, I didn't require much more. I was open to new experiences, and my little five-year-old girl was "open" to it, too. Throughout our trip, she'd never seemed to find anything odd or, what would've been more worrisome, scary. I took that to mean that if we were game, so was she. Feeling safe and protected, children can adjust to a lot. They trust their parents. I couldn't have asked for a child more adaptable than Nanao.

I didn't meet up with Billy again until dinner. Lining up to take trays on which food had already been placed, I said, "Where did they put you?"

"I don't actually know. It must be the room where the men sleep, but where that is I'm not sure."

I knew what he meant because I hadn't the slightest idea where we were either. In the hours before dinner, Nanao and I had explored and found the dojo was laid out like a puzzle in a maze. Large corridors led into small rooms; wide staircases ended in walls. A door that looked as if it'd been built for a dormouse opened on an enormous room. One staircase, shiny with black paint, ascended to a room it was somehow clear we shouldn't enter.

The building was so irregular it wasn't even clear what floor you were on. All the windows—and there seemed to be a disproportionate number of them on one side of the building—had opaque glass with patterns embedded in it. Rather than the soft diffused light of paper screens and lanterns that I imagined when I thought of Japan, there was only the relentlessly cold light of overhead fluorescent bars. The straw mat tatami were the only sign of a traditional interior in the entire building. I could overlook my disappointment for the lack of design aesthetic, feeling it was a tradeoff for having a place to stay. My requirements weren't just simple, they'd been stripped down to the bare basics: clean water and a safe place to sleep.

I'd later learn that there had been a fire at the original dojo a year before we arrived. This replacement building had gone up in prefabricated haste. Attention to aesthetics was of no concern to the builders. The structure was a place for shelter and practice, nothing more.

"Do you know where you'll be sleeping?" Billy asked.

"In that big room where Noda took us."

"Is it all right?" His face showed the same concern he'd shown on the bus in Afghanistan. We were now an itinerant small family, organically close. Physical proximity meant security. I couldn't imagine sleeping apart from Billy, not sleeping together as a family. This would be a new experience entirely. And whether I was ready for the experience or not, immediately upon entering the dojo I could tell it was a place where I didn't make the rules.

"Yeah, it's fine," I said. "Ito told us all the women stay there."

"Ito is a woman?"

Ito's hair was short, and style was obviously not a consideration when it was cut. She didn't wear earrings or makeup and wore the same blue athletic training suit Noda wore. With a flat front and back, she showed no single physical feature that distinguished her as a woman.

"Yeah, she's a woman," I said. "She's nice."

"Papa, Ito said she's going to take us to the *ofuro*. That's the bath," Nanao said.

"Why?"

Excited at the idea of a bath, Nanao couldn't wait. "Ito told us everybody takes a bath in the evening."

"What's that supposed to mean?" Billy said, turning to look at me.

"That you do what everybody does."

The walls and floor of the bath were tiled in black, gray, and green. A large window with opaque glass opened on a yard covered in weeds. Steam rose above the six women who sat in water that was obviously boiling hot, yellow, and smelly—Ito told me sulfur had been added to it. She didn't tell me how to bathe, but it was clear there was a method to it, and that I should imitate her every move.

Painfully thin, the bones in her back stuck out sharply, looking as though they must hurt the skin. All of the women in the bath had little more than nipples for breasts. A number of them had deep maroon blotches the size of Nanao's palm all over their bodies. They'd step out of the bath and take turns scrubbing each other with hard bristle brushes. For a fast, scary moment, I wondered what I was doing with my child in this torture chamber, where bony, abused-looking women boiled themselves in sulfur. Would they now sleep in coarse gowns?

Nanao tried to get in the bath, but it was much too hot, so she sat on a low stool washing herself from a small basin. Ito got out of the bath, and carefully and gently washed Nanao with a soft sponge from head to toe. Nanao's wide eyes were locked on the blotches on Ito's body. Ito faced me and said, "Treatment. Medicine." I'd soon learn they were all on fasts and the blotches were from suction therapy, cupping.

Ito's eyes, soft and dark, were incongruous above her hard, bony cheeks. Every time I said something, she looked at me as though just by looking she could reach in and come out with understanding. She smiled as if to say *it'll be all right* as I slowly lowered myself into the green-tiled bath, careful not to stir up its scalding contents. I'd never been in water so hot, but my body quickly adjusted. I'd only known bathing as a time to wash, to get clean, but this was therapeutic. A nightly bath. If this is a ritual, I thought, it is a restorative one and I embrace it.

"Kyaren-san," a co-bather said, after Ito introduced me.

"Kyaren-san," Ito repeated, as if correcting her.

"Karen," I said.

"Kyaren-san" I would hence be known.

I'd scrubbed off layers of skin, the hot water had melded my muscles with my bones, and it was deeply relaxing. Lying down that night in a room full of unknown women, I felt enveloped in comfort. The thick futon and clean cotton coverings felt as good next to the body as custom-made clothes.

The women talked the entire time in voices just above a whisper. It wouldn't have mattered if they'd shouted. The sounds were the same as those in the airport. Not understanding a word, it was no different than silence.

In the morning, I woke up to Ito saying, "Kyaren-san. Time." Hardly twenty-four hours had passed since we'd arrived in Japan, but already it was clear that adding -san when saying a person's name was not just polite, but required. Her voice was as soft and low as if she were whispering a secret—it hardly seemed waking me was her intention. It was five thirty. When we went out in the corridor to wash, trainees were already scrubbing the dojo floors. We followed Ito to breakfast, and no sooner had we sat down with our miso soup and brown rice than Ito had finished hers. Obviously not a meal we should linger over, I hurried Nanao and we took our bowls to the large stainless-steel sink where three trainees, their heads bent industriously, were doing the washing up.

Ito took me into the kitchen to introduce me to the women who were already preparing lunch. There was much nodding of heads but barely a word said. The woman who had tried to say my name the previous night in the bath smiled broadly, showing incredibly crooked, gold-capped teeth. One tooth, larger than all the rest, came out of the upper gum, which must have made closing her mouth a conscious action.

"You will work in the kitchen with the women," Noda said.

He'd come up behind us and stood at the door of the kitchen. As quiet as a mouse, as small as a mouse . . . all mouse ways described him. "We all do a work," he said. *As busy as mice* was my unspoken thought. It had never been made clear what I'd be doing at the dojo, but working in the kitchen suited me fine. Although it would be institutional cooking like at the school in Denmark, I wouldn't have anything like that responsibility.

By the end of the first week, my life had become a routine I'd never imagined possible. Regimented and scheduled, from early morning until late at night, everything we did was planned. There was no time that could be called leisure. I was fine with it. After having had essentially a year of leisure as we traveled—I fell in line, did as all the trainees did. Rising at five thirty, I joined the others cleaning the dojo. Then it was meditation time. That was followed by jogging to a small waterfall down a narrow unpaved road just behind the dojo. All day long there were classes: yoga, judo, karate, aikido. Afternoons we'd put out trays of needles for acupuncture and prepared mugwort for the moxibustion treatments the senior instructors gave to trainees. From the beginning, it was clear I was expected to join in, to participate and become part of the group. When not scheduled to work in the kitchen, I was supposed to be in a class. Nanao was supposed to be there right beside me.

During our year of travel, no day was like the one that had preceded it. I seldom knew when or where we'd sleep, what we'd eat, who we might encounter. Now, with no expectations of what living in the dojo would be like, the prospect of an ordered life with parameters didn't seem particularly onerous. Our clothes, worn out from travel, were soon replaced by the unofficial dojo uniform, the blue "training wear." And wearing what everyone else wore indicated we could be identified. We had our place in a group, in a country where nothing mattered more.

Like an orthodox religion with codes of eating and dress predetermined, everything was decided for us. It was easy. We left our lives as individuals at the entrance to the dojo and transformed on the spot, without a word being spoken, into the disciples of Master Jun Yoshida. We were taken under Yoshida-sensei's all-encompassing wing—a wing with an eagle's span. His philosophy of living and personal development covered all aspects of our daily lives. Absolute obedience was a given.

"Sensei will return today maybe," Noda said about two weeks after we arrived.

We were in the little room that could've been called the foreigners' room because the six foreigners at the dojo were the only ones who ever went there. Except for Noda. He was in charge of us, kind of. Kind of, because everything about him was timid, and I sensed he was intimidated just by our size. But Noda clearly enjoyed his measure of control and power. When the small group of foreigners met every day at the appointed hour, three o'clock, he would make some pronouncement, always spoken like a warning: "Come to all classes." "No eating in the room." "Do not use the car if not the business of the dojo." "We meet at three o'clock with promptness."

It was Noda's business to see that we knew where to be when, and what rules to follow. That must have been as hard for him as it was for us, because although some rules were spelled out, most weren't. However, it was clear that transgressions would not be tolerated. It was also, apparently, Noda's personal responsibility that we learn Japanese, and during those daily three o'clock meetings, he taught us however he could. He didn't have a textbook, but came to every class with copious notes and a tattered Japanese-English dictionary. He seemed to be under severe stress—not because of us but because of his relationship with his sensei.

"Wake up! Everyone to the third-floor dojo. *Kyoukataiso!*"

The voice calling out was not Ito's, who gently plied me out of sleep every morning saying, "Kyaren-san. Time."

Standing at the dormitory door, the male instructor yelled, "Everyone up! Now!" I could hear him repeat his message in the men's dormitory. There was command in the voice, but also appeal.

"Sensei has returned," Ito said. In the same manner she dispatched her food, not a thing to pay more attention to than necessary, in seconds she was out of her sleeping robe and standing before me dressed. "We must go quickly."

It was midnight. Although I already knew not to question anything, I was surprised by this late-night order.

"What about Nanao?" I asked. Would they really demand I wake a five-year-old child in the middle of the night for exercise, for *kyoukataiso*?

"You must bring her. All people must go."

Yoshida-sensei and I were the same height, 170 cm or five feet, seven inches, and in Japan, that was singularly tall. At any height, he was an imposing figure who moved no other muscles in his body than the ones required for a particular action, and every action appeared to be one of exquisite precision and impressive control. He never gestured, and I swear his eyes blinked less than the average person's. In his presence, other people were mere twitching souls, unconscious tics and mannerisms governing their every breath. When Yoshida-sensei spoke, his voice started in a deep well, and the wooden floors and tatami mats of the dojo absorbed and added tone and depth. When angry, the voice boomed.

Every day for at least an hour, or until he felt like stopping, we were put through his "hard exercise" class. We ran, jumped, hopped, climbed ropes. Fasting women had to carry healthy men the length of the dojo floor on their backs. *Kyoukataiso*, while a strengthening exercise, seemed to have no other lofty purpose than to move the body to complete physical exertion. That midnight, sensei taught us the class usually taught at noon, without modification.

Although we could not understand even one sentence, we were required to attend Yoshida-sensei's lectures, held in the evenings three times a week. Noda, small and fidgeting, instructed to do simultaneous translation, desperately clawed for words to convey sensei's message: *Through the practice of yoga, breathing exercises, meditation, natural foods, and mastery of martial arts and understanding of Zen, one can attain perfect health and spiritual equilibrium.* Or something like that. Noda, fearing to miss one word of this message, was equally fearful his small voice wasn't small enough, and he might be disturbing sensei's talk.

During these lectures, we were told of Yoshida-sensei's exploits as a spy in Manchuria during the war. We learned of his mastery of Budō, some of these martial arts were familiar to us and some not. Striding around in his dark *hakama*—the traditional Japanese garment resembling long culottes, the wide legs made broad arcs as he threw someone in a demonstration of aikido. Although I was skeptical, it was possible to believe this man had, ninja-like, crossed borders, escaped custody, dispatched enemies.

Yoshida-sensei was an attractive man. His dark hair was thick and combed straight back, revealing a sculpted brow that shaded steady ink-black eyes. He had the grace and posture of a dancer, the gait of a samurai. He saw no man as his equal, and certainly no woman could ever be. Much later, when I could understand more than they were aware, I heard the dojo women talking among themselves about sensei's exploits with the ones who were not so thin and bony.

Yoshida-sensei had developed his own form of yoga, and we practiced that every day along with traditional yoga. A wide variety of martial arts were taught, and we'd have regular demonstrations by Bushido masters showing their skill in karate, judo, *Shorinji Kempo*, aikido, *naginata*, *iaido*, and Tae Kwon Do.

Billy threw himself into all this training wholeheartedly. On several occasions, he went to do *sesshin* (intensive meditation) at Ryutaku-ji, the temple of the Rinzai sect of Buddhism just a short walk from the dojo. I saw him regularly, but sometimes regular just meant passing him in the corridors like he was any other trainee. Those early months at the dojo we slept in dormitories, so our chance to communicate was usually in the dining room (you didn't dare talk in class) where we could exchange a few quick words.

There was no one at the dojo I could call a friend and I just got used to being solitary. Although we were all supposed to attend classes when we weren't working, I found it was possible to skip them. I didn't want to do martial arts, and when I wasn't scheduled to be in the kitchen, I'd find a corner in the dojo's maze to hide and read. But no corner in the maze was secure when sensei taught his exercise class. Anyone's absence was conspicuous, and there was never an acceptable excuse. Before the class began, the teachers-in-training, acting on Noda's orders, scoured the dojo to make sure all able bodies were present. In Yoshida-sensei's estimation, there was no such thing as a dis-abled body.

. . .

At the end of every month, there was a celebration for the people who'd had a birthday. The low tables from the first-floor dining room were passed up hand-to-hand to the third-floor dojo. Also passed up was the dinner—fifty plates with an identical food layout. Sitting with our legs bent at the knees and tucked neatly under our behinds, the formal *seiza* position, we waited for sensei to begin the festivities, which he did by handing out small birthday gifts.

"Yamada!" sensei called out one month. He never used the honorific. Then again, "Yamada!"

When no one came forward, the teacher to sensei's right, Mihara, leaned over and, in a voice not heard by anyone else, reminded sensei who Yamada was. Yamada had been in a really bad car accident. He'd arrived at the dojo several months earlier, carried out of the taxi on the back of his elder sister. Similarly, he was carried into the dining room three times a day by two trainees who propped him against the wall at the back of the room. His sister would leave her work in the kitchen to go feed him with a spoon. A sturdy woman whose body appeared to compensate for her brother's, she was the only woman in the kitchen who could lift by herself the giant pressure cookers, valves hissing, and heavy with brown rice.

Unlike Noda, who was more like Yoshida-sensei's flunky, Mihara was his right hand. And we'd heard he was as skilled in the martial arts as sensei. Now sensei ignored him, and bellowed from deep within the well: "YAMADA!"

Yamada then crawled across the long dojo to the place where sensei sat. No one moved or spoke the ten minutes it took him to do it. At first I thought it was cruel to have Yamada crawl that entire way, and wondered why someone didn't just take the present to him. But that thought gave way to thinking, *This is perseverance.* And patience, which we were all required to demonstrate. Sensei handed him his present with no more fanfare than the others had received, and in the silence of the dojo we could hear Yamada say, "*Arigato gozaimasu.*" Thank you.

. . .

The total population of the dojo might have been about sixty. The trainees, I'd learn, might stay a week or a month. Trainees were men and women, but all the instructors were men. I'd guess we were all in the same thirty-years-old age range. Sensei, then about fifty, would have been the oldest person at the dojo. Billy and I were the only couple, but Nanao was not the only child. Ito's daughter, Kyoko, also lived there.

Kyoko, though eleven, was not bigger than Nanao, then just six. She had a congenital condition that affected her muscles— when she walked she dragged her legs. Ito had come to the dojo because of Kyoko. It was a penance. During *kyoukataiso*, sensei yelled at her, slapped and pushed her. It was clear he thought anything wrong with the children was the fault of the mothers: they were weak, careless, irresolute. Even without under- standing what he said, I disliked that his tone was harsh and dismissive when he spoke to her. I never saw her complain and couldn't understand that she wasn't just resigned, but accepting.

At first, we viewed Yoshida-sensei's behavior as unusual, but after a while we too accepted, to some degree, what everyone accepted. Following the rules as laid out by someone else had become simply a new and different experience. It was embraced. We were seldom outside the dojo walls, and within the walls the dojo was a world unto itself. It felt good to be just another member of the group. We'd stood out and been pointed and stared at for most of our journey, and now in our characterless blue athletic suits, a variation on the uniform theme, we had the illusion we fit in and were like everyone else.

Although Nanao was permitted to stay in the women's room with me, Kyoko had to stay in the children's room whether there were other children at the dojo or not. Telling me Kyoko said she was *samishii* and explaining that meant lonely, Nanao began to sleep in the children's room with her. Kyoko was her one and only playmate, and I liked that she was so caring. When Kyoko received her acupuncture treatments from Yoshida-sensei or Mihara, Nanao would remain in the treatment room, separating the bent needles from the rest as she'd been taught. Other American children might play by taking care of their dolls and stuffed animals with make-believe medicine, but she told me Bearie was "getting a treatment" the day I went into the women's room and saw her bear on my futon with bent needles sticking out of its wooly fur.

One day, staying behind in the dojo after *kyoukataiso*, I doubled a length of rope, giving one end to Nanao for Double Dutch. We turned for a minute until we got the rhythm, and then I called Kyoko over and put the rope in her hands. Bending to take some inches off my height, I jumped in, hopping from foot to foot in my favorite childhood game.

"Oh. What is this?" Yoshida-sensei had come back up to the dojo and his deep voice, without the warning of footsteps, caught us by surprise. "This jumping?"

"Double Dutch. A girls' game we play in America," I said, speaking to him directly for the first time.

Kyoko had dropped the rope ends at her feet. I picked them up and Nanao and I turned. Sensei stood watching the ropes and, without preparation, jumped in. He and his *hakama* were tangled at once—and this ninja, caught in a child's game, laughed heartily.

And this was the enduring paradox, because on the other side of his hearty laugh and broad smile was a scowl, dark with a wrath that sent an unmistakable message of fear.

While Billy became adept at aikido, I became adept at avoiding classes. I didn't mind being at the dojo, but it had never been my intention to practice martial arts, and I'd never been a fan of meditation. I made up my mind I'd do yoga, and work in the kitchen. That's it.

Since the foreigners were only in the gaijin room (room for

foreigners) from three to four in the afternoon, it was free the rest of the time and I used it as a hideout. But my cover was blown one day when we'd been at the dojo about three months and Noda came running into the room, winded, telling me, "Get ready!"

Ready for what?

I was told to change (into what?) and bring some things (for what?) and that I, and Cathy, the other foreign woman at the dojo, would be going out of town with Yoshida-sensei (for how long?). And, oh yes, I must bring Nanao. Having not been out of the town yet, and almost never out of the dojo, I welcomed this surprise. I was hopeful I might get to see something more of Japan. I saw Billy just long enough to tell him we'd be leaving with sensei. I got a bag ready and was in his car on our way out of town, with Mihara driving, within minutes.

In the car, we learned we were headed to the north, the Japanese Alps, where sensei would present lectures and demonstrations of his yoga technique. Cathy and I were not told why we'd been singled out to go on this trip, but I sensed he wanted to show us another side of Japan, treat us to a new experience. I couldn't even imagine what life in Japan was like outside the dojo, but whatever his reason for taking us on this trip, I was excited.

The first night we stayed in the city of Matsumoto in a *ryokan*, a traditional Japanese inn. We were ushered into our room by a kimono-clad woman, where another woman, also in kimono, sat waiting for us, on her knees. She served us tea. We changed into *yukata*, a cotton kimono, and there was a child-sized one for Nanao. Following her to the bath, taking small steps in our *zori* (thong sandals), we went down a pebbled path, through a garden of bamboo and pine, and over a little bridge. I was now accustomed to the *ofuro*, but this bath, part inside and part outside, part stone and part wood, was special. Immersing myself in water heated to perfection, with the soothing scent of hinoki (Japanese cypress), I could only think,

At last, I am in the Japan I've read about, seen in books, dreamed about.

Back in the room that Cathy and I were sharing, we were served a meal that was the very essence of *washoku*, Japanese cuisine. The dishes had maple and ginkgo leaf motifs, and the food served on them was astonishingly beautiful, and reflected the season. There was not a lot of anything, but each morsel we put in our mouths was a new and satisfying taste sensation.

Every place we went, everyone seemed to know Yoshida-sensei, and he was treated like a king—or, more aptly, a *daimyo* (Japanese feudal lord). And it was no different the second night we stayed at Mihara's home. His family was obviously not well-off, but the table was covered from end to end with food. There may have been twenty different dishes, all prepared by Mihara's mother, and all so prettily arranged I wanted to preserve rather than eat them. Mihara's parents and grandparents were there, and his sister, and they barely ate. After the meal, a real feast, they laid out a pristine futon in what was no doubt the best room in their small house. It was my first experience of welcome in a Japanese home and I was overwhelmed, especially that poor people could show such munificence.

What a contrast the whole experience was to dojo life, where the atmosphere wasn't just austere, but strained, and the general facial expression dour, almost grim. Mihara's mother's warm smile warmed your inner being. Bowing and saying *"Arigato gozaimashita"* when we left couldn't possibly convey the gratitude I felt.

A month after our trip to the north, I was told Yoshida-sensei was sending me, with Nanao, to Korea. As before, I wasn't given much information, just that a friend and colleague, Park In Lee, was opening his own dojo in Daegu, Korea. Yoshida-sensei was "lending" me to teach modern dance classes as a kind of opening bonus attraction.

Soon after we'd arrived at the dojo, Noda had asked me point-blank, "What can you do?" In addition to cooking, I said I knew modern dance. For all the fact that it was strict, the dojo also had an eclectic side, so it wasn't completely out of the ordinary when this little interview ended with Noda telling me, "You will teach classes." I taught a few modern dance classes on a few occasions. Only the trainee women joined the class, and I remember trying to tell them in elementary Japanese how I'd been inspired by Yuriko Kimura and Takako Asakawa, two of my favorite dancers in the Martha Graham company. I couldn't believe these countrywomen, extraordinary dancers, weren't well-known names in Japan.

I had no idea where Daegu was. When I learned I'd be taking an overnight ferry from Shimonoseki to Busan to get there, I was less than thrilled. Next to flying, boats are my least favorite form of transportation. I was nauseated the entire voyage, and could only just keep my eye on Nanao, who ran up and down and all over the place. Just looking at her added to my seasickness.

As an emissary of Yoshida-sensei, arriving in Daegu, I was greeted like a dignitary. Nanao and I stayed in the home of Master Lee, a martial artist on the level of Yoshida-sensei, and his wife Madame Lee, a yoga teacher. We stayed for two weeks, and teaching just two dance classes a day gave me a lot of time to wander around the town sampling the food in small shops and stalls that lined the streets. I loved the Korean food, and ate kimchi whenever it was served, which meant starting at breakfast, and with every meal. But I could not swallow a cup of thick sugary tea I was served with a raw egg in it.

Korea was evidently much poorer than Japan, but people were so generous. Nanao and I were given *hanbok*, the Korean national dress, and all the accessories that go with it. Since South Korea is so close to Japan, I thought Koreans might be similar, and was pleasantly surprised the difference was so great. They were open, warm, quick to laugh, and even the women could be boisterous.

One evening, we went with Park In Lee and his wife to the temple of a Buddhist priest to pay Yoshida-sensei's respects and give a gift sensei had me carry from Japan. The priest was very old, easily in his nineties, and being presented to him was a solemn experience. While we sat with him, he summoned a monk to bring him paper, an inkstone, and brushes. As we watched, he did an ink painting of birds and cherry blossoms for Nanao, writing her name along the side in hangul, Korean characters. For me he did a calligraphy of my name—Ka (flower) Ren (lotus)—writing the bold characters in *reisho*, the ancient clerical script. Madame Lee later had them mounted on silk scrolls. Nanao and I treasure them still.

Returning to the Lees' home in a taxi, Madame Lee began to hum "Arirang," which is effectively the Korean anthem. Master Lee and the taxi driver soon joined in, and they all three began to sing. It's a beautifully simple and melodic song, and when I first heard it at her home, she taught me the words, so I sang along with them the parts I knew. By the time we reached their house, our solemn experience with the venerable Buddhist priest was way behind us. The sounds from the taxi were like a party on wheels. We said goodbye and thanked the driver as though the party had been at his home.

Returning to the dojo, it was clear I was having my best experiences when I was away from it. In that strict environment, where so much was limited and proscribed, I'd almost forgotten there was still gaiety in the world, still beauty, still liberty. Even fun. Those things didn't exist in dojo life.

15

Contradiction epitomized dojo life. There was the mind-numbing daily routine of knowing where I was supposed to be every minute of the day, while at the same time not knowing if I'd be told to pack and leave town, or leave the country.

Twice we'd been given space to live in as a family. Once a small room in the dojo, and later three large prefab rooms that had been built as an annex on the north side of the building. And twice, too, we'd been ordered to move, on the spur of the moment, and told sensei wanted us back in the common women's and men's rooms, that he didn't want to make exceptions of us, and that the simple life of trainees could not be one concerned with comfort.

Our living arrangements were capricious to the point I thought it might depend on sensei's mood on a particular day. While I could adjust to the changing circumstances, increasingly I found the dojo wasn't so much unpredictable as inconsistent. There's a difference. And that difference made it an unstable place to be. Yoshida-sensei's erratic behavior only added to the instability. We'd gone from living in a car for a year to living for almost the same time like students in a dorm. I was sick of this "simple life" and sick of the dojo's ever-changing trainee population. I wasn't a trainee. I didn't want anyone telling me where and when I should sleep, what to eat, when to exercise, and if and when I could have sex with my husband.

Now that I was back in the women's room, Billy was always asking me if everything was all right. He wanted to know if anyone bothered us. Although it must have been a relief for him that we were living in a safe place, he hadn't quite let that sink in. He always seemed a little worried, just uncomfortable enough to never relax. A big part of that is his personality, but the other part was he clearly recognized the dojo was not a suitable place for us to live.

Trainees were supposed to wash up and leave the dining area immediately after meals, but this day as we sat in the dining room, Billy looked around uneasily to see if Noda, who sneaked about on slippered feet, was around. Now, I didn't think twice about breaking the rules. What could they do? Nobody was going to put us in jail or hurt us.

"Yeah, we're doing fine," I told him. "Nanao's doing great. Can you believe how fast she's learning Japanese?"

"Do you think she likes doing all that stuff sensei tells her?"

"Like? She loves it." And she did. Naturally agile and with a child's pluckiness, Nanao could do the exercises better than many of the adults.

"We're going to have to get her in some kind of school soon," Billy said.

"Yeah. We'll take care of it. There's plenty of time. We're not on the road anymore."

No doubt there are parents who'd be concerned their child was missing school, but Nanao would've been in kindergarten. And I felt, especially during our time on the road, she was learning lessons she might not ever learn in school. I was convinced her experience of traveling would stay with her, and even with her young eyes she'd see that people are basically alike—not in our cultures, surely, but in our humanity. And I hoped she would see the world as I did, and find, as I had, that most people are kind and helpful and that the world we call Earth is a wonderful place full of endless lessons.

We'd been in India in April, which is when the school year starts in Japan. We waited until September and enrolled her in the local kindergarten thinking the stress-free and plenty-of-playtime environment would be the best way for her to begin her education in Japan. And by that time, she was already functional in Japanese, and could read the children's books Ito gave her.

Nanao joined in all the dojo activities and nothing seemed to be surprising or unnatural to her. She sat in meditation, ate brown rice and seaweed every day, and did yoga. Yoshida-sensei favored her and always chose her to demonstrate exercises for the other children. In *kyoukataiso*, his voice boomed "Nanao!" and she'd scamper to his side and do as she was told, run across the dojo floor or climb a rope as well as a monkey. Sensei was openly proud that Nanao already had a handle on Japanese. She was the perfect example of the core of his teaching: A strong flexible body in harmony with a calm mind could accomplish any goal and achieve spiritual equilibrium.

During our travels, I'd carried a notebook of lessons I made up for her and was still teaching her to read and write. Now she could write Japanese and read Kyoko's books, and she had absorbed Japanese effortlessly. Without a doubt, Nanao's Japanese was the best of all the foreigners' at the dojo. There were four foreign men, all with bald heads, living at the dojo by the time we arrived. A Dutchman and three Americans who, after a year of study, had only made elementary progress with Japanese. Several times Yoshida-sensei publicly (there was no private anything at the dojo) berated Noda—doing it in Japanese for the Japanese, and in English for us, saying it was Noda's fault we weren't all fluent.

. . .

One cold, rainy day it had taken me half an hour to warm up the foreigners' room with the small stove. Trainees weren't permitted to use heaters, but it didn't look like the gaijin were going to survive the winter without one. After the bald-headed guys had gotten sick one after the other, taking turns with fevers, Noda got permission to put a heater in the room, telling Mihara "foreigners are weak against cold."

"Are you coming to judo?" Billy asked me.

"No." I was so obviously comfortable no one could have imagined I was going to leave that room and my book to jump barefoot around a cold dojo. I was reading Tanizaki's *The Makioka Sisters* and enjoying their prewar Japan and its depiction of traditional life more than the one I was living in.

"Just be careful Noda doesn't see you," Billy cautioned.

He didn't have to see me, but I knew he knew what I was doing. I was spending all my time in the gaijin room. Although I continued to help in the kitchen, I'd lost interest in the classes, and I went to the room to read and write. I'd also taken to making myself tea and toast in there. I found an old hot plate in a room full of discarded dishes, teapots, and sake cups. On the days I'd forego the usual breakfast *ojiya*, brown rice gruel cooked with miso and leftover vegetables, after cleaning up in the kitchen, I'd go in the room for a ten o'clock brunch. Billy told me he'd caught the aroma of hot buttered toast wafting up to the dojo floor just when they were in the middle of an exercise.

I knew the other gaijin were on to me—the bald guys, and Cathy. She kept saying she was leaving to return to her commune, though I was sure her commune buddies would never see her again. Cathy was enamored with Japan and all things Japanese. If she could snare a Japanese husband, her life would be perfection. None of them ever said anything, but they seemed to regard me with quiet disdain. I was not following dojo rules, or the macrobiotic way.

. . .

"How do you know Japanese cooking?" Ito asked me one day.

After I'd been in the dojo six months, she began to talk. We often stood side by side in the dojo kitchen, a place as makeshift as a camp kitchen set up by kids. I was aware Ito watched me cut vegetables to see if I knew *sengiri* and *mijingiri*, thin slicing and mincing. I'd hear her knife stop hitting the cutting board and know those dark eyes were turned on me. I never looked up. The other women would chime in, their heads nodding in approval, "*Jozu desu ne*"—"She does it well."

"Billy taught me," I said in minimal Japanese. I listened closely as the kitchen women chattered though seldom attempted to join in. A long time had passed since I'd had a conversation in English with a woman friend. I was learning to live without that, but I would have welcomed it. It was impossible to have an intelligent conversation with Cathy. She was fanatically macrobiotic, and any talk with her was peppered with unsought advice: "This is good for your lungs . . . this will cleanse the kidneys . . . that will putrefy in your intestines."

Aside from Billy, those kitchen women were the only adults I spoke with. The bald-headed guys acted as if they'd taken a vow of silence, giving me beneficent smiles when we passed in the corridors. At meals, they chose to sit with the Japanese, chewing their brown rice with annoying intent. With pale shaven heads, they walked around in a cloak of Zen mystery and Buddhist pretensions. I didn't think of them as impostors, but they were so thoroughly devoid of personality I had no interest in them and didn't mind being ignored.

"Oh, can Bill-san cook?"

"Yes, Ito-san. He can cook very well." *You could find out for yourself if you would allow the men in the kitchen, because those bald-headed guys can cook, too.*

Billy originally thought he'd be cooking at the dojo, but almost as soon as we arrived, sensei issued an edict saying no men could be in the kitchen. They were to do martial arts, yoga, and meditation exclusively. And study Japanese. Although macrobiotic cooking was supposed to be one of the "healing arts," sensei strictly forbade the men to do it. Noda was the only man who ever came in the kitchen. Although he spoke English, I seldom talked to him. I thought of him as merely an instrument of sensei. And the longer we were at the dojo, the more I thought of him as that relative of the mouse, the rat. He often watched me. He'd come in the kitchen and, with some pretense of looking around or giving orders to the other women, come over to the pot I was stirring, and with distaste evident through the screen of his face, he'd say, "Hmm. I don't think this is Japanese taste."

Noda spoke of what he didn't like about "the West" as if it were a place the size of Tokyo. He seemed to despise all foreigners, and the rare times he smiled was when he quipped about our size, the amounts we ate, and our poor Japanese. This latter was a matter of personal concern and frustration for him because our failure was his failure. Sensei eventually gave up on Noda teaching Japanese and had him arrange for the men to go to Tokyo to study.

I'm sure it never occurred to sensei to send the women, meaning Cathy and me. We had to stay in the kitchen, and Cathy, an excellent cook who wore an apron like a badge, had no interest in learning Japanese because she believed she was fluent. Several times she told me about her technique for "language acquisition," although all she ever spoke was English with a Japanese word thrown in now and again. Mainly she giggled, expertly hiding her large yellow teeth behind her blue-veined hand.

That Yoshida-sensei was despotic, first, last, and always, became his most salient characteristic. He was a dictator above all else. As long as his rule was followed, there weren't any problems. When that rule was tested, there were.

Yoshida-sensei usually had his meals brought to him on trays in his rooms, but on occasion he would surprise everyone and sit among the trainees in the dining room. One evening when he had so honored us with his presence, one of the men in training to become a teacher went to sensei's table to pour his tea. I heard afterward his mistake had been to not sit in the formal *seiza* position as he did it.

As swiftly as a samurai drawing a sword to detach a head, sensei threw the cup of hot tea in the errant teacher's face. The teacher-in-training bowed and made apologies. The following day, when he came in the kitchen for a second helping of rice, I could see one side of his face was still red. I wanted to say something, but there was nothing to say. He totally accepted the mishap as his fault.

Yoshida-sensei was increasingly violent, becoming furious during *kyoukataiso* when someone didn't execute an exercise properly. Often now we'd hear the loud "Whack!" of his bamboo stick as it landed across someone's body. Although sensei was usually indulgent with the children, these days they were crying more because of his disciplining. Strict to a fault, his behavior with the general dojo population was now pathological.

"You don't think he'd hit Nanao, do you?" I said to Billy when he returned from Tokyo one weekend.

I already had any number of plans for what I would do if he did, and fantasized what I would do if he even hit Billy. Although Billy was now quite skilled in judo and aikido, I saw myself jumping in the fray to help. I didn't have to think about what I'd do if he were to hit me, knowing I'd instinctively protect myself. The day wouldn't come when I'd be on my knees before him asking for his forgiveness for some unintended offense.

Billy often spoken of Yoshida-sensei as a "charismatic character" and was without a doubt impressed by him. A true acolyte, he attended classes reliably, and applied himself to learning Japanese. But he wasn't blind and knew I was just putting up with being there, sticking it out so he could fulfill his one-year commitment.

Ever since Billy went to the language school in Tokyo, I was taking my futon to the gaijin room. Noda knew but never said anything—I guess he thought it was all right to have conjugal visits since the dojo wasn't supposed to be a prison. But this Friday night when Billy returned, instead of making love like any normal couple would do after being separated, we lay in the narrow futon drawing up contingency plans in case Yoshida-sensei hit one of us.

"I'll grab him and jump out of the window with him," Billy said, completely serious.

"Billy, don't be nuts."

"It'd be more nuts to try to fight the dude." We both had to laugh as our "contingency plans" went on into the night getting funnier and funnier—and more and more desperate.

It was time to leave.

And this incident sealed it.

It was Christmas and sensei said all the foreigners should prepare a special meal. There were now two Europeans and four Americans—us, Cathy from the Midwest, and Paul, a baldhead from the South. We had different ideas of what constituted holiday food, but for the first time since we'd all been living in the dojo, we worked together good-humoredly, cooperating to pull it off. We'd just finished the breakfast cleanup when Noda came in the kitchen with three trainees behind him carrying the provisions we'd asked for.

"These are the things for the grand party," he said. "They were sent down from Tokyo. There will be many guests. You must prepare for one hundred."

Christmas isn't a holiday in Japan, but still, after cooking together for two days, we were in a festive mood and thought the meal we'd created was a proper holiday feast. The aroma of pumpkin pies with clove and nutmeg and stuffing with sage and thyme that now permeated the dojo, replacing the usual smells of brown rice and broth made from kelp and dried fish shavings, had the trainees waiting in anticipation and uncharacteristic excitement in the large third-floor dojo.

I was bold enough to tell Noda, "We dance at parties in America," and he'd arranged for music to be played since, he said, "This will be a foreign party." And dancing after the meal would be in order because there was no chance of anyone saying they were "stuffed." All the plates were prepared beforehand with the same modest amounts for everyone and no seconds.

When Yoshida-sensei stood up after the meal and said simply, and loudly, "Dance!" in seconds the dojo was a sea of blue-training-suit-clad bodies moving to *The Best of Sam & Dave*.

All of a sudden, in the middle of "Hold On, I'm Comin'," there was a crashing sound, and Yoshida-sensei started his bellowing.

I looked around and saw a teacher-trainee with blood dripping down his face. Next to him lay a broken sake bottle, its contents spilled on the tatami floor. No one moved, no one dared, as sensei ranted on for what seemed like an eternity. Once again, the trainee sat before him, on his knees, as the blood dripped freely down his bent, contrite head.

Park In Lee, the Korean martial artist I'd stayed with in Daegu, was a guest. Sitting in a place of honor next to sensei, he tried his best to calm him. As soft-spoken and humble as sensei was brash, Yoshida-sensei didn't listen as Master Lee tried to reason with him. At one point, sensei brushed him off so brusquely I thought he might attack him too—and imagined the specter of those two martial artists in battle at a party.

Only after sensei was well bellowed out did he stop ranting.

He then stood up and again exhorted us to "Dance!"

Although any joy I felt dancing was gone now, we danced. We were obedient. Yoshida-sensei was in full control. It wasn't fear that kept us all dancing. Having given up all autonomy, we wouldn't have known what else to do.

. . .

I never found out what the teacher-trainee had done.

It didn't matter. What regard I had for sensei was wiped out after that evening. He was out of control and I didn't trust him. I didn't fear him, but I no longer wanted to be any part of his tyranny. Our year was about up anyway. We were free to leave, but leaving was no simple matter. We'd already learned that this business of "face" in Japan was very important, and if it appeared we were leaving because we were dissatisfied, or were in some way critical of the sensei, it would have been a great affront. We had no points to make. We didn't have to save anyone at the dojo; they were as free to leave as we were. Although, for the Japanese trainees and teachers, their relationship to sensei could not be so easily terminated.

Yoshida-sensei was charismatic all right, but it occurred to me that might be a distinguishing feature of a lot of maniacs. The sake bottle incident confirmed it, but it'd always been an unsettling fact that he was practically licensed to hit, beat, slap, or kick the trainees and instructors. He would never change. Arrogant in the extreme, he must have been convinced if not of the rightness of his behavior, at least his right to it.

Even without the events of the Christmas party, that one-year commitment started to drag, and both Billy and I longed for real freedom and simple pleasures that simply didn't exist in dojo life. The dojo wasn't a cult, and we weren't forced or coerced into doing anything. Still, we had no independence and our movements were so proscribed, the last thing we thought we had was freedom—real or otherwise.

"We've got to get out of here," I told Billy the day after the Christmas party. And I didn't mean eventually.

We didn't know anyone in Japan, and we had no contacts and not the slightest idea where we would or could go if we left the dojo. As a practical matter, we figured we'd better get married, as it would give me spouse visa status. We'd started scheming right after the Christmas incident, but months went by before we managed to get away long enough to go to Tokyo, where we quietly married on May 21, 1976.

We set aside time to come up with a plan of what to do once we left the dojo. "Planning for the future" sounded like the title of an article for a family magazine, not something for us to do, certainly not anything we'd ever done. Just thinking about the future was like throwing a ball in a big park—you could throw it anywhere. Probably when other couples were thinking about homeownership and mortgages, investments and insurance, we were camping out on the outskirts of Kabul or Katmandu.

But our hopes for the future did include having another child.

Nanao had been born just before my twenty-fourth birthday. When I tried to get pregnant a second time, I was in my early thirties. I was not exactly old, but it was no easy thing trying to conceive. Before Billy and I started out on the overland journey, while we were in London I'd been examined by a Harley Street specialist who told me I had a cyst on my ovary, and that I would definitely not become pregnant unless I had it surgically removed. The scolding manner and harsh tone in which he told me—*was I personally responsible for an ovarian cyst?*—had the effect of my neither believing nor trusting him.

I waited until we reached India so I could see an Ayurvedic doctor, and I was sure I was in good hands when I was told this physician also administered to Indira Gandhi. The doctor's amiable manner and almost melodic mention of "imbalance" left me feeling confident to take the powders he dispensed. At the dojo, I continued to take the Ayurvedic powders, the dried bark of the banyan tree. I followed a strict macrobiotic diet—which dictated no sugar, no meat, and no refined or spicy foods. And I was in a dietary quandary, as Ayurveda recommends consuming dairy products, and macrobiotics rule out dairy of any kind. I also had regular acupuncture treatments that were supposed to stimulate fertility, and they were not having any effect. Uncharacteristically, I went to see an obstetrician—who instructed me to take my daily basal body temperature, which I did, to the point of distraction, and tears.

Yes, I wanted to have another child, but the dojo was the last place I wanted to do that.

"I'm ready to get out of the dojo, but I'm not exactly ready to leave Japan," Billy said. "We've only glimpsed this country."

He was right. Although we hadn't arrived in Japan with the expectation that we might hear the sound of "one hand clapping," we knew there was more. But more of what, we weren't at all sure. I had become fond of the area where the dojo was located. Surrounded by rice paddies, I was sure the view of Mt. Fuji was unrivaled. I wondered if we'd find another place in Japan as beautiful. If we stayed in Japan, we both wanted to remain in the region of Shizuoka.

"Let's stay a little longer," Billy said.

And with that, we agreed we'd stay in Japan. A little longer.

Billy told Yoshida-sensei we were going back to America for a few months and that we would be coming back to Japan. By lying and saying we were first going back to the U.S., the break with the dojo would be clean. This move was purely to save sensei's face. We hadn't even discussed returning to the United States as one of our options. We didn't have a home there.

We could tell Yoshida-sensei was behind Noda telling Billy, "There are more foreigners coming to Japan with each day. More will come to the dojo. You will be able to teach. Your Japanese has become good, you would be able to do translation for the foreign people."

I had to wait until after Noda left the room for Billy to translate for me all he'd said to him, but I could tell Billy had handled it skillfully when he ended the conversation with the noncommittal "*Chotto* . . ."—"It's just that . . ." In the Japanese language, explanations are often not necessary. Discussing matters deemed personal can be ended with "*Chotto*…," and you are not expected to say more. It's considered rude to pry. This is part of the beauty of the culture.

Noda had been at the dojo longer than anyone else. A true devotee of the Yoshida Yoga Dojo, he participated in all the exercises, but he never appeared to benefit from them or from the health foods. Thin and pale, his back curled, he was hardly the dojo poster boy. He couldn't get through the day without napping, which he was doing when we went to say goodbye.

Cathy came out of the kitchen just long enough to beg me to mail a package to Iowa once we were "stateside." I took it, deciding I'd rather pay the postage from Japan than trust her with the secret that we weren't going to the States.

Ito-san bowed many times, and though I knew she was sorry to see us go, she appeared to be without sentimentality, simply accepting this necessary parting. She'd told me her husband had walked out of the door one day, abandoning her and Kyoko, and I wondered if she'd seen him to the door, bowing with this same detachment. Nanao wrapped her arms around Kyoko, who, after first bowing, let her thin arms hug Nanao around the waist.

Going to sensei's room to say a formal goodbye, I felt uneasy about how he might react. But he was in a calm mood, almost meditative, and earnestly wished us well.

"Ah, Nanao," he said, beckoning her to come around to his side where he sat at his low table. He embraced her, and in a display of emotion that showed equal parts gladness and sadness, he said, "You're a good girl!"

Yoshida-sensei's broad smile showed his strong ivory teeth. His dark eyes glowed, I think even glistened. In that moment, I could feel affection for him, and remembered his laughter jumping Double Dutch. In Japan it is enough to bow, so there was no need to tell him I was grateful for the haven the dojo had provided us after our travels.

Now, having experienced a disciplined, almost monastic life, I knew it was not for me. I did not want to be living in a dojo. I was glad to be leaving.

16

We went straight from living in a dojo to living in an old, isolated farmhouse at the top of a mountain.

I'm not sure what made us think we could plop ourselves down in the middle of a Japanese farming community and make a life there. But that's what we did.

We'd heard about the farmhouse from Ito-san. The owner was a relative, and she was adamant in impressing on us that no one at the dojo should know that she'd told us about it. No one ever did. After we left, we never saw her or anyone from the dojo again.

Meeting the owner, he told us it had been his childhood home, but none of his family wanted to live in it now.

"It's pretty far out in the country."

"Great," Billy said. "Where?"

"It's about one hour away."

"Great," Billy said again.

"You like to be in the country?"

"Yes, yes, we like it."

"I heard you're from New York City."

"We are."

He drove us to the farmhouse, driving on narrow paved

roads that turned into unpaved ones with steep drops, until finally we came to Futokoro Yama—Breast Pocket Mountain.

Taking one look at the place, Billy and I said simultaneously, "This is it."

The farmhouse had been vacant for years, but we could tell with a little cleaning and fixing we could make it not just livable, but nice.

"How much is the rent?" Billy asked.

"Oh, you can live in it for free," the owner said, adding he'd rather have people living in it than leave it to be destroyed by mold and mildew, insects and weasels.

It was now two years since we'd left the States and paying jobs. We'd managed, seeming to require little money after our basic needs were met. Our "savings" amounted to the small allowance we were given at the dojo. And although "free" sounded good, Billy insisted he accept $50 a month.

We were charmed by the old house—traditionally simple, every room had tatami, the windows were paper-screen shoji, the doors sliding screen fusuma. The view—not quite the word to describe a panorama of bamboo groves, tea plantations and rice fields, mountains and endless sky that gave you the feeling you were not just at the top of a mountain but the world—was spectacular.

Traditional simplicity also meant the house didn't have even one convenience. The kitchen, situated on the cold dark north side, had a beaten-earth floor. There was a small, rusty, two-burner stove for cooking, and a *kamado*, a hearth built into the kitchen. Later I'd find its huge pots were perfect to boil dough for bagels.

There was no plumbing system. Water came into the house through a length of split bamboo connected to a tank on the hill above. It was running water, but it didn't run in hot. Every night we needed to build a fire to heat the bath, and if we wanted hot water during the day, we had to boil it. The farmhouse toilet (*benjo*) was the old squat-style Japanese type and unsurprisingly, it didn't flush. But a more significant fact was the vacuum trucks that usually empty these toilets couldn't reach it. Because of the location of the house, at the top of a mountain and perched on the side of a hill, the only access was by walking down a steep path.

One of the first things we learned from our neighbor was how to empty that *benjo*—and Billy and I easily agreed that would be his chore. Not just because it was an unpleasant job, but the waste had to be scooped into two buckets that were then balanced on a beam and carried on one shoulder to the fields or the woods. Those thick wooden buckets were heavy even before they were filled.

The almost primitive living situation didn't faze me. I'd lived on the road for a year, camping most of the time, and then in the dormitory at the dojo. The mountaintop location made emptying the toilet a chore, but in exchange we got not just a soul-satisfying view, but a home.

On that first day, the owner introduced us to our closest neighbors, a family named Ōishi. And then we went a little farther uphill to meet another family also named Ōishi. I'd learn that almost all the families in that area shared the same last name, and they were not all related.

The Ōishi family up the hill had three children, and it was our good fortune that the eldest, Hiroko, was a girl Nanao's age, and also a first-grader. Hiroko's mother and I soon agreed we'd take turns driving Nanao and Hiroko down the hill to catch the morning bus to the local school. They'd walk back. Nanao did that for all of her elementary school years. Arriving home rosy-cheeked, she never complained once. She may have thought most children walked more than an hour uphill to get home from school.

I didn't think I'd ever get used to calling our next-door neighbor Ōishi-san, and his wife the same thing without variation. I learned that because she was older than me, I could address her as Oba-san (aunt). I could also call her Oku-san (wife). Since many people in the area shared the same last name, it was also permitted to call her by her first name, Setsuko. Nanao called her Obaa-san (grandmother).

Ōishi-san, the husband, a man of perhaps sixty, was up long before daylight. Agile in a pair of *jikka-tabi*, the split-toe shoes farmers wear, he plowed fields, climbed trees, and carried farming implements up and down the stone path our houses shared. Setsuko didn't appear to be quite as old, but she moved slowly, deliberately, as she carried out her myriad daily chores. As if too much at one time wouldn't do us any good, Ōishi-san would every now and then give us bits of information: The stone path is treacherous, especially when wet. Weasels can get in through the roof and we should make sure there are no openings. And he promised Billy he'd take him to dig for *jinenjo*. This fabled mountain potato, an alleged aphrodisiac, could be found in the nearby woods—its distinctive heart-shaped leaves pointed to the unseen roots.

When Ōishi-san saw we were using an electric brazier like most city people used, he told Billy he should uncover the original one under the floor in the central room. I'd seen the one his family used and it seemed pitiful, just a small charcoal fire in a pit. I doubted it could keep them as warm as the modern electric ones. Since Nanao was a regular visitor at Ōishi-san's house, sitting with them watching television and snacking to her heart's content (I was certain these kind neighbors were undoing years of my feeding my daughter conscientiously) I asked her if their brazier was warm.

"Brazier? What's that?"

"You know, the table with the fire under it."

"Oh, you mean the *kotatsu*."

"Yes," I said, aware it wasn't the first time she'd taught me Japanese.

"Warm? Mama, it's hot."

And so, following Ōishi-san's instructions, Billy reconstructed the *kotatsu*, lining the pit with red clay he first mixed with straw. Ōishi-san made all the sumi (charcoal) his family used, and in an arrangement reminiscent of earlier times, with no money changing hands, we established a fine barter system. In return for keeping us supplied for our *kotatsu*, we drove him on his occasional errands, and sometimes took his elder brother to doctor appointments.

With our savings from the dojo, we'd bought a used car. Called a "minicar" with good reason, the only thing the 1000cc car had going for it were a steering wheel and brakes. Before we arrived, Ōishi-san's transportation had been a wheelbarrow or a motorized bicycle-cum-wagon. We were happy to take him wherever he wanted to go—and our trips with him were always excursions of learning old roads and new shortcuts. We met his family members in other villages, and often the end of a trip included some treat like *unagi no kabayaki*. This grilled eel dish, a specialty of the area, was soon our favorite.

Before Billy started to rip up the floor for the *kotatsu*, I was a lot more than dubious we'd be warm enough without a heating system. I had unhappy visions of being in that old drafty farmhouse with a big hole in the middle of the floor of the main room. Once it was finished, I could endorse the *kotatsu* as more than just an effective way to keep warm. The ledge surrounding the *kotatsu* was the perfect temperature to place jars of yogurt to incubate and whole wheat bread dough to rise. The *kotatsu* is where we sat for meals and anything else we might do at a low table. Ōishi-san and Billy played shogi (Japanese chess) there. While sitting wearing the traditional *hanten* (quilted jackets), our deep, clay-lined *kotatsu* kept us toasty during our first farmhouse winter. But step away from the *kotatsu* even for a minute and you'd be cold, as the *kotatsu* is designed to keep the person, not the room, warm.

During that winter, we developed an enduring appreciation for the *ofuro*, the deep Japanese bath. Getting into our tile wood-fired bath on cold evenings, sitting in hot water that comes up to your neck, heating our bodies to the core, was what kept us from freezing in that farmhouse through which winter drafts passed freely.

Billy building the *kotatsu* was our first test of succeeding in the countryside on our own. But we were not succeeding in my getting pregnant. At one point I gave up and decided we should consider adoption. I managed to contact a Japanese adoption agency, but they would not consider us: We were a foreign couple, in Japan just a year, speaking minimal Japanese, and living in a farmhouse on minimal funds. Their response was a polite but definite, "No thank you."

Totally exasperated, I wrote to Jean Pearce, who wrote a column titled "Getting Things Done" for *The Japan Times*, which I'd read daily in my hideout in the dojo. I knew she regularly researched and gave advice to hapless expatriates trying to navigate Japan's bureaucracy and arcane ways, or who were simply at a loss to find something as ordinary as oatmeal in the age before the Internet.

I thought twice about asking her for fertility advice when she was more accustomed to publishing information about where to buy peanut butter and how to file Japanese taxes. But I did write her, and no doubt sensing my desperation, she answered immediately, with the name of a fertility specialist in Yokohama. I was soon able to secure an appointment with Dr. Rihachi Iizuka, who I'd later learn was an internationally recognized specialist. Dr. Iizuka took one look at my basal chart, and, unlike other doctors who'd appeared baffled, he said my problem was simple: my hormone production during ovulation was deficient. The next thing I knew—and I was alarmed—a nurse was standing next to me with a syringe. I told Dr. Iizuka if there was any chance that the treatment might result in a multiple birth or abnormality, I would choose not to have it.

"No, no, no. You misunderstand. This injection will just boost the normal functioning of your hormones. There is no danger," he assured me.

He gave me a medical letter of introduction so I could be monitored at a hospital in our area, which would relieve me of the need to travel back to Yokohama, at least five hours of travel time from the farmhouse.

"Let's wait and see," were his last words to me.

I never had a second treatment, I never went to that other hospital.

I was pregnant within the month.

I was determined my second birth wouldn't be like my first—clueless, and under the delusion that because I lived a "natural" lifestyle, "natural" labor and childbirth would be a snap.

This time around, I read Lamaze and Leboyer. I did the breathing exercises, and Billy did them along with me and was diligent in seeing I practiced on a regular schedule.

In line with our simple and traditional Japanese lifestyle in the farmhouse, I thought it'd be perfect to have our baby born at home on a futon on the tatami mats. Midwives are common in Japan, and I had no problem finding one willing to attend my birth. But the one nearest us didn't drive, which meant Billy, or I, would have had to drive an hour over narrow mountain roads to pick her up, and then take her back after the delivery. I abandoned this "perfect" idea as impractical.

My due date, February nineteenth, was also Nanao's birthday. It was fast approaching, and my concerns were not about birthday cake and party favors, but that we hadn't figured out who would look after Nanao while I gave birth.

Nanao's second-grade teacher stepped in and said she could stay with her and her family the days prior to the birth, and the five days I'd be in the hospital. Totally unexpected, this was a personal act of kindness and consideration I could only have imagined coming from a family member or close friend.

Throughout my search for a maternity clinic or hospital, I found that childbirth in Japan was full of contradictions. Ages-old common sense ran parallel with bureaucratic thoughtlessness and downright foolishness. I knew the labor room was not the place to try to get my ideas on childbirth across to the doctor and assisting staff, so I wanted to have a meeting of the minds beforehand.

I spoke with several obstetricians, all of whom answered my questions about delivery procedures and practices with annoyed, condescending answers. Believing he was reassuring me, one doctor said, "Don't worry. I'll take care of everything." When I assured him that I was not worried but concerned, and that I did not want him to take care of everything, it was immediately and mutually obvious that I was in the wrong place.

Japanese doctors are well known for their imperiousness and quasi-godlike status. Although it's no longer true, at that time it was common for doctors to dish out unlabeled medicine with aplomb, simple instructions, and no talk of potential side effects. Commonly lacking in anything that could be called bedside manner, they appeared to believe it was beneath them to talk with, let alone explain anything to, a layperson, and they certainly didn't think it was necessary for them to answer questions. When I think about it now, it's probable they had little more than disdain for a foreign woman barely functional in Japanese. Indeed, my Japanese was rudimentary, and it wasn't easy for me to get the information I needed. But I did get it, eventually finding an obstetrician to go along with my natural birth plan. I interviewed him, and he basically agreed with everything—although he was resolute in his refusal to lower the lights in the delivery room, as natural birth guru Leboyer commanded.

In 1978 Japan, no one talked about "natural" childbirth

because no other scenario was contemplated. It was assumed all women would go through labor and delivery without any aids. The hard work of labor was simply that, and there was not a palliative in sight. While I was in labor, I was definitely not paying attention to what the other woman in the lying-in room next to mine was doing, but Billy told me afterward that he heard her being chastised (by the nurses? the doctor?) for making too much noise. He could hear her being told not to disturb the woman (that would be me) in the next room. Typical Japanese thinking and behavior: consider the other person and take care not to cause a disturbance or any unpleasantness. Birthing a baby does not alter this dictum.

I could not have cared if she were screaming bloody murder. I had my own labor to get through. Billy stayed with me throughout the labor and delivery (a first at that hospital) and told me after (I wasn't listening to anything during) that at one point I'd yelled, in mistaken Japanese, "*Itakunai!*"—"It doesn't hurt!"

I thought it a great paradox that although the majority of births in Japan could be deemed natural, as in not induced, aided, or given the benefit of modern medicine, babies were removed from their mothers almost instantly. Although I'd obtained the doctor's permission (it was more like I'd twisted his arm) to keep my baby in my room, because I did, I was regarded as a heretic by the nurses and had to invoke the doctor's name every time they changed shifts. I did get most of my demands met, and was even catered to, but the necessity to be so watchful was wearing. And while the doctor agreed to go along with my demands, and had even appeared affable, I later heard that he'd referred to me as "a foreign nut."

· · ·

We named our second daughter Mie—in kanji it means "beautiful branch."

Our first child born in our adopted home was a branch on a tree we were in the process of planting, the family we were growing.

17

A lthough I'd become a familiar figure, it was clear that the simple people I lived among were not accustomed to seeing someone who looked like me. I just had to accept the fact that at no time and nowhere would I go unnoticed.

When I walked on back roads and the narrow paths that cut across tea fields and rice paddies, I learned to announce my coming with a cough or audible footstep. It seemed unfair to appear all of a sudden in front of some old farmer tending his fields and minding his business. I was often reminded of that time in Yugoslavia when my sudden appearance in the store brought everyone to a standstill.

I was generally content with our country life, but its limits were glaring. My entire world consisted of farmhouse domestic chores and the care of children. Social interaction, such as it was, took the form of joining the other women for such community obligations like cutting roadside weeds. My only access to an intellectual life was buoyed by the few books in English I could get my hands on, and the full extent of any cultural activity was the summer folk dance festival.

At the dojo, instruction in every martial art was offered, but not any of Japan's traditional arts I wanted to study like *shodo*, calligraphy. I'd inherited the love of writing from my father who lived at a time it was considered an accomplishment to have good penmanship. A shopping list written by my father was something you'd want to keep. Early in my childhood, I'd learned to love the technique, art, and joy of transferring words from pen and ink to paper. Now I wanted to learn to do that practicing *shodo*, the way of writing.

Odagi-san, a woman who took English lessons at the school where Billy was now teaching, said she'd introduce me to her teacher—if, that is, I wanted to be a "serious student." I had to ask myself, how serious was I? How serious did I have to be? I'd heard that the sensei, Oki Roppo, well known and highly esteemed, was referred to as One of the Five Fingers of Japan. Just hearing that was daunting. Although I was grateful for the chance of an introduction, I was hesitant: Could I possibly meet the expectations of this eminent teacher? And, more practically, I had to consider the travel time: driving to the central station in Hamamatsu, taking a local train to Shizuoka city, then a bus, and then walking to his home. It added up to four hours one way. I attended one class with the idea that if I were accepted, I'd make my decision whether to join or not afterward.

My mind was made up the minute I stepped into his studio.

Eighty-three years old, Roppo-sensei sat at his writing table surrounded by his *fude* (brushes) and timeworn *suzuri* (ink-stones) and an aura of tranquility.

I presented him with a loaf of bread I'd baked. He received it, telling the students present how pleased he was to have a home-made gift. He told me he'd be glad to accept me as his student, and said that although I might not realize it, I was fortunate in not having ever studied before, as I wouldn't have any mistaken preconceptions. He then gave me an *otehon*, a practice book. Although most of these books are printed, Roppo-sensei wrote the samples himself, in front of us. I was told to bring my finished writing the next week to be corrected.

Stealing time from the children and chores, sitting at a low desk, I practiced at home every day the simple characters I'd been given. After a week of effort, I felt I couldn't get a handle on it. When I returned to class the following week, I sat in the formal *seiza* position and watched while Roppo-sensei checked the work of the students before me. I thought their writing was beautiful. I'd later learn that most of the students, including Odagi-san, were teachers of calligraphy themselves.

By the time it was my turn to show my work, I was so embarrassed and ashamed by its primitiveness, my eyes filled with tears. Roppo-sensei made the corrections, said a few inaudible words, and wrote the samples for the next lesson. Oddly, I felt encouraged. How unlike Yoshida-sensei, I thought, who in the same circumstance might have humiliated me and told me to never come again.

I continued to study with him, and for a long time I felt handicapped by my lack of knowledge of kanji and the techniques of calligraphy. He'd said I was "fortunate" not to have studied before, but I had the distinct sense of being disadvantaged when I compared my writing to the other students'—knowing it's common to start calligraphy lessons while in first grade.

And I could not reconcile myself to his method of teaching. He rarely spoke. He didn't explain anything. I wanted desperately to be told and instructed in very definite terms, as I was accustomed. I couldn't see the point of traveling so far just to watch him write. But after a while it all started to come together, and I could see that his method, teaching without words, new to me at the time, had its merits. The student was expected to observe and endeavor, in the truest sense of those words. It was instructive to see how he sat, how he held his brush. It was an inspiration to watch him writing and see how one brushstroke followed the other—flowing in perfect order.

Roppo-sensei taught me discipline. It was self-directed discipline, not imposed as it had been with Yoshida-sensei. The meditative aspect of calligraphy was calming, and the concentration it took to write with a brush trained me to focus. Providing a welcome respite from the domesticity of my life, studying calligraphy enabled me to block out thoughts of the mundane—diapers to be washed, meals to prepare, the fire to be built for the bath.

Now, after more than thirty years of study, during the hours I practice I can enter the world of the legendary Chinese calligraphers I admire, principal among them Wang Xizhi and Huai Su, whose works I learned to write.

Three years after Mie's birth, I was happily expecting my third child.

Now I had it down. Where to give birth was no longer a conundrum because I'd found the Mizumoto Maternity Clinic. Gentle in his manner and unlike many of his colleagues, I felt Dr. Mizumoto respected me for being prepared for my baby's birth. Reassuring me he would not intervene unnecessarily, he asked only that I trust him to use his best judgment.

By that time, my expectations for the kind of birthing experience I wanted had changed. I'd raised my own consciousness about what "natural childbirth" meant. What could be an *unnatural* childbirth? Did a woman who chose to have an epidural or some other procedure or aid have a plastic uterus? Hadn't she carried her baby around for nine months, straining every bone, muscle, and ligament—or did she have a stainless-steel frame? I never required any intervention, but I would've seen no shame in it if I had.

This was birth number three, and I was relaxed about the whole process. My contractions started while we were eating dinner.

"Okay, Billy. I think it's time to go," I said, I guess a little too nonchalantly.

"What?!" He jumped up from the low table where we'd just been enjoying a nice dinner. He blurted out a series of questions:

When did the contractions start? How many minutes apart were they? Why hadn't I said anything?!

I'd made couscous (I didn't avoid spicy foods and ate anything I liked) and just wanted to finish eating.

On an exquisite morning in April, I gave birth to a son.

From the window of my room, I could see a field of clover just beginning to flower. My baby boy lay in my bed sleeping, nestled in my arm, small and snug under a quilt. In the earlier morning hours, Nanao and Mie had held their brother while his age was still being measured in hours.

Mrs. Mizumoto, a midwife and registered nurse, had worked side by side with her husband since their twelve-bed clinic opened. She was responsible for the clinic's interior furnishings, floral-patterned wallpaper, and the fresh and wholesome food served on beautiful dishes and lacquer trays. During my five-day stay, I was able to get some much-needed rest, cared for by attentive midwives and nurses who dispensed tidbits of advice along with massage. I had to reflect that had I given birth at home, per my original plan, rest would have been out of the question. We were still living in the farmhouse, and I would've had no choice but to resume house-hold chores.

Mrs. Mizumoto brought sunshine itself every time she came in my room, and one day she brought a large bunch of red roses, presenting them to me with a big smile and a simple, "For you!" Later, when Nanao and Mie visited, she had fresh strawberries and *sembei* (rice crackers) for them. Her gestures of kindness were more than generous; thoughtful, she knew I didn't have a *jikka* (family home), which meant there could be no doting grandparents and solicitous relatives.

The morning I left the clinic, I was served a cup of *sakura-cha* (tea made from preserved cherry blossoms) and given *osekihan* (rice steamed with azuki beans) to take home. These delicacies, served to wish health and prosperity, are offered on occasions deemed auspicious: graduation, marriage, the birth of a child.

The total cost of two thousand dollars we paid for the delivery and my five-day stay in a private room would be reimbursed through Japan's national health insurance system.

With Mario swathed in a soft gauze cotton kimono, presented to us as a gift, Dr. and Mrs. Mizumoto and the entire staff saw us to the door, a courtesy extended to all new parents. I left the Mizumoto clinic feeling I'd been a well-treated guest at a traditional Japanese inn—a deeply pleasing experience for which this country is deservedly famous.

I also left with the realization that Dr. and Mrs. Mizumoto had succeeded in defining the connection between hospital and hospitality.

No, I didn't have a jikka, and my circumstances around my babies' births couldn't have differed more from that of my Japanese friends than if we had been living on two different planets, in two different dimensions of reality.

A month or two before Japanese women gave birth, they'd return to their jikka, the family home. When that wasn't possible, their mothers came to stay with them. During that time, my friends were free to rest in preparation for the birth, confident any other children were cared for. Their rest continued when they returned to their jikka for a month or more after the birth. Nurtured by their own mothers, these new mothers only had to nurse the baby.

Women in Japan are urged to rest after childbirth as it's considered essential to a full recovery. Rest is deemed so important to restore and rejuvenate a woman's body that Japanese women are cautioned not to even brush their hair (much less do housework) following childbirth as it's regarded as "brushing away" crucially needed energy that should be kept in reserve at an all-important time. In maternity clinics—I've seen it for myself and it's kind of funny—generally meticulously coiffed ladies look like unkempt wild-haired madwomen.

I was once scolded by the midwife who attended Mario's birth when she "found" me reading in bed: "Anton-san. You will strain your eyesight and it can have a lasting adverse effect. Please stop." Her warning was firm, a directive to be followed. You would've thought I was sneaking a cigarette or drinking whiskey from a bottle, in a bag.

Dr. Mizumoto told me "new mothers take longer to recover from childbirth than most people think." And he said that physical and emotional problems related to the postpartum state have always affected women, but now since most women go back to work after having babies, "It's almost as if they need permission to take time to recover."

I surely wasn't going to have time to rest and recover once I got home after Mario's birth.

Billy picked me up at the Mizumoto clinic and drove me, Mie, and Mario home. He left me at the door. He'd cleaned the house and prepared lunch and dinner. He'd aired the futon. He'd cut and stacked the wood. The cooing and clucking of grandparents seeing their just-born grandchild would've been balm for my still-sore body. But what greeted me was a house so empty it felt abandoned. Stepping into my dark, primitive kitchen, I was overcome with the reality that there was no one but me to tend to the needs of a five-day-old infant and a demanding toddler, and that tired or not, things had to be done. Sure, the wood to heat the bath was cut and stacked, but I had to build the fire.

Billy wasn't a bad guy, a good-for-nothin' husband. He had to go to work. He was now teaching English at a small language school in town that could best be described as fly by night. Not only did the owner of the school not give him any time off, we would find out later that he'd cheated him. Telling Billy he held back some of his salary to pay taxes, in fact the owner had pocketed it.

There was no paternity leave in Japan at the time, and even if there had been, I doubt there was a man in the entire country who felt he had any particular role to play when his baby was born. Because mothers went to their mother's, and men generally did not take care of children, the new-father role was nonexistent. During my early child-raising years here, any man caring for young children would have appeared radical, if not insane.

In the early days on Breast Pocket Mountain, sometimes someone would come to our door to tell me something I only partly understood. Half the time I wouldn't even know what it was about, but if they asked for money, I gave it, and if they told me to show up someplace, I'd be there. One thing I understood for certain: I was expected to cooperate.

One morning, Hiroko-chan's mother came by and said that it was her and my turn to clean the local shrine.

"Oh?" I said, surprised.

"I put the notice in your box. Didn't you read it?"

"Er, yes . . . the notice . . ." I said without making any mention of reading. It was hit and miss what got deciphered and what didn't. If I forgot to ask Nanao to read and translate for me, the message was lost for all time.

This Shinto shrine was pretty defunct, maybe used once a year for the autumn harvest festival, but the village people were committed to its upkeep and keeping it clean. I brought a bucket, a wiping cloth, and a scrub brush and spent the morning on my hands and knees. With dusters made of rags attached to a stick, we dusted the shrine as high as we could reach.

Not a week after my labors at the shrine, Billy got a call from his friend Ron Koetzsch who'd studied at Kyoto University and continued to visit Japan regularly. Ron, who gave me a translation and beautiful edition of *The Tale of Genji* on his first visit to our farmhouse, would forever remain in my good graces because he'd show up and help Billy with the toilet-emptying chore.

Ron told Billy he was traveling for a couple of weeks and would like to visit us for a few days—with a friend who needed to get off that track so often called beaten. Our farmhouse was definitely the place to come—you couldn't be further off the track if you were trying to get lost. Where we lived, a place that didn't show up on local maps, was not a place anyone went unless they were going to see someone they knew.

The traveling companion turned out to be John Denver. And he turned out to be traveling with a small entourage that included his personal natural foods chef, his masseur, and our friend Ron, who acted as his interpreter.

The farmhouse was large—we seldom ever used the rooms on the second floor. Like most Japanese households, our closets had stacks of futon, always ready to spread out on the tatami for guests. But I didn't want any guests just then. Mario was three months old and Mie, a toddler, had, among her many demands, the insistence I take her to visit a neighbor's goat every afternoon. I said as long as they were willing to eat simple food and not be treated like guests, they were welcome.

I barely recognized John because he didn't fit his well-known image of wire-rimmed glasses (he wore Ray-Bans) and shaggy blond hair (it was blond but well styled and brushed firmly away from his eyes). In place of an embroidered hippie wristband, he sported a thick gold Rolex. The first evening as we sat at the *kotatsu* eating our typical dinner of brown rice, miso soup with wakame seaweed, and natto (fermented soybeans), I told him that I knew who he was, but I honestly couldn't name even one of his songs.

"What about 'Jet Plane,' " he said. "Ever hear that?"

"Oh I love that song!"

Although I didn't associate them with him, I loved "Annie's Song," "Sunshine on My Shoulders," and "Country Roads," too.

John had just wrapped up his tour of Japan, and when word

got out (we never found out how) that he was at our house, television cameras, interviewers, and fans showed up at our door. It's hard to believe the commotion that descended on Futokoro Yama out of nowhere. John was very popular in Japan. And he was gracious. He told us he wanted to apologize to our neighbors for the hullabaloo (they loved it), and to show his sincerity and appreciation for the village's hospitality, he offered to put on a little concert. The village elders said they had the perfect place for him to perform: the shrine. And it was clean and ready.

I was delighted when before he sang "Country Roads" he said, "This one's for Karen."

Although he had a big following in Japan, our old neighbors had no idea who he was. During the concert, the eldest Ōishi said, astonished, "Well, this boy can really sing."

John stayed with us about four days. He clearly enjoyed the simplicity of our lifestyle, the plain food, the rustic farmhouse. Whenever I was occupied in the kitchen or with some chore, he'd take Mario, rock him and sing to him. The weather was warm and we spent afternoons by the river just a short distance from our house. Surrounded by birdsong, clear water, wild azaleas, and bamboo, John took it all in. He also took a lot of photographs and said he'd send prints when he got home, which he did.

"You've got a piece of paradise here," he told me.

The real world has a way of intruding on paradise.

It was July, maybe a month after John left. Typically we would've been in the middle of the rainy season, but now it was just hot. I fanned Mario, who couldn't sit or roll over yet, while he lay contentedly on a *zabuton*, a large cushion, as I practiced calligraphy.

When the telephone rang, I knew it was from overseas the minute I put the receiver to my ear; that faraway sound was unmistakable. I thought it might be Johnny. He'd call on occasion—"Just checking on you," he'd say, reminding me of our father. Always generous and looking out for his sister, when Mario was born he'd sent me a check.

It was Mollie. She loved talking on the phone, could talk for hours, but she didn't call me and I didn't call her either. It was expensive. She'd only be calling if there was something wrong.

"You've got to come home now."

Johnny had been shot. He was dead.

It's not possible to convey the shock. I only remember wanting to shut it out, pretend it didn't happen, that Mollie had never called. This was a nightmare and I would wake up. But this nightmare was real. I was awake, and I had to go back.

We didn't have anything approaching the money needed for the cost of a ticket to the United States. Stim Harriman, one of the few foreigners, an American, living in Hamamatsu at the time, offered to cover the cost, unasked, saying we could pay him back whenever we could.

I took Mario with me, and could only think how happy Johnny would have been to see him. Mollie bought Mario a baby "suit" to wear for the funeral, but I refused to dress him in it, would not consider taking him to the funeral. Miss Fannie, Mollie's mother-in-law, looked after him. As I put him in her arms, dressed as he always was, in a soft white cotton baby kimono, I felt he was safe.

Johnny was shot in the head by someone who stood next to him. Someone he knew. It had been done "execution style." I know that because the police told me, but I'll never know why.

Many of his friends were at the funeral. Guys I knew from around the block, boys I'd grown up with on 159th Street but hadn't seen in years. Was the person who did it one of them? Was the murderer among the mourners? I was as overwhelmed by fear as by sorrow. It was a horrible feeling to be scared of people you know. My anguish was making me crazy. I wanted to run. To scream. To attack someone. But I didn't do any of those things. I sat in the funeral, tearless, gripped in grief.

Here I was again, in the middle of a New York City horror story. My little village in Japan no one had ever heard of seemed not just far away, but unreal.

Embracing Mollie as I prepared to leave, the softness that was always folded up into lacey layers of what she called "feminine attire" was now rock hard. A hard line crossed her mouth.

With a missing mother, we'd started out a small family.

"Now it's just you and me, Karen."

Months and, without my marking it, years passed. The daily strain of trying to make a life in the Japanese countryside weighed on me. The hardest part was trying to do it without relatives. We were the only "nuclear family" in our area; if that expression ever sounded like a curse, it was then.

So many times I wished our children had grandparents—next door, down the road, in the same country. People, family, they could turn to, who'd always be there when Mama and Papa were too weary or distracted. My days, and nights, too, were spent soothing cries, wiping tears, responding to whines. Mie appeared to need a piece of me every moment.

Aside from being the only foreign woman in the middle of a Japanese farming community, I felt further alienated knowing none of the women could relate to my situation. Although I knew some despised their mothers-in-law (the feeling often mutual), there was at least another adult around, whereas I was mostly alone, babbling with the children.

Some days when the mail was delivered, I'd grab the kids and run to the door so I could waylay the postman in the yard—I didn't want him to just deliver the mail and leave. If I missed my chance to talk to the postman and comment on the weather, it might mean missing the opportunity to talk to another adult that day. Billy, who left the house early in the morning and didn't return until late at night, six days a week, was hardly ever around.

I joked to myself that if three people walked up our road at the same time, I would think it was a parade.

It was around this time, and for the first time in my life, that I thought I understood my mother. Young herself, she had the care of three young children, and only one year separated me from my brother and my sister from me. Also for the first time, I thought, or feared, I might become like her—might not be able to take care of my children. I might lose my mind.

Stuck in the farmhouse, I was cracking at the seams. I was trying my best, but with no relief in sight, I didn't have the least confidence I'd make it. I told myself I'd never give up, as I believed my mother had, because I assumed I was in control. And while I came to appreciate why and how my mother lost her mind, it took me some years more to actually appreciate that my father didn't lose his.

The countryside lifestyle was so obviously not viable for us anymore. There were too many problems and frustrations. I believed it couldn't even be healthy to be without adult company so much of the time. Still, despite being alone and isolated, I wasn't dying of loneliness. Although having young children is antithetical to having solitude, I could get some time in my day, quiet time, when I could do something I wanted to do: write.

The children's nap time hours were the most precious hours in the day. I might have been tired and in need of a nap myself, but the second I confirmed they were down for the count, I'd take up my pen. While we lived in the farmhouse, I wrote articles, though I didn't know if they'd ever get published. I kept a diary I variously called "Diary of a Mad Housewife" or "Journal of the Plague Years," because I only wrote in it when I was depressed. Some passages from it turned up in the novel I wrote ten years later.

I wrote a lot of letters. Picking up my Montblanc Meister-stück, a gift from Don and a fountain pen I've now had fifty years, I wrote letters to friends, making sure I had commemorative stamps when I mailed them. These letters, my connection to civilization, enabled me to use a language I could speak fluently, and express myself. Although the best part of letter writing is correspondence, few friends proved capable of that. Tamar was an exception, and so was Felix. I've been friends with Felix Arts since we met on Ibiza in 1965. When Billy and I went to Holland to buy the VW in Amsterdam, we first stayed with Felix at his home in Rotterdam.

In any case, from my secluded perch on Breast Pocket Mountain, I went on writing letters, confident no one I knew would go to their grave saying, "Karen owes me a letter."

The day in May 1982 Dr. Mizumoto informed me I was two months pregnant with my fourth child, I suddenly couldn't understand Japanese. He repeated it in English. I went home and threw up. I'd wanted a big family, and I would have welcomed another child—but just not then.

Just starting to get my waistline back after Mario's birth, I'd visited the Mizumoto clinic to inquire about options for birth control. Now too late for that, I had to abruptly stop breast-feeding and contemplate an impending birth. Billy and I talked that evening, and he was easily as disconcerted as I was.

"Whatever that doctor turned on," he said, referring to the fertility specialist I'd seen years earlier, "get him to turn it off."

We got a laugh out of that before I vomited again. I'd never had morning sickness to the point of vomiting with any of my pregnancies. I'm convinced I was overcome with stress hormones.

The next day I called my friend Satoh-san, totally despondent, and I guess she could detect my despair.

"I'll come see you," she said before hanging up the phone.

She lived more than an hour away and did not drive, and before she could knock on my door, she'd have to take a bus, a train, another bus, and a walk, uphill. When she called in the morning saying she was on her way, I was overwhelmed with gratitude, and I felt better the minute I saw her.

Kazuko Satoh, a professor and activist for women's rights, lectured all over the country and had been a delegate for Japan at the world conferences for women in Mexico City and Copenhagen. It was hard to believe she could make time to spend the afternoon with me. But she did, saying simply, "Support should not be an abstract notion."

Never mind my waistline, I wondered if I'd be able to accept Satoh-san's offer to introduce me to an editor who wanted someone to write a regular column, in English. I'd been seeking just this kind of opportunity, but had found it elusive. Frustrated, I watched as Billy—a professor, and a man—was regularly approached and asked to contribute essays for publication. He'd always turn them down, saying, "Please ask my wife. She'd love to do it."

I was able to get a few guest spots, but for all the encouragement I received, it didn't look like I'd get much into print. Now I had the possibility of becoming a regular columnist for a regional edition of the national newspaper *Chunichi Shimbun*. Bewildered, I'd called Satoh-san; I'd come to rely on her for advice, guidance, and counseling. No question ever flummoxed her, she was as passionate as she was practical minded, and I found her clear thinking uplifting. Her confidence in me helped me develop confidence in myself at some of my lowest points. I didn't want to turn down this offer. Satoh-san saw no reason I should.

"Another child shouldn't stop you from doing what you've yearned to do."

We spent the afternoon talking about topics I might want to write about. I had so many ideas I felt like they were boiling in my head.

The panic passed. By the time Satoh-san left, I was happily looking forward to having another baby, and starting to write a column.

It's common in Japan to have a third person, a go-between, to address matters that might be considered delicate. Which is why, after I was hired by the paper, it was Satoh-san who told me the editor was surprised I'd given my banking information as an account with Billy's name. We'd always shared a bank account, and any earnings I received went into the account under his name. It was never a problem.

"I'm sure you have it worked out," Satoh-san said, "but it would be good for you, psychologically, to have your own money. That's important for women. It will help your self-esteem, your confidence. It costs nothing to open an account. Takes no time. Do it."

I didn't get it at first. Our "financial system" worked fine for us. I had a bank book and could access our joint account freely. But I came to see what she meant. Having financial independence is a must for women. The fact that our money was in the same account also meant I wouldn't have the satisfaction of seeing money I'd earned adding up. I wasn't earning a lot, but whatever money I did earn was an indication not of my worth, but my ability to be compensated: for my time, ideas, writing.

The first thing I did with my first paycheck from the newspaper was buy a desk, the handmade no-nails Matsumoto Mingei Kagu I'm sitting at now.

Becoming pregnant with my fourth child brought our life in the countryside to an end.

As I got bigger, things I'd done daily for seven years seemed to get bigger, too, and too much. And I mean, why was I building a fire to heat the bath, and who, in Japan in 1982, didn't have hot running water?

The farmhouse toilet, which you had to straddle and squat over, was hard enough for me in late pregnancy, but I had to accompany Mie every time she went to be sure she didn't fall in. Funny, yeah, but it was no joke. It was a serious concern, and nerve-wracking. What had appeared charming about living in a traditional Japanese farmhouse became, over time and with the addition of babies, just too rough. Whereas our neighbors shared chores in their extended families, Billy and I did everything ourselves, and we were barely managing.

Billy had left the language school when he was offered a position at a small university. Their first foreign English professor, it seemed they couldn't get enough of him. In addition to his regular schedule of classes, he was required to attend endless meetings, participate in student festivals, judge English-speaking contests, plan excursions, arrange international homestays, and visit high schools for recruitment. Add his hour-and-a-half drive early every morning to the city and then back again at night and our "lifestyle" wasn't making any sense.

His absence, the inconvenience, and daily chores aside, I was simply fed up with the isolation. I could only see it getting worse with a growing family. It was impossible to get help in the countryside, and in the circumstance where all families were multi-generational, I'm sure there was no one in our village who even thought about the need for outside help.

I remember the time a neighbor, something of a busybody, saw me sitting on a bench with Mario just weeks old and wrapped in a blanket while Mie played in a sandbox.

"We don't take babies out when they're so young," she said disapprovingly.

I got that. But I wondered if she got that I was alone and had a three-year-old who needed to go out. I didn't have a lot of choice and chafed at being chided.

"This is it. We have to move," I announced to Billy at the beginning of my third trimester.

At a minimum, I needed to be able to get help, and that could not happen living where we were. Billy got right on board. He did better than that: within the month he'd found a large house in the city, and we prepared to move. Although we'd been living in the farmhouse seven years, I'd always been cautious about acquiring things, and we didn't have a lot of stuff. That, along with the fact that a traditional Japanese house has very little furniture, I was packed in no time.

Six women neighbors (five shared the last name Ōishi) invited me for a farewell dinner at an inn famous for serving a local specialty, wild boar. I didn't even eat meat at the time but would have never mentioned it. I ate the *inoshishi* while sitting around with them chatting and trading stories about the kids, the school, all the while thinking the kind of relaxed socializing time we were having, just as I was leaving, was what I'd always wanted.

I'd resented that none of them were ever available for a cup of tea, never had an hour to sit down to knit and chat together. So much in need myself, so self-absorbed, I couldn't see my expectations were unrealistic, and I unreasonable. They were all farmers, the daughters of farmers, the wives of farmers. These women didn't spend their days sitting around chatting. Up before dawn, in the fields and then in the kitchen, they might not have had time during the day to sit at all.

I know living in those multigenerational households that I envied wasn't a cakewalk. The tensions and stresses of sharing a house in Japan with in-laws, especially mothers-in-law, are well chronicled and considered just the way things are, especially in farm households. They may have envied me.

. . .

A few carloads, and our move to the city was complete.

The house Billy found had ten rooms. We didn't need ten rooms, but after living in a spacious farmhouse, it was impossible to imagine living in one of Japan's notoriously small apartments. I could imagine a couple and two kids making it work, somehow. But I couldn't conceive of doing it with four children —and we had a cat and a dog.

Billy had entered a low-residency program for a Master of Arts in teaching. After completing the degree and publishing several papers, he was promoted to full professor at his university. This made it possible for us to pay what seemed to be the exorbitant rent, ten times what we'd been paying for the farmhouse.

The house, located in one of the oldest neighborhoods in the city of Hamamatsu, was part of an estate, the owner living in a still larger house on the other side of the garden. Our house, we were told, was famous for the fact that Empress Teimei—the mother of Emperor Shōwa, great-grandmother of the current emperor, Naruhito—had once spent a night there. Imperial legend or not, the house was perfect for making the transition from country to city living. It was surrounded by a garden and closed off to the street by an imposing gate. Although located in the center of a densely packed neighborhood, no other house could be seen once behind that gate. What we could see was the pond at the back, and we could get a glimpse of the renowned wisteria trellises of Seirai-in, the Buddhist temple next door that held the remains of the wife of the Edo-period shogun Tokugawa Ieyasu.

Our new neighborhood was much like our neighborhood in the countryside: everyone knew everyone else and had lived there a long time. There were no apartment buildings, and new people did not move in and out. The mom-and-pop store on the corner was the kind of place you sent your child to with your purse and a note. When I went to the store myself, it wasn't just to get fresh tofu, but to get the lowdown on the weather, listen to neighborhood gossip, or ask in which direction Mie, who treated the store as an outpost, had gone. Mie was now enrolled in a local kindergarten run by a Buddhist temple. Every afternoon after she got out, she'd skip over to Kuroda-san's store, where she was welcomed like a regular customer.

The house was exquisite—a fine example, a relic really, of traditional Japanese architecture and skilled craftsmanship now rarely practiced. While I tried to make the house comfortable for our family and modern-day use (we put in a new kitchen), I also did my best to maintain the integrity and beautiful aesthetic of its traditional design. With the exception of one room off the spacious entrance hall, all the rooms were covered with tatami. The large room I chose for my study had the best view of the formal garden. I'd find out how formal when I woke up one morning to see two men in the pine trees directly outside my second-floor bedroom appearing to manicure the trees as they clipped pine needles with fingernail-sized scissors.

There were no screens on the windows, and when it got warm, we had to have screens custom-made since the dimensions of the windows were of a size no longer in common use. When it got very hot, we removed all the shoji (paper-screen panels) and replaced them with *yoshizubari*—screens made entirely of bamboo that provide shade while allowing cool summer breezes to pass through. The owner told me those bamboo screens hadn't been used for years because they were so bothersome to take out and put away. When I removed them from their storage place, the newspaper they'd been wrapped in when they were last put away was revealed. It was from the 1930s.

Today a large black Mercedes-Benz parked in the driveway can indicate affluence, but there was a time in Japan, not so long ago, when the wealth, and more importantly the prominence, of a family could be deduced from the outside by the size of the stone lanterns in the well-kept garden and the number and size of carp in the pond on the path to the entrance. My calligraphy teacher Roppo-sensei had such a garden and entrance.

One day a saleswoman came through the front gate, and from my study I could see her glance around in admiration at the garden before ringing the bell and stepping into the entrance hall. It was common then (we still do it) to leave the front door unlocked for the convenience of delivery- and salespeople.

"May I help you?" I asked.

"Who lives here?" she wanted to know, seeming to forget her manners along with her original purpose in coming to my door.

"Well I do," I answered, and smiled. I could easily understand that she could not have expected to see anyone who looked like me answer that door.

"But who"—and she began to stutter—"who, who—who decorated the house?"

In a Japanese house, the *genkan* (entrance hall) is the first thing any visitor sees, and most people make a point of keeping it neat and attractive. Our saleswoman was now looking around in bewilderment at my idea of ikebana (flower arrangement) on top of the *getabako* (cabinet for shoes) and staring at the calligraphy scroll Roppo-sensei had given me, in gratitude for that loaf of bread I'd baked for him.

"I did, of course. Now, what can I do for you?"

It felt good to establish I was the woman of the house. I wasn't passing through; this was not a place I was just stopping. This beautiful place was my home.

We were in the new house just two weeks before I went into labor.

It was the shortest labor and delivery I'd experienced, but far from feeling like I wanted to kick back like I was in a hotel, I was anxious to get home. I had three other children waiting for me, and a deadline. Concerned that I'd be overwhelmed once home,

Dr. Mizumoto practically begged me to stay the full five days. "You're older [I was thirty-seven]. Mario is not yet two years old. Please rest. Let the nurses look after you."

I'd developed a good relationship with Dr. Mizumoto and was inclined to listen to him. Always personable and genuinely caring, he was also respectful, and would never have called me, as the other doctor had, "a foreign nut." It's not surprising that now, more than thirty years later, his eldest daughter is my gynecologist. The youngest daughter, a general practitioner, is married to my orthopedist. They named their firstborn Karen.

I stayed the five days, and thankfully when I arrived home with Lila in my arms, I had help. Years before I met Satoh-san, she'd established a support and discussion group called the Feminist Salon. The Salon was made up of women professionals, as well as those women who, as homemakers and caregivers, had never worked at a job outside of their homes in their lives. The day Satoh-san told me Kiyoko Izuka, a fellow member, told her if we moved to the city she'd help me with the new baby and in the house, I caught my breath. Now, what had been an impossible dream—having help—would make it possible for me to take care of my family, run a household, and meet deadlines.

Izuka-san told me she'd come three mornings a week until Lila entered nursery school, and that's exactly what she did. I didn't just rely on her, I could not have done half the things I managed to do without her help. When she came to work in our home, her own three sons were still in school. She'd passed the stage of being a full-time, all-hands-on-deck mother, and working outside the home part-time was her way to prepare herself and her family for her move back into the workplace.

People who don't do it are not aware of the skill it takes to run a household well. Not everyone can do it competently. Like a lot of women who have run homes, her managerial and organizational abilities could've placed her at the top echelons in the business world—which makes it all the more a wonder so few Japanese women ever find themselves there. Aside from her general ability as a homemaker who could prepare healthful Japanese meals, on a budget, she could sew and came to my aid on several occasions when I needed to show up at a wedding or some other affair for which I had some fabric but "nothing to wear." She also had a beautiful voice, and sang chanson as she went about her tasks.

Aside from the help I received from Izuka-san, I was also no longer the young, freaked-out, I-don't-know-what-I'm-doing mother. When Nanao was an infant, I couldn't imagine having a second child because I was up to my neck just trying to deal with one. With the birth of my fourth child—and as Satoh-san memorably told me, "Lila is the prize"—I could see that not only could it be done, but I could be good at it. And while doubts about managing the day-to-day after a first child is one thing, I know I'm not the only parent who has thought, *How is it possible to have a second child when I love this child so much?*

Now I had four children. And what I learned from them was that I had endless capacity for loving.

I had no idea.

A big bonus of moving to the city was that I could regularly meet and talk to other foreign women. There weren't many living in Hamamatsu, and I knew, or would eventually meet, all of them.

That big bonus came with the big drawback that these foreigners never represented a community. It was a transient group, and trying to build friendships could be frustrating. I became cautious, shying away from those foreigners, women and men, who I knew were only in Japan to work, and who would be leaving. Aside from it being tiresome having to constantly repeat your life story, I found it emotionally draining always having to say goodbye.

But I won't deny that knowing other foreigners, women especially, with whom I shared a common cultural background, and familiar points of reference, was one of the best things about moving to the city. We'd meet in each other's homes, and as my house was bigger than everyone else's, I'd often offer to host our get-togethers. Our group of women, mostly mothers, was a mix of Americans, Danes, Finns, Brits, and Filipinas. Any room we were in would virtually hum as women almost desperate to speak their own language talked without taking a breath.

Time would fly and conversation never stopped as we recommended dentists and pediatricians and travel agents. We traded magazines, lent and borrowed books, exchanged recipes, gave away children's clothes, and offered information on immigration laws. Experiences of pregnancy and childbirth were shared, along with the nuts and raisins we'd ordered in bulk. At a time when cheese was not readily available in supermarkets, we'd divide a huge wheel of Gouda bought from a wholesaler friend of Billy's—I'd pick up the cheese at this friend's parents' fish store on the outskirts of Hamamatsu.

We talked about our children born here, and how they viewed their foreign mothers. Sigrid, tall and blond, told us her son said he was embarrassed she stood out among Japanese mothers like a "yellow mountain." I could report Mie didn't shy away from dark brown paint and crayons to color me in her drawings, forgoing the *hadairo* ("flesh" color) all her kindergarten classmates used to color their mothers.

I think many of the women would have agreed with me that after an initial period of trying hard to fit in, we'd had to make adjustments. We'd succeeded in some ways, and now could sanguinely accept the differences and limitations. I know I was seasoned. I had come to that point of hard-won confidence to be who I was, a foreign woman in a foreign place. I'd always be that.

By this time, Billy and I had been living abroad almost ten years, and although we did not yet have permanent resident status in Japan, our visas allowed us to live here without impediment. It was unlikely we'd be going back to America to live.

．　．　．

We'd taken our first trip back to the States to visit after we'd been away about five years.

Billy's parents made room for us in their small apartment downtown. Felicia, a woman who'd get on an airplane with not much more than a shopping bag, had come to visit when we were still living on Breast Pocket Mountain. She was game and undaunted by the primitiveness of our accommodations. I'd been pregnant, and now the two-year-old Mie was meeting her grandmother for the first time. Harold Anton, ever irascible, hardly played the adoring grandfather role Daddy had, but rather could be heard calling out to Mie and Nanao, "Don't break the floor!" every time they ran around the apartment.

I stayed with my sister Mollie for a week and could only marvel at how she kept it together. Teaching full-time, having full responsibility of three sons, she was always stressed. She worried constantly, mainly about the safety of her children—something I never had to think about in Japan. She'd shepherd her two youngest boys to and from schools out of the neighborhood, adding another task to her already busy day. At home Nanao could walk home at night after volley ball practice without my giving it a second thought.

One evening when I returned to her apartment in the projects without calling first, she actually got mad at me, yelling, "Don't you know you can get killed!"—on the street, in the elevator, in the stairwell. No, I didn't know that. Or rather, after all these years in Japan, I'd forgotten. Fear was now no part of my life.

I knew Mollie's neighbors from when she first moved into public housing, and now they welcomed me not just warmly, but with plates of collard greens they knew I loved, and missed. They came over to her apartment after spending hours cooking for me.

"So how you like it over there, Karen?"

"I like it a lot."

"Is it all Chinese people?"

"Japanese."

"Japanese. They ain't no black people?"

"Not where we are."

"You in the country, right?"

"Yeah, it's a village in the mountains."

"How you come to be in a place like that? I hear it's happening in Tokyo."

"Yeah. Maybe it is. I've only been there twice." When we got married, and when I registered Mie's birth at the embassy. Billy registered Mario's.

"Karen, is the food good?"

"Yeah, I like it a lot."

"And you cooking that Japanese food, too?"

"She ain't got to cook it! They eat everything raw!"

I loved being with these women. The repartee easily resumed even after years of not seeing each other. Miss Fannie, always flamboyant, was a woman who wore her Sunday hat every day, and she could crack me up just by a *way* of talking. Though our time together was filled with laughter, troubles were also openly spoken about, shared: Delores was plagued by a drug-addicted husband, Loretta was looking after the son of a sister then in her last fight with pancreatic cancer.

That visit reminded me how open Americans are. And how friendly. Whether talking with an unemployed Vietnam veteran on a Manhattan bus, or conferring with a woman in the changing room of Bloomingdale's about her choice of an outfit for her daughter's second wedding—Americans struck me as people who were willing to reveal details about themselves, their vulnerabilities and struggles. There were people I'd known in Japan for years about whose personal lives I knew nothing.

On the following page: *Photograph of the farmhouse at Futokoro Yama (Breast Pocket Mountain)*

Billy playing shogi (Japanese chess) with our neighbor Ōishi-san, while sitting at the kotatsu *(charcoal brazier).*

Ōishi-san (the wife) holding Mie, Nanao sitting on wall, me with our dog Koko.

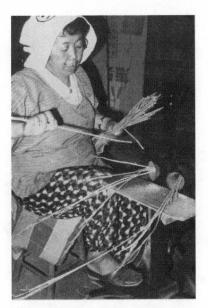

Ōishi-san spinning straw to make sandals and baskets.

Ron and Billy emptying benjo *(traditional toilet).*

Billy's shakuhachi *(bamboo flute) class holding a concert at our farmhouse. That room was our bedroom—example of the versatility of traditional Japanese design.*

I'm in foreground wearing yukata *(summer cotton kimono) for Bon Odori (summer dance festival).*

John Denver enjoying a cup of sake with our neighbors after he gave an impromptu concert at the local shrine.

John holding 3-month-old Mario and 3-year-old Mie.

When I first started studying Shodo (calligraphy). On wall, my first piece for exhibition, Shunpu (Spring wind).

With calligraphy class members.

Practicing weekly lesson.

Relaxing after many hours of writing.

18

I began to build relationships with Japanese women when Satoh-san invited me to join the Feminist Salon. The Salon was where I met my children's doctor, my Japanese language teacher, and Izuka-san, my nanny-housekeeper.

At the time, I recall the feminist movement in America didn't think much of women like me—a mother who admittedly found domestic life challenging, but who also admitted to finding in it a great deal of fulfillment. I was astounded that a prominent spokesperson for the American women's movement, a woman I'd greatly admired, could state that it was "folly" for a woman to have more than one child. Through my participation in the Feminist Salon, I saw the women's movement here could embrace all women, showing as much regard for those women who had chosen professional careers as for those who had chosen to be mothers—whether of one child or four.

Satoh-san started the group to meet what she saw was a real need for women to get together, share, and openly talk about the many issues they faced. At the Salon, they would find encouragement to seek solutions for what for many had become intractable problems. We'd discuss challenges we faced raising children, running households, trying to find suitable work. I was the only foreign member of the Salon, and during our monthly meetings I'd learn about the other women's situations, plights, and predicaments. The Salon helped women obtain loans at a time—and it was not so long ago—it was virtually impossible for a woman in Japan to get a bank loan. I recall one woman who wanted to start a shop selling items made from reformed kimono was helped sourcing used kimono as well as finding a store to lease. No matter what project you had in mind, with Satoh-san at the helm, the women as a group encouraged you to get started.

Once I told Satoh-san I was looking for a modern dance class to join, and she scoured the city of Hamamatsu before she felt certain she could tell me there were no classes.

"I guess you'll have to teach it yourself."

That wasn't my plan at all. I told her I wasn't a modern dance teacher.

"Apparently you know it better than anyone else because there is no one else around," was her quick response.

She found a studio I could use, and until I found a babysitter —in her support-should-not-be-an-abstract-notion style—she pushed Lila around the neighborhood in a stroller the mornings I taught my class. That's how I ended up teaching Martha Graham technique to a group of Hamamatsu women—a core of whom studied with me for more than ten years.

At the Salon, many mothers spoke of feeling isolated and desperate for companionship and opportunities outside of the home. Because of the lack of childcare facilities, babysitting, and playgroup alternatives, it wouldn't be too much to say they felt trapped. Women who lived far from their extended families found themselves isolated, not on a depopulated mountaintop as I'd been, but in the middle of cities. These women could not have imagined anything like the playgroup arrangements I'd had in Vermont—nor would they have availed themselves of them. Each mother saw her child as her charge to bear, alone.

. . .

Satoh-san was a true advocate for women and families. Not long after we'd met at a women's conference, she arranged a series of talks for me to give to women's circles, civic groups, and PTAs. For a full year, I went before groups large and small, in cities and towns, talking mainly about education, women's roles, family life, and the cross-cultural experience.

When Satoh-san asked me to speak at the prefectural head-quarters for a symposium titled "Japanese Women in the Twenty-First Century"—years before the century started—I tried to decline. After all, I wasn't a futurist. But the organizers pleaded with me, saying they simply wanted me to share my ideas, experiences, and perspective on women and child raising in general. Agreeing to speak, the first thing I told that group was about the elaborate arrangements I'd had to make for my baby, Mario then a year old, in order to get away that day and look toward the twenty-first century with them.

Satoh-san told me afterward that she was sure that when I first stood before them, there had not been even one woman in that literally provincial audience who would have guessed that we had so much in common. And that few would have thought that by the time I took my seat again, she'd identify with me. I also spoke at many *kominkan* (community centers) in rural areas. I'd walk into halls full of people who looked like my old village neighbors. Their chatting would stop, murmuring would begin, and then total silence would envelop the hall as they took in my whole person.

With these groups, I'd begin by telling them:

"You might not know anyone who looks like me. But how I look and how you look is only a superficial matter as far as I'm concerned. Although I may look very different from you, my life is very similar in many ways to your lives.

"Like many of you mothers here, I wake up early every morning to prepare my children for school. While they get dressed in their school uniforms, I make their breakfast and very often, that breakfast is miso soup and rice, which is the breakfast my children prefer. On the days it's required, I make their *obento*. Some days I buy fresh tofu and sashimi for our dinner. In the evening the whole family goes in the *ofuro* before we sleep—and yes, we sleep on futon.

"If you were to pass me on the street, you'd never suspect that I make my own *umeboshi* and *rakkyo*, and that I know how to make *o-zōni*. In fact, my neighbor Yoshibo told me he liked my o-zōni better than his mother's! Common dishes like *nimono*, *oyakodon*, *oden*, and *sakana no shio yaki* that are served in homes around Japan every day, I serve in our home, too.

"I have practiced *shodo* (calligraphy) for many years, and my favorite styles are *gyosho* and *sosho*. I love Japanese folk crafts, and in my home I have many pieces I've collected over the years. Like many foreigners who have adapted Japanese ways, I wouldn't dream of walking in my house in shoes.

"Please try to imagine that I was the *kodomokai no fukukaicho* (vice president of the children's association). [I tell them this because it is such a typical Japanese-mother thing to do—and nothing I do will ever make me appear to be a typical Japanese mother.]

"You'll probably have difficulty believing my children's first language is Japanese—and they speak no differently than your children. In fact, they speak Enshu-ben, the dialect of the area where we live.

"I hope you'll see that whether we are different or alike in how we look, what we eat, or even what language we speak, these are superficial matters that cannot tell us what is significant about anyone."

I admit I was calculated in mentioning *umeboshi*.

All Westerners are familiar with sashimi and tofu. But *umeboshi*, a pickled plum said to aid digestion and eaten almost daily, is what every woman, every grandmother, in my audience could relate to, and I knew it. At the mention of homemade *umeboshi* (not many make their own anymore), some in the audience would gasp. Just letting the word *umeboshi* come out of my mouth, I could see them relax.

I easily imagined that they, like many others, were in the habit of judging people by how they look, and saw them as different from themselves—no doubt making assumptions that just don't apply. I wanted to make it clear that types of food eaten and daily customs are cultural concerns and learned behaviors. Once learned, this behavior is ordinary. I had long ago accepted the flexibility of culture. I had no desire to be seen as Japanese or even acting Japanese.

I would stand out in Japan, always. But I could also fit in.

19

B ringing your wife to Japan is like bringing a bag lunch to a
smorgasbord."

That's what an American man who lived in Hamamatsu told
Billy some years back. I recall thinking that this was the most
outrageous thing I heard this person, who I'd always thought
obnoxious, had ever said.

"What's that supposed to mean?" was my icy response to
Billy. I wasn't asking a question, but I got an answer.

"He said that since foreign men here can choose among so
many available, beautiful Japanese women who are willing to do
anything for them, why come to this country with a wife."

Well! I never!

I forget the context in which Billy told me this, and certainly
his repeating it held no significance as he knew I was inclined to
disregard rather than comment on this man's utterings. He was
an ex-Marine, a tragic figure who abused his wife, abandoned
his son, and later committed suicide.

When I arrived in Japan all those decades ago, Western women
(American women in particular) were perceived as demanding

harridans who exacted a stiff domestic price from their husbands. This perspective even came with its own word: *kakadenka*. Translated as "henpecked," it seems to have gone out of fashion, like *spinster*.

Apparently, Billy was henpecked, because he participated in the activities of raising a family and took on some of the chores of running a house. His chores (airing the futon, taking out the garbage) could be seen by others. Although I usually carried our babies on my back, if he pushed the baby in the stroller, it seemed the world—at any rate, the neighborhood—took notice. While I didn't think of Billy as having "a hard act to follow," having been raised by a man, I surely knew men could be as capable as women in the house. Billy never had to iron dresses as Daddy regularly did, but with three daughters, I did see to it he knew how to braid their hair.

I once caused a stir around here because of something I said in an interview with a local newspaper. Long before I saw a copy of the interview, I heard about it—from Mario's Shorinji Kempo sensei, my dentist, neighbors, a gas station attendant, and a deliveryman. Mo-chan, a friend from our old village, telephoned me, saying, essentially, "Right on!"

The thing that stood out for everyone in this lengthy interview was my statement that "I expect my husband to be home for dinner." Not exactly revolutionary stuff. I'd just said that the short time in the day when the family can sit together at the dinner table and eat a meal I've prepared for us all to enjoy is important. And I wasn't forgiving about giving up a minute of it to the office, the school, or even traffic.

My friend Sachiko, a dentist, told me she couldn't recall when her husband last had a meal with the family. A businessman, he tended to disappear around dinnertime. On his day off, he'd leave the house early and do whatever he chose. Contrary to the then commonly accepted notion that Japanese women didn't care if their husbands are never at home or stay out drinking and carousing, it really upset her. She said she felt she was raising their three children single-handedly. "Sure, he provides a comfortable living, but that's not all I want from him." Given that she was financially independent, that was evidently not all she needed either.

Satoh-san once told me, "Japanese men are holding on to ideas that are no longer viable. In present-day Japanese society, women and children are changing. Only men do not appear to change."

Sachiko was one of those who'd called about the controversial interview. She said her husband had also read it, confessed he'd been "remiss," and announced he planned to "review" his entire relationship with the family. I remember thinking maybe he would change. Maybe *kakadenka*, a word I never hear anymore, was gone for good.

I didn't know anything about being a wife and was figuring out as I went along how to be a mother. I adopted any number of Japanese customs, like *ombu*. Although I had foreign women telling me I had "gone native" by this practice of having my babies take their naps on my back, I saw having my hands free as practical.

I did look to other mothers for clues, and I found that many were way out of my league as they could claim competence as gardeners and dressmakers, bakers and accountants. A lot of them were tutors, too, and I was glad I could rely on Izuka-san to tutor Mie in mathematics.

Cajoling kids to eat was not a habit I was going to pick up. I've seen Japanese mothers chase a toddler around a room trying to get them to take a bite of a rice ball. I prepared and served food I thought was good, and ate it myself. The kids were free to eat it or not, as they chose. I never offered alternatives. I assumed they'd eat if they were hungry.

Although I had nothing but respect for those mothers I saw settling sibling disputes, employing skills any diplomat would envy, my own way of handling this was not to—I never inter-vened. If I heard crying during playtime, I ignored it. I figured either they would come to me if they needed me, or I'd go when I saw blood.

In Japan, I felt that a mother was not just a private role within one's family, but a public one as well. There were ways you were expected to behave, speak, and yes, dress. This was all news to me as my mothering style, mirroring my general lifestyle, could probably have best been described as "freewheelin'."

One of the few times I rebelled against what I saw as insuffer-able conformity was when I wore a beige dress to Nanao's elementary school graduation. I knew—I'd been told—all the mothers would wear black. I'm sure it seems like a small thing, but when you see that graduation photo, it's obvious I was announcing, loud and clear: *I'm an iconoclast. I'm a rebel. I not only march to my own drummer, but the last thing I will do is what everyone else is doing just because that's the way it's done.*

Ah, that was the early me. I later fell in line, at least to some extent. Lest my children pay the price for my showing up at PTA meetings and on open-school days, not as their mother, but as the Foreign Woman Who Is Obviously Different, I had to stop with the I'm Doing My Own Thing stance. The first things to go were my dangling earrings. Later, the long skirts I'd bought in India were only worn at home. I remember Nanao telling me that when I went to the PTA meetings, I should "be sure to dress like the other mothers," innocently believing I'd blend in. I showed up dutifully, making no effort to blend in, just not stand out.

And I had to learn that as a mother, there are always duties, and no escape, nowhere to run or hide when my card came up. Although it took years for this to sink in, I did come to see that it was impossible to live in a Japanese community and not accept this basic fact: Your turn will come. It may be for the children's association, the neighborhood association, or any of the many slots to be filled in the PTA. But as sure as the rainy season, seldom would a year pass when you were not called on to be an official in this or that group—and it wasn't unusual to be in several groups at the same time.

Every time I was chosen for something or told that I'd been selected for yet another committee, my first reaction was, and without fail: *No way.* But this was followed, and with lightning speed, by the realization that it was my turn. I wasn't even dreaming of saying, "No. I won't do it."

One day, a woman in our neighborhood, a mother who knew she'd soon have to hold the staff of office, stopped me in the grocery store and said she knew I'd already served a term as vice president of the children's association.

"Did you volunteer for the position?" she asked.

"Are you joking?" I'd only agreed to it when I saw there was no way out.

"Yeah, nobody ever *wants* to do it," she said.

"But you're all used to participating as a group, no questions asked. No one seems to mind."

" 'Seems' and reality are different," she said. "We just know there's no getting out of it and we accept it. But believe me, everybody is dragged into it."

So I adopted this attitude: Do it now and get it over with. No matter how busy I was at the time, I reasoned, I might be busier later. I did whatever was asked of me, and likened it to making a deposit in the bank. The time would come when I wouldn't be available to do something, and then I'd have a little cushion and could draw on my deposit.

There were always various responsibilities in the public school, and we mothers were all obligated to participate. There'd be a meeting to outline what positions had to be filled. Some mothers, I noticed, would volunteer immediately, deciding it was best to get it out of the way. Then there were the others who'd try to fade into the edges of the group until they had no recourse. I'd tried the blank I'm-a-foreigner-I-don't-know-what's-going-on look, but it didn't work at all. Everyone was more than happy to explain it to me.

One year I was chosen (I can't say elected since there was no democratic process involved) to be a representative in Mario's first-year junior high school class. In the hall on my way to the classroom to assume my new position, I met the woman who would be the co-representative. I had my work cut out for me, let me tell you, trying to convince her that she should be the leader and I the assistant.

"Oh no, Anton-san, please. Oh, won't you be the leader?" she pleaded.

"Oh, I beg you," I said. "Not me, please."

"*Onegaishiamsu.* I implore you," she said.

Have a heart, I'm on bended knee, in the name of all that's good, I ask your indulgence. I was running out of ways to beg.

"Oh, I beseech you," she went on, "I don't know anything. This is my first experience with junior high school."

Now she had me. I had the dubious distinction of being her *sempai* (the senior or superior) in this circumstance because I'd already had two kids in and out of junior high school and was on my third.

"Don't worry," I said, "I'll be right by your side. I just don't want to be the leader," who I knew had to read long notices to the assembled—and there would be no time to decide if you did or did not know a kanji or to check electronic dictionaries.

But she wasn't giving up. "I've been ill," she told me. "I don't know if I'll be strong enough to attend all the meetings."

I wasn't going to be outdone in the illness department. I had a few stories of my own, and at the time could even say I had been hospitalized and had only recently been discharged.

Wouldn't you know it, she too had been in the hospital, and for something worse!

We both went on, exchanging stories and vivid descriptions of our various symptoms and ailments, delineating clearly and to what degree we were debilitated. We mentioned our prescribed medications by name. Although we were—*okagesama de*, "thanks to you"—much improved, we were still under a doctor's care. (Saying *"okagesama de"* is a common expression in Japanese. It essentially means you are giving the other person credit that you, or a family member, are in good health— although that other person does not, in fact, have anything to do with the good state of your health.) I think if we'd had surgical scars, we would've shown them!

Finally, we both just laughed and said, "Okay. Let's do it together."

I got to know local women, other mothers, through the many community and school activities we were all active in. Reliably, we could be found cutting weeds along the roadside or working as early-morning traffic monitors when the kids boarded the bus for school. We were an army.

The time I told my kids I'd been appointed *fukukaicho* (vice president) of the Children's Association, they thought I must have gotten the message wrong. Could their mama really be in such a lofty position? I called the *kaicho* (president) Maeyama-san to check (after all, it wouldn't have been the first time I'd misinterpreted a message in Japanese) and she reassured me.

"Oh yes, you're *fukukaicho*. I told you on the phone."

"Yes, I know," I answered, and told her that my kids didn't believe me.

"I wonder why not?"

And yeah, I wonder, too. My father had been head of the Community League of 159th Street numerous times. I should've let them know I come from a solid line of community leadership.

These neighborhood women were the same ladies I once got together with for a year-end party. I've been to many Japanese parties, and the simplest thing I can say is: we don't mean the same thing when we use that noun. Sitting around a low table eating and chatting, with no music and definitely no dancing, is just not my idea of a party. But this particular party turned out not to be just a fun get-together, but a total blast.

Housewives and mothers one and all, our "women only" party was a potluck dinner. And it was a delicious, if somewhat mixed-bag, feast of pizza, cream corn stew, fried oysters, salads, baked stuffed fish, chocolate cake, and custard pudding. I was the only one to bring a traditional Japanese dish, *oden*. Simple and hot (and what I'd fed the family before going to the party), this clay pot stew of boiled fish cakes, *konnyaku*, and daikon was eaten up immediately. Along with the beer and wine there was, you guessed it, karaoke. Later, someone put on a tape and all my sister housewives started to dance to a song that had the refrain "Popeye the sailor man!" I recalled the song was popular with Nanao when she was in second grade.

"Do you have any dance music?" someone asked me.

Dance music? I couldn't conceive of a party without dance music. I was home and back in a flash with Hammer, LL Cool J, Salt-N-Pepa, Tina Turner, Third World, Marvin Gaye, Prince. I put on the cassette, and within minutes the fluorescent lights were turned off and someone had plugged in a thing that looked like a crystal ball with garish lights that rotated at a dizzying speed. One woman stood on a chair twirling a flashlight while calling out, "Let's disco!" With a lot of loud laughing and talking, it got positively boisterous. There was sweating, taking off of sweaters, and general letting down of hair. And well we could —there wasn't a man in sight.

"We could never act like this if our husbands were around," Ogo-san said. "If they were here they just wouldn't like it, and we'd never feel so relaxed. And even if our husbands pretended to enjoy it, you can be sure they would complain about it the next day. And in any case, we wouldn't be comfortable acting like this around them."

Considering the degree to which they were letting it all hang out, I asked her if they didn't feel pent up all year long. After all, *year-end party* means just that.

"Oh no, no. Our husbands expect us to be meek, quiet, and well-behaved, and we're used to it. It's no problem."

I couldn't have been more different from these women. What they could accept in their marriages I would have found not just stifling, but unbearable. Yes, we were very different, but here we were, women on the loose, escapee mothers, housewives gone to hell, partying our butts off. Like I said, it was a total blast.

With other mothers and co-officials of the Kodomokai (children's association).

My nanny-housekeeper-friend, Kiyoko Izuka in kimono, (I'm barely visible but she's so beautiful I chose this photo anyway).

With members of the modern dance class I taught in Hamamatsu for ten years.

With Roberta Flack after one of her concerts in Japan. Her personality matches her voice—beautiful and unique.

(L to R) Lila, Mario, Nanao, Mie.

The family at new year 1988. Rear: Karen, Billy, Nanao. Front: Mario, Mie, Lila.

Family photo with our dog Kuku.

At home in Tenryu – with grandsons Isaiah (rear) and Luka

20

I began writing for *The Japan Times*, Japan's largest and oldest English-language newspaper, in 1979 when they published an essay I wrote. Jean Pearce, the columnist who'd rescued me when she gave me information about the fertility specialist, told me the paper planned to start a new column titled "Living in Japan" and that they would invite readers to contribute essays about their experiences. Knowing I was a loyal reader and that I'd written essays, she urged me to contribute something.

In those days, Billy regularly borrowed a typewriter from a friend's office in town. Over the weekend I'd type up anything I'd written and he'd return the portable Smith Corona on Monday. I sat down to write my essay for "Living in Japan"—which had a five-hundred-word limit—and when I looked up, I had two thousand words. I submitted it anyway.

Fortunately for me, they liked it, asked for photographs, and published my essay—not for that new column, but as a Sunday feature article.

I had no other purpose in writing that article than to tell people about the beautiful place where we lived—where we live still—

in Tenryu, Shizuoka Prefecture. A place that is a vista of bamboo stands, terraced rice paddies, and rolling green tea bushes. Here mountains meet the sky, outlining the foothills of the southern Japanese Alps.

The Japan Times readers are longtime foreign residents as well as those newly arrived. And naturally there are many Japanese readers, many who are curious about those foreigners who have chosen to live on their crowded island. This is the readership I addressed as I told them about the people we were settled among, farmers who lived and died in the houses they built from trees cut from their own land, people whose simple lives were carried on in a quiet continuum with the seasons.

I wanted people to know about my nearest neighbor, Ōishi-san, who grew everything she ate, and who on a rainy day, when she wasn't in the field, could be found spinning straw for baskets and sandals, or making futon. (It was common for traditional Japanese women to create their own futon.) In her house, the wood in the entranceway had the sheen like that in Buddhist temples from the daily wiping.

I thought readers might like to hear about the time a fox came to nibble at a pumpkin pie I'd put outside to cool, and how when I told this story to Ōishi-san, she was more curious to know about what I'd done with the *kabocha* (squash) she'd given me than the fox.

In that essay, I wrote that if you walked in the woods around our old farmhouse, you might be surprised by a bevy of quail, or perhaps one lone mushroom, shooting up from the dark forest floor, ivory white and twenty centimeters tall.

Gyo Hani, then the managing editor of the paper, praised my essay and encouraged me to continue to write. I was grateful and, putting it on the back shelf of my mind, hoped I'd be able to write something else *The Japan Times* would print.

Mie, not yet a year old, kept me busy running after her in the yard as she chased lizards and sat in mud puddles eating rocks, and when in the house, supplemented this diet by tearing out and eating the rice paper of the shoji screens. I'd had my easy ride with Nanao. Mie was on the go from sunup, and as soon as she could speak, she made demands. Billy used to tell me, "You've met your match." I can't blame my lack of literary production at the time on my "match," but I can say she did not contribute to a supportive environment for writing and certainly had no interest in my authoring aspirations.

I'd read *The Japan Times* from the first day we arrived in Japan.

In those first days, when there was not one word of Japanese that was intelligible, I found solace in being able to read. Period.

And I didn't just read the paper. I read every word. Every evening, the paper was what I most looked forward to after dinner, and after the end of another day of being unable to use language to communicate. Doing the crossword puzzle was my dessert.

In those early years, it was more than a newspaper to me, it was company.

Sometime around the mideighties, the paper announced with regret that one of its regular columnists had died suddenly. I was sorry to hear the news. I knew the writer through her column, which I'd enjoyed and would miss reading. Putting aside all thoughts of being an opportunist, it occurred to me that newspapers must always be seeking to fill space. I'd noticed too that most of the columns in the paper had a Tokyo dateline. I didn't know Tokyo at all at the time. I thought of it as a place to renew my passport at the American Embassy. I was living proof that not every foreigner living in Japan was living in Tokyo.

Several years had passed, but Hani-san was supportive when I asked the editors to let me write a column with a dateline from Hamamatsu, where we were then living. Hamamatsu is the place people pass when they speed by on the Shinkansen ("bullet train") to Tokyo, or Kyoto in the opposite direction. We knew it not only as our home, but the home of Yamaha, Suzuki, and Honda, those giants of Japanese industry and pillars of Japan's "economic miracle." I wrote the column "Hamamatsu Highlights" for seven years, introducing readers to people and places, artists and events, and facts, like Hamamatsu having more sunny days than any other place in Japan.

I started writing a column I titled "Crossing Cultures" shortly after we bought land and built our current house in 1990.

Having made that commitment, I realized there were few foreign families (I didn't know any) who were settled quite as firmly as we were. Deciding to stay in Japan after that first year at the dojo, we'd simply thrown in our lot with the people of this country. As an American couple living and raising a family in rural Japan, we were a rarity.

We had no Japanese family members—though I often wished we did. I think it must be the single most desirable element to live in Japan. As part of a Japanese family, our children would have grandparents as well as an extended family of aunts, uncles, cousins. Family would give us occasion to participate in Japan's many cultural rituals, and help open some of the doors to this culture that influence many aspects of daily life. A family would be both informant and guide, shedding light in some of those arcane corners that might otherwise forever remain in darkness. Having a family would give us a haven, a place we and our children knew we were always welcome. It would be our *jikka*, a home we could always return to.

I suggested to my editor at *The Japan Times* that readers might be interested to read about life in Japan from the perspective and experience of a foreign woman participating in society here at every level. Not especially enthusiastic, she responded dryly, "Let me see something."

That something was my first column, published November 8, 1990.

Immediately, the column proved popular. And what a joy it

was for me to share my life and experiences with such a large and receptive audience. I still keep the many letters of appreciation I received, and not least because these handwritten and typed letters are now relics.

The Japan expert and writer Donald Richie, who would become not just a good friend but a supporter, told me my column was the first thing he read on the days it appeared. Men and women from all over Japan, as well as from Ireland, Austria, Ghana, Hawaii, Poland, and Sri Lanka, to name a few countries, wrote telling me that through my column and my eyes, they felt they were experiencing the "real" Japan.

The "real" Japan for readers meant our *inaka* (countryside) lifestyle. How "lucky" I was to have experienced the rustic life, they told me—though I think few would've wanted to be as "lucky" as I'd been to build a fire to heat their bath, have no plumbing, and empty their own toilet. In the column, I didn't romanticize these aspects of our country life—by that time I had come to see them as deprivations.

Deprivations notwithstanding, I noticed and observed everything, and enjoyed immensely telling my stories of raising a family here and the children's school life, as well as my interactions in the neighborhood and community. I reported on what amused me, like that time the other mother and I were prepared to show surgical scars we didn't have.

I shared my sadness as I experienced the unrelenting depopulation of the countryside. A tragedy in so many ways for Japanese society, it hit me personally as it accompanied the deaths of my old neighbors, Ōi-san, Arai-san, and Ōtani-san—farm women who'd kept me supplied with green tea and shiitake.

Japan was full of surprises, and lessons, and I never ran out of things to write about. Now into my fourth decade, I continue to uncover new aspects of Japanese life and culture. This unending discovery remains one of the things I find so appealing about living here.

To have a forum and outlet where I could openly express my ideas and feelings greatly enhanced my experience of living in Japan. Sharing my thoughts with an appreciative audience was more than beneficial: it sustained me. I have often wondered, and doubted, if I would have remained in Japan as long as I have without it.

I came up with the title "Crossing Cultures" for the column thinking I was entirely original. I didn't know anything "official" about the acculturation process. Still, I knew my cross-cultural experience was as valid as any.

Readers often wrote wanting to know my "coping strategies" for living in Japan. The very term "coping strategy" always sounded to me like there was some mechanism that you could put into action as soon as you faced some cross-cultural difficulty—and that it would get you through until the next time you had to "cope."

I bet there are coping strategies—ways of getting by, managing, surviving. But in all my years of living abroad, I've had to deal with problems, face obstacles, and remove barriers, only to find another, higher barrier down the road. I've had to do my best to *overcome* difficulties. I am not familiar with coping.

The column never proposed to be an advice column, but that didn't deter those many readers who wrote asking for advice. I appreciated the confidence readers had in my opinions and responded, thoughtfully, to each query. Almost all letters seeking advice were from people dealing with some problem of living in Japan. Sometimes these problems reached crisis proportions, which appeared to be when a person would take the extraordinary step of asking for advice on personal matters from someone they didn't personally know.

An outstanding example of this occurred some years ago when *The Japan Times* telephoned me saying they'd received a call from an American woman, an expat, who wanted to contact me. They told her to write to me at the paper, but she insisted she needed to talk to me. Since it was the newspaper's policy not to give out the telephone numbers of its writers, they asked if I'd call her, saying "she seems desperate."

The moment the woman heard my voice on the telephone, she began to cry uncontrollably. Calming down, she told me of her troubles—she had quite a few, of varying degrees of gravity. She wanted to meet me in person and I would've met her, but when she understood that I didn't live anywhere near her, she was close to despair. I suggested she contact a counseling service in Tokyo—which she'd already done. Although she found them helpful, she said she wanted to talk with me because she read my column regularly "and I really know you."

We talked for a long time and later corresponded. I was also able to talk with her husband. After further crises and intervention, I learned she and her family left Japan. I cannot be sure I was any help, but I was glad she felt comfortable contacting me, and that readers of my column thought I was a person who was available, willing to listen. It meant a lot to me knowing I connected with my readers.

Most requests for advice were more mundane, reflecting some aspect of the challenges of cross-cultural living, generally negative experiences with accompanying undesirable outcomes. One woman, a longtime resident, wrote saying she was having problems with her neighbors. Stating that because her opinions corresponded "pretty closely" to mine, and since she agreed with "almost all" my views, she wanted to know my day-to-day strategy for dealing with "the Japanese woman."

Because my life and relationships in Japan haven't been without problems, I hardly thought of myself as an expert or role model. I have stepped on toes, rubbed, and been rubbed, the wrong way. But I could tell her this: it would serve her well to see Japanese women for the individuals they surely are, and not a species.

Should I/should I not leave/return to Japan was a recurrent

theme of letters seeking advice. But in that category, this following letter was unique:

"This is my first letter to you. I'm reading your column in *The Japan Times* every time. I'm thinking whether I shall move back to Japan or not. I am Japanese and came to school in the U.S. and met my husband, who is a Japanese American. That was eleven years ago. We filed for our divorce and it was final last year."

The writer went on to say that although she had a good-paying job, there was nothing to keep her in the States.

"But I don't know if I can fit into Japanese social life since I have been in the U.S. since age of twenty-three. I should admit that I've been influenced with American culture." In the next paragraph, she wrote that since she considers Japan to be a male-dominated society, she didn't know if she could remarry a Japanese man.

She concluded: "I really need your opinions about Japan and what you think."

What I think? *Wow* is what I thought when I put her aerogram on my desk. The cultures have certainly crossed and the tables truly turned when a Japanese woman was asking me if she should return to Japan to live and, possibly, marry a Japanese man.

How do advice columnists do it? I wondered. Did they always feel confident they were right and had given good advice? Did they lie awake at night burdened with the responsibility of advising people about matters of consequence? Were they comfortable guiding people toward decisions that might significantly affect their future lives? Did they enter into a dialogue with the people they advised or just write and tell them what to do?

If advice columnists typically responded right away, I knew I wouldn't make a good one, because I thought about what this woman asked me for two weeks before I felt I could give her a well-considered reply.

. . .

Nothing piqued readers' interest more than the matter of how we were handling our children's education. For many foreign parents living in Japan, the necessity of sending their children to Japanese schools was simply the critical crossing point: the time to leave.

There were no international schools in our area, and even if those schools had been a geographic possibility, they would not have been a financial one. The exorbitant tuition is most commonly covered by an employee's company. Our kids went to local public schools.

Readers wanted to know if our kids were bilingual, and if so, how did they get that way?

It's a well-known fact that young children have an incredible ability to learn languages. While adults struggle to learn a foreign language, children can have native fluency in a relatively short time. Billy and I were amazed how fast Nanao learned to speak, read, and write Japanese—and in Japanese, these are three very discrete skills.

We arrived in Japan on June 1, 1975, and when Nanao entered kindergarten on September 1 that year, she was functional in Japanese. She didn't have any special lessons or tutors; we didn't do anything to augment her exposure to Japanese. Her Japanese language acquisition appeared to be a seamless process. I still remember the afternoon at the dojo she ran up to me saying, "Mama, listen! I can read this," and proceeded to read from a children's book Ito-san had given her.

"Yes, yes. How wonderful. Now run along and play, dear." To myself I thought: *Sure, sure. Nobody can read that stuff. It looks like Chinese.*

Once we were living on Breast Pocket Mountain, Billy and I relied on Nanao to read notes from her teachers, school announcements of upcoming events, and the *kairanban*, the neighborhood bulletins that circulate door to door, informing you about everything from local recitals to the proper disposal of garbage and where to evacuate in the event of an earthquake.

Mie was the test case for us. Although she was born in Japan, we weren't confident she'd learn Japanese since it wasn't spoken in our home and we didn't have Japanese relatives. At the time, we didn't know that children will naturally speak the language of the society they live in. We would've had to go out of our way for her to *not* speak Japanese. Of more concern should have been her speaking English.

During those early years, I tried to find out what I could about raising bilingual children, and I would've welcomed sharing experiences with similar families, but I didn't know any families in similar circumstances. I searched everywhere for information, and the best I found was the *Bilingual Family Newsletter*—a six-page brochure published twice a year.

Growing up, Mie spoke to us in Japanese, exclusively. We spoke to her in English, but she always answered in Japanese. I would later learn that if you want your children to be bilingual, you must *insist* they *only* speak to you in *your* language. We understood her, and she understood us, and we felt that we were already different enough in our community—we didn't want to put pressure on her. I read to her in English, sang children's songs—and hoped for the best. Whenever we could, we visited the States and sent the kids to summer camps. I trusted she'd speak English, eventually, and naturally. She did. And she studied Chinese.

Nanao had attended a Montessori preschool in Vermont, and Maria Montessori's statement that "A student is not a vessel to be filled, but a lamp to be lighted" could describe my educational philosophy.

I had only been in Japan a short time before I realized how very conformist schools were. I was sure children were not encouraged to develop individually, and I simply dreaded the idea Nanao would become just another little "vessel" with information being poured into her head eight hours a day. I felt at a loss, and began to think the years of raising my daughter according to the principles of a progressive education would all come to naught.

I considered home schooling, but decided it was not desirable. It just didn't seem to be the best choice in a society where group participation carries so much importance. The home-schooled children in Japan I knew were all the sons and daughters of missionaries. These families were in Japan at the behest of their church. Their purpose in being here was not to participate in Japanese society but to convert it—at least this is what a friend, a Charismatic Evangelical Christian from Alabama, told me.

Pragmatism is what permitted me to let Nanao go to Japanese public school. It wasn't easy to accept at first, but I realized I would simply have to let go of my education-has-to-be-this-way-and-no-other attitude. Nanao, of course, didn't balk at going to public school, and was as enthusiastic as any kid her age. She entered elementary school when we moved from the dojo to Breast Pocket Mountain. On her first day, the principal, a simple, no-nonsense kind of man, made it plain that he didn't intend for the one and only foreign child in the school to have a hard time. As Nanao, Billy, and I stood beside the principal in the schoolyard in front of the entire school body (about a hundred kids), he introduced her and said, "We are a group. No one is to be left out."

Nanao was the first foreign child in her kindergarten, elementary, and junior high school. All four of our kids were always the only foreign children in their schools and our community.

When Mario and Lila were in elementary school, our prefecture conducted a special survey of foreign children in public schools to find out what problems they were having. The principal of their school was asked if they could be interviewed, and he'd answered, "Why? They certainly don't have any problems. And they're not 'foreign.' "

During those initial years in Japan, although I often complained about Nanao's long school day, the many tests, the six-day school week, the short vacations, the uniforms—Nanao never complained about any of it. She'd essentially never gone to school anywhere else, so adjusting to public school in Japan wasn't a big deal for her. Far from paying attention to my disdainful cries of "school on Saturday!" I bet she thought I was nuts.

Still, I was open in my criticism of Japanese education, especially what I saw as its stifling conformity and overemphasis on rote learning. An early essay I wrote, published in translation, criticized Japanese schools for being institutionalized mills of processed learning. That essay, appearing in the book *Gaikokujin no Shizuoka Mita* ("Foreigners View Shizuoka"), was illustrated by the editor with a drawing that showed a teacher removing a sign saying "Elementary School" and replacing it with one saying "Factory." An army of identical-looking children, their eyes glazed with the same empty stare, march robot-like past the teacher and through the school gate.

I came to adjust my view, and can say now I've never regretted our decision to send Nanao, and then Mie, Mario, and Lila, to public school in Japan. It helped them to be socialized in this country, and of course, it was the best way for them to learn Japanese.

Yes, they were always the only foreign children in their schools and our community, but they didn't see themselves as different, in any significant way, from their friends and classmates. For little kids, it can't be easy being the "only" anything, and no doubt there were challenges. The one big challenge I remember Mie facing in elementary school was when she came home and told me a kid "called me American!" I had to inform her that she was indeed American, and that in any case, it was not an insult.

Not being born rebels, they accepted all the school rules of behavior (which are legion) just like their classmates. They were generally eager to go to school (if I'd wanted to punish them, I would've said "You can't go to school")—had many friends, enjoyed their activities, and liked their teachers. They did their assigned homework every day during summer vacation. All three girls were stars on their volleyball teams, fast runners, and good swimmers, and Mario excelled in every sport he played.

I can now look back and say that for all my criticism, I recognize and commend Japan for its educational accomplishments. Its high rate of literacy, which is virtually 100%, is an achievement anyone anywhere can appreciate.

And the equality of educational opportunity in this country is something that should be emulated by all countries that claim to be democracies. Our kids have always gone to school with the children of doctors, engineers, carpenters, office and factory workers, shopkeepers, hairdressers, dentists, and farmers. The property tax a student's parents pay does not dictate the kind of school available to them. There are no leaking roofs in Japanese schools. There are no schools that don't have sufficient textbooks. No teacher in Japan has ever had to "chip in for chalk."

Just after the beginning of the school year in April, public schools in Japan start their program of *katei homon*. Although this translates as "home visit," I don't think we have anything comparable in the U.S. Of course, I was in elementary school so long ago that all I can remember are the wooden desks, inkwells, and globe lights, but still, I have no recollection of any teacher ever visiting my home.

No matter where their students live, nor how many students they have, teachers go to the home of each one for this annual visit. They came to our out-of-the-way farmhouse. They came to our home when we lived in town and our children attended the city's largest elementary school. I don't know what the original purpose of these home visits was, but I don't think there is any hidden agenda. The teacher usually spends twenty to thirty minutes at each home—and although it's not an inspection tour, they probably get some idea of the child's home environment after visiting the house and talking with parents.

Some mothers have told me they're always full of anxiety before one of these home visits. Anxious to be courteous and to make a good impression, they might spend the day before cleaning the entire house or baking something to serve with tea. But the teachers, equally anxious not to impose, will offer to talk in the entrance, and generally refuse all refreshments.

The title of sensei (teacher) carries so much weight and importance that some parents find just that intimidating. But I always got the feeling the teachers were glad to meet parents outside the confines of school when the conversation could easily slip away from the academic. I spent part of one visit talking about sushi. The teacher's family ran a sushi restaurant and as a result, apparently, the teacher had hated sushi all his life.

Another time I was amused when the teacher said, in respectful tones, that he had been wanting to ask me about the braided band of colored embroidery thread Lila wore tied around her left ankle. When I told him it was just something she'd made in a day camp when we visited America, that all the kids were wearing them, he appeared relieved. It seems when he'd asked Lila if it could be taken off, she'd said "Oh, no." She'd meant that it was tied in a tight knot. Her teacher thought her colored braid might have some religious or cultural significance and he didn't want to offend.

The teachers impressed me with their detailed observations of their pupils. They typically had thirty to forty students in a class, and after saying something positive about a child's individual traits, they could tell you how your child socializes as well as they could recall their scholastic record. If a teacher thinks a pupil needs help, they may suggest extra drills, which they'll give with your permission. In all the years our children went to public school here, no teacher ever recommended we hire tutors, or send them to *juku*. These coaching schools that help students keep up in class or prepare them for entrance examinations make up a big part of Japan's huge education industrial complex.

With their long hours, short vacations, and endless tests to grade, and the many extracurricular activities they participated in or supervised, when teachers showed up at my door, I was simply astounded they could find the time. And, as demonstrated by the following incident, teachers were also amazingly caring.

Mario was always athletic. He's run in marathons since he was little, and when he wasn't combing Barbie dolls' hair with his sisters, he played team sports and did martial arts. In junior high school, he bicycled to school and back twelve kilometers every day, reaching our home on the steepest hill at night.

I'm sure that day of the sports test he'd put his all into the fifty-meter sprint, before crumbling at the forty-five-meter line. His teacher's calm voice told me over the telephone that he'd had an accident, he was all right, and I should come to the hospital immediately with my health insurance card and seal. Not known for lingering in the mirror, I was fully dressed and in the car in eighty-nine seconds. When I arrived, he'd just been X-rayed and diagnosed with an avulsion fracture of the thigh bone. This type of fracture where ligament tears away from the bone taking a fragment of bone with it, occurs commonly among adolescents, when their muscles are stronger than their still pliable bones.

"I'll see to it he takes it easy," I said to the doctor, as I was trying to figure out how he'd be able to climb the stairs to his second-floor bedroom, and the ladder to his loft bed, when the doctor said, "He'll have to stay in the hospital."

I actually gasped. Leave my third child and only son in a hospital? The only time any of my children had been in a hospital was when they were born. Patiently, the doctor explained Mario would have to stay until he could lift his leg. Mario, writhing in pain, couldn't lift anything.

Our local national hospital (and I note: in Japan, if you say an institution is national or public, it implies it's the best) is a ten-minute drive from our house. I could visit often, but I was stretched as I'd just started writing for another newspaper, and now had five deadlines a month.

It was helpful knowing the school principal visited Mario often, and that Umebayashi-sensei, his homeroom teacher (who'd also been Mie's teacher), went every day. Umebayashi-sensei was also his math teacher, so on some visits he tutored him. On many days, he sat by Mario's bedside until he fell asleep.

This was more than diligence—and this caring attention was something I came to deeply respect in teachers here.

A consistent feature of Japanese education that was so different from my own experience was this: every student was expected to learn.

I remember the year Lila's teacher asked if it was all right with me if she gave her extra drills in mathematics. She said that soon new concepts would be introduced and she wanted to be certain Lila had a firm basis in the work that had gone before, and that if she didn't, she would be "lost."

This was arresting information, because "lost" is just what happened to me around the same time in my early education. In my case, however, my father was not told that I needed help and that I was at an important crossroads in the subject—but rather, that I had no ability in mathematics. My teacher told my father not to even expect me to learn mathematics—and that with luck (and luck is what it would take), I would get by. This information was given to my father when he visited the school for "open-school week." The teacher also told my father—and I remember his exact words still: "Karen will never be able to do more than count her change."

The devastating effect of this teacher's words—and more than that, the lack of confidence, lack of expectation, and total absence of belief in my ability—was immediate. I lost interest in learning and I no longer expected myself to learn—mathematics or anything else. I had loved school, loved learning, and had good enough grades, but soon all of my grades began to suffer.

It was not until a junior high school teacher took an interest in me that things started to change. She seemed to think it was peculiar that although my records showed I had been a good student, all my grades had gone into a precipitous decline at the same time. One day after class, she asked me why. This was a very long time ago, and I don't remember exactly what I told her —probably I said I was just stupid—but I do remember what she told me: "Don't talk such nonsense. You are a smart girl. I know you are. If you're having difficulty with mathematics, I'll help you. There's no reason why you cannot learn mathematics, or any subject."

As can be expected, I went from being the class dolt to being thought of as one of the "smart kids." This teacher encouraged me to apply to the Bronx High School of Science (I had to take a science aptitude test to even be permitted to take the entrance test), one of the most prestigious high schools in New York City. I didn't get in. But what's telling is that I never thought of it as a failure. I'm sure she wanted me to know that I could have the same goals as the "smart kids." My teacher wanted to reinforce in me the idea that I was capable. She expected something of me, so I could expect something of myself.

Indeed, the "luck" the other teacher spoke of did play a part. My luck was having a teacher who cared about me. But I don't think any child should have to depend on luck for an education.

Still, and always, I thank you, Mrs. Josephine Jones.

· · ·

My biggest concern about Nanao attending Japanese public school was my certainty she wouldn't be encouraged to develop as a creative individual. I was convinced she wouldn't learn to express herself, think for herself, have her own opinions and ideas. And I was right on all counts: no part of her education in Japan prepared her in that way. And in junior high school, students are put on a conveyor belt of education they never leave, as the focus is not on learning, but testing, and memorizing facts and figures. It became increasingly clear Nanao would not be nourished in the one-track Japanese educational system that kills curiosity and so utterly restricts the minds, imaginations, and spirits of children.

My concerns were all brought into sharp relief the day Billy returned from a parent-teacher conference in Nanao's second year of junior high school. He was livid.

"Not only did this guy [her teacher] not get that Nanao's bilingualism and biculturalism were a plus, he called it a *handicap*—and I know that word in Japanese."

It was discouraging, to say the least. But by that time, I'd come to accept that we'd chosen to live here, and that educating our children in Japan was our fate. I told Billy Nanao would just have to avail herself of the education available.

"Oh no," he said. "That's not going to happen. They don't deserve our daughter."

And from that moment, he set about finding a school that did deserve her—and ensured that she'd get the education she deserved. In over forty years of marriage, we have argued about everything in the cosmos, but never these: money and child raising. I knew he had Nanao's best interests in mind.

Yes, we'd chosen our life, but we were united in thinking we should equip our children to be able to choose theirs, too. And probably the best way they'd be able to do that was if they also had an English-based education. The time had come, and we'd soon have to make a decision about high school. Billy went to America to find a boarding school for Nanao.

Traveling from the West Coast to the East, he talked with educators, telling them about our situation, the unusual circumstances of our life. It was gratifying that all of the schools said they'd welcome a student like Nanao, and several offered generous scholarships.

Nanao had early on shown ability and talent in art, so we picked a boarding school where her work in art was as important as her grades in mathematics. She thrived in that environment where her creativity was encouraged and she was treated as an individual, not a number representing her class standing.

Buxton School in Massachusetts, then with a student body of seventy students, was a place she was given individual attention and could talk with teachers, if not as equals, as adults who not only respected her opinion, but expected her to have one. One of the first reports home we received were her teachers' comments that she did not speak up in class, did not offer her opinions. In her application I'd attached a detailed description of her education. I guess the teachers didn't take me seriously when I wrote that in her school in Japan she was *never* expected to speak up and give her opinion.

Nanao had resisted being sent away to school, but Mie, totally impressed by the transformation of her *ane* (elder sister), couldn't wait to copy her. Nanao had returned home with a whole new mindset and style, one that came complete with retro clothes and a whole lot of piercings in her ears.

And I think Mie's worldview was starting to change. She was in her second year of junior high school when I let her skip school so I could take her to Tokyo to hear Nelson Mandela speak. He'd only recently been released from prison, and as part of a worldwide tour seeking funds and support, he came to Japan. I told Mie who Mandela was, and I told her what I told her teacher when I explained why she would miss school: "It's important to experience being in the presence of this great man."

Mario and Lila would later follow their older sisters in

attending an American boarding school, in their case the George School, a Quaker school in Pennsylvania.

In 1982, I began writing a column I titled "Another Look" for the *Chunichi Shimbun*. I took on this job just after learning I was pregnant with Lila, my fourth child.

Writing for a regional edition of this national newspaper, I knew my audience was exclusively Japanese. So from the beginning I wrote about those things I thought they'd be interested in knowing from the perspective of a resident foreigner—making it clear I didn't speak for all foreigners, certainly not all Americans, and that indeed the average American might hold opinions different from my own.

My editor, Narita-san, had the idea to start a page, a pilot project, where Japanese and English could appear side by side. He was aware many Japanese who don't speak English have a perfectly good handle on it as a language they can read, and quite a few are adept at writing it. Readers were invited to translate my column, and the best translation, chosen by Narita-san (formerly the paper's senior correspondent in London and New Delhi), appeared in the next issue, along with my new column. (I called it the "double whammy"). The idea took off, and for every column published, more than a hundred translations, sometimes more than two hundred, were submitted.

When I first started writing that column, I decided that since I'd been told I could write about anything—indeed, Narita-san repeated it several times, saying "anything at all" (though he once cautioned me not to write about the Yakuza, Japan's mafia, which would've never occurred to me)—I'd do the mature thing and take care not to alienate and antagonize readers. I chose to forego knocking people over the head with my "message" in favor of seeking a positive way to share my views with an unknown audience.

. . .

When I began the "Another Look" column, I realized I was in a position to make a difference. I realized too that my reason for writing was that I wanted to be a voice for positive change in Japanese society—and that the best way to do that was to create common ground with my readers.

The subject I wrote about most often was education in Japan. Being critical of it, I kept and regularly updated a file of statistics and damning facts to bolster my criticism. Although I was critical, regular readers understood that if I complained about the schools, it wasn't because I wanted to report it in a comparative study, but rather because my children, and theirs, went to those schools. At the time I was writing, many of the subjects I took up, like the need to encourage students' critical thinking, creative capacities, and individuality, and the importance of seeking their opinions on such practical matters as school uniform designs and mandatory hairstyles, were being discussed for the first time. While I was openly critical of various aspects of Japanese society, no one could think I was apathetic, or an anthropologist writing from an academic distance.

On several occasions, the *Chunichi Shimbun* arranged talks for readers that were also open to the public. At one talk, after I said something critical, a woman spoke up and asked, "Why do you live in Japan if you don't like it?"

I replied, "I never said I didn't like Japan. As there are no countries that are paradise, I'd probably have something critical to say about any country where I lived." And, politely, I reminded her, "You live in Japan because you were born here. Your husband has his work here and all your family members live here. Although you tell me I don't like Japan, I might like it more than you because I live here purely as a matter of choice."

Her riposte: "I guess you're right about that."

It's gratifying to think that through my writing, I played a part in contributing to progressive change in my adopted country—which is what I was told when I was invited to join a committee first convened by Prime Minister Keizō Obuchi, and later, Prime Minister Ryutaro Hashimoto, on the theme of "Children's Education, Internationalism and Society."

I continued meeting my bimonthly deadline, at first mailing my columns in A4-sized envelopes, and later faxing them, for fourteen years, until Narita-san retired.

Not long after I began writing the column, my mentor Kazuko Satoh, who'd introduced me to Narita-san, told me he'd asked her if she thought I'd be able to continue. He knew I had a large family and thought it might be difficult for me to meet regular deadlines.

Satoh-san told him: "When Karen started writing the column, she'd just moved from her home in the countryside where she'd lived for seven years into a large house in the city, in the middle of winter. She'd had the flu, and her fourth child was due almost the same day as her first deadline. If nothing prevented her from meeting the deadline under those circumstances, then nothing should prevent her from continuing to do so."

And nothing did.

Until Jonathan, my eldest nephew, telephoned to say my sister Mollie was in a coma after collapsing suddenly, and I had to rush to New York City.

21

When Mollie died from a ruptured aneurysm, she was forty-three years old. She and I were the last members of of the family we were born into, and her sudden death was devastating. But there was no time to be devastated. She was the divorced mother of five boys, three of whom were minors at the time. Leaving my own young children at home, I got on the first available flight to New York City to be by her bedside, where she remained in a coma for five days before she died.

I now had permanent resident status in Japan, but it was still necessary to obtain a reentry visa before leaving the country so I'd be able to return. I saw this troublesome bureaucratic piece of paper (the nearest immigration office was a two-hour drive from my home) as just one more thing I didn't need to deal with before rushing to my sister's deathbed.

I was more than grateful to learn that in mitigating circumstances, such as sudden death in the family or other emergency, bureaucracy could bend, and it was possible to get the reentry permit at the airport at the time of departure.

. . .

Mollie had been a teacher in the New York City public school system for almost twenty years. Thus her children were entitled to the full benefits provided by her membership in the teachers' union, as well as Social Security and life insurance. It was a given these funds were not going to be immediately available, but forthcoming or not, even in the face of death, the rent and utilities had to be paid, the children fed. Ever supportive and generous, Tamar came down from Vermont almost as soon as I arrived and pressed a fistful of dollars in my hand.

Mollie was eulogized as someone who had "enriched the neighborhood and touched the lives of the people who knew her, and even the people who didn't." She was active in her Harlem community, from the Cub Scouts to church. In the days following her death, her neighbors brought home-cooked meals and went from door to door collecting contributions in a brown paper bag.

Certified to teach in any school, she'd chosen to spend her entire teaching career teaching children with learning disabilities and special needs. During one visit, when I brought Mie to summer camp, she'd taken me to her school, and I watched as she affectionately interacted with students who greeted her with hugs in the hallways. When we sat down with one group at lunch, Mollie introduced them in turn. Some had such severe disabilities that my overwhelming feeling was one of pity. I was overcome with the same feeling I'd had when I'd visited my mother, and could barely swallow my food. Mollie warmly chatted with them.

The administrators of my nephews' elementary and nursery schools were understanding and waived all fees due. Although Mollie had managed to raise five sons in Harlem at a time people could speak of young black men as an "endangered species," I was concerned about what would become of her middle son, then a teenager, without his mother's loving care and guidance.

I decided to contact Buxton, Nanao's boarding school,

knowing Mollie had considered sending him there. I had no reason to think they could do anything—I just was not afraid to ask and let them know my need. In an act of incredible understanding and generosity, they gave my nephew financial aid, and accepted him for immediate admission even though the school year was already well in progress.

These people cannot be repaid. They can be remembered. And I remember them for stepping out of the mold, for not just breaking rules but changing them, because life doesn't always go by the rules. They put bureaucracy to the side and compassion to the forefront, and let the institution they represented care about one boy in need.

As manifested by their many acts of kindness and thoughtfulness, Mollie's neighbors and colleagues clearly respected and admired her, and they stood by her family in its worst hour. It was these neighbors and fellow teachers who let me know the children were entitled to emergency relief in the form of food stamps.

This is where the bureaucracy began.

I went to a local welfare office, where I was told I could submit an application for food stamps. I filled out the form and, when my number was called, I approached the counter. After answering several questions, I was told to come back the following day. Saying to the clerk that I'd been told emergency food stamp relief could be issued on the same day, she shot back, "I don't know or care who told you what, but you're not walking out of here with any food stamps. Who do you think you are coming in here at four o'clock demanding food stamps?!"

Already reduced by the circumstances to that humble state where poor people reside, I couldn't have demanded the time of day. I couldn't have contemplated "demanding" anything from this female agent of the government of the United States of America. While waiting my turn, I'd watched the clerks behind the counter. They were so generally rude you would think they'd been trained to act in that manner. With unveiled contempt, they openly and verbally abused the people who beseeched them as though it were a routine part of their job.

As for the woman who now barked at me, I wanted to inform her, with pride, that my sister, Mollie Marie Hill Dowling, was a teacher and employee of the Board of Education of the City of New York, and a taxpayer who had worked every day of her adult life. I wanted this woman to know that we weren't destitute and that my sister's surviving dependents were *entitled* to aid. I wanted it made clear to this civil servant shrew, whose very existence exuded scorn and derision, that I wasn't begging for anything. Indeed, I wanted her to file it away in her little bureaucrat's brain that I did not *need* to beg for anything.

Instead of this harangue, however, I refocused and reminded myself that this was not to be a contest between this woman's ego and mine—that my mission was to act on behalf and in the interest of my nephews, children who could not represent themselves. I held back tears and quietly answered that it'd taken me the whole day to get the required documentation—Mollie's death certificate among others. She'd been in a coma almost a week, and although it was clear she wouldn't make it, when the call came saying she'd passed away just after midnight that day, I was inconsolable. But I kept that under wraps because I had to console her children.

Speaking with officious finality that made a mockery of the Christian cross hanging conspicuously around her neck, this official said, "Everybody's got a hard-luck story. But no food stamp authorization is going out of here today and that's that."

Although the office was supposed to be open until five, Mollie's neighbor Loretta had warned me "they hate to process applications after three o'clock because they're always trying to leave early."

I couldn't help but note that the woman who spoke to me was dressed like she was on her way to a club, and I could not see that she'd made any concessions in attire for the time that would elapse before she got to the dance floor. Her supervisor, reiterating they wouldn't issue emergency food stamps, was himself dressed like he was off to the gym or about to go for a jog.

I returned to the office the following morning and was one of the first people waiting on line, outside in the cold, in front of the building. When we were let in the waiting room by the security guard, it was soon crowded with old men and women, and mothers with crying babies. I saw one child, pregnant with a child, holding another child's hand. A man on crutches, cataracts clouding his old eyes, spoke in a loud voice to no one in particular: "When you get old you really in trouble."

Noticing one lone yuppie, complete with suit, briefcase, and horn-rimmed glasses, I could only wonder what cruel twist of fate had brought him there. He got up when his number was called and stood in line behind an old woman wearing mismatched shoes. The young woman sitting next to me wore a thin jacket, and I saw her hand shiver as she filled out a form. In that room full of coughing people dressed in ragged clothing, I felt self-conscious in a warm woolen coat and solid shoes.

Although the waiting room was completely full, clerks clustered in groups behind the counters idly chattering. When my name was called (I felt better about not being called by a number), I walked across a soiled carpet in a room full of dirty old office furniture and sat down at a social worker's desk to be interviewed. While she wrote down the information with one hand, she ate a donut with the other, indifferent to a cockroach that crawled across her desk.

I was told I would have to go to a downtown office to be issued the identification that would permit me to obtain the food stamps, at yet another location.

Okay.

But I couldn't help but think that while I was fit enough for all that running around, what about the old woman with the two different sneakers, the man on crutches, the young pregnant mother and her child? They'd all have to make the same trip, a forty-minute subway ride. Later I'd remember someone telling me that many people preferred begging and sleeping on the street simply because it's less dehumanizing than the welfare system.

What a sight to see the name of the wealthiest and "greatest country on Earth" attached to the dilapidated office building downtown where the identification cards were issued. The windows were so dirty you couldn't see out, the ceiling vents were taped on, the chairs we were required to sit on filthy. Crude signs tacked all over the walls warned people of the consequences of fraud in obtaining government aid. There was not one person there, I would vow, who had the wherewithal, the energy, to engage in anything that could be called fraud. The desperately poor Americans who crowded this room could not have been discerned from the denizens of some struggling nation where people could expect nothing at all from their governments.

I almost didn't recognize my name when it was mispronounced over a PA system so ineffective as to be all but nonfunctioning. Smacking gum in my face as he spoke, the clerk produced an identification card with my photograph and said loudly, "Sign here, Karen."

Japan regularly nourishes its bureaucracy with papers to sign that also require the stamp of your *inkan* (registered personal seal). I've waited on line in Japanese offices and city halls, places thick with that bureaucratic institutional pall that's the same no matter what country you're in. I've had to give up entire working days to feed the bureaucracy-monster what it wants—papers, papers, and more papers.

I have, however, been treated with respect—even if that respect comes prepackaged with the required honorific "san" attached to my name—and no civil servant dare utter my name without it. It's a small thing, but it guarantees you can hang on to your dignity, in every situation, no matter what.

Oh, how I longed to tell this last bureaucrat, "I am accustomed to being quietly and respectfully addressed as Anton-san."

22

I first sought out Dr. R for marriage counseling.

Sitting opposite her that first time, I told her I'd gone to see her because I wanted to have professional advice about obtaining a divorce.

"Oh, that's interesting," she'd said.

" 'Interesting'? Really? Why?" I thought she delivered that line with a little too much coolness.

"Because people who want a divorce don't usually come to me," she said, "they go to a lawyer."

I suppose I must have worn my problems like a badge, because when I said I felt I was "coming to a wall" in my marriage, she responded, "No. You're at the wall."

If we hadn't settled in Japan, I doubt that Billy and I would still be married.

Let me restate that: I'm sure we would not still be married.

Some of our worst problems occurred right along with the wave of divorce that swept so swiftly across America in the seventies and eighties. It would've been easy, too easy, to split up if I'd been in the States. All of the members of my family had died, but there were many friends—themselves divorced or soon-to-be divorced—I could've gone running to for consolation. By that time, I knew not to look for "perfect" but good enough, and I bet I would've found it. Before the divorce was final, I'd probably have met a man, at a party, in a library, in a class, with whom I felt I could make a life. Billy, according to the statistics, would've found a woman even sooner.

We had problems, and I don't expect anyone who's an adult to think otherwise. If I could have said "I'm going home," I would've gone home. It's precisely because I had nowhere to run with my problems that I had to face them. Although I thought about it later, I didn't think then that our relationship had the compounded strains of raising young children in the absence of close friends and family, not having enough money, trying to do meaningful work and not always succeeding. And I didn't calculate the many hurdles there are living in a country and a culture as different and unfamiliar as Japan's.

My extreme isolation found me trying to seek everything in one relationship, and that clearly wasn't working. During the years we lived on Breast Pocket Mountain, added to the daily isolation was the isolation, deep and unseen, of wanting to build connections, and finding that might take a very long time, and still then, might not happen.

It would be years later before I would acknowledge the utter defeat I could feel because I couldn't communicate in my own language, and the daily challenges that presented. My Japanese was improving, but only very slowly. On an average day I talked to no one. Had no one to talk to. It was so quiet on Breast Pocket Mountain, I found in the loneliness the quiet could be haunting, the sound of the wind almost unnerving. I thought the loud cawing of the crows mocked the silence that enveloped me. And I remember feeling there was a chill that ran down my back and said, *You're alone. And don't forget it.*

In my journal from November 1982, I write:

... isolation, aloneness, alienation, that's all I feel anymore. I've got to be at my lowest possible mental and physical state. I don't feel like doing much more than crying and sleeping. Maybe the worst thing is that I know there is no escape. There's a commitment whether I feel committed right now or not.

At the end of that passage I add, with hesitating optimism unable to crowd out the truth:

Of course this will all change, and things will be better. Oh, but when? The now of it is so horrible.

There were times when I thought, *Who is this man that I married?* Sure, we were friends, but learning to live together as husband and wife came with all the challenges all couples face. I'd wanted to live in the countryside, but I could not reconcile myself to the reality that living where we were guaranteed I'd be alone day after day, with no more company than young children. I seriously thought I might lose the ability to communicate in anything other than simple sentences, that my brain might atrophy. In those days, Billy and I seldom had dinner together, as he'd arrive home from work after I, totally weary, had gone to bed. Returning to a dark house, he'd find a note directing him to leftovers. When he was around, it seemed it was just long enough for us to have an argument.

Without a doubt, the Japanese general attitude toward divorce had an influence on me and an impact on our marriage. If Billy and I got divorced, "What would the Suzukis think?" I'd say to myself and laugh. Yes, it was laughable, but it wasn't a joke. The opinions of neighbors and the censure of society served as a checkpoint. Not only were we living in a country where divorce was not common, we were living in a community where it wasn't considered a scandal but a tragedy. The afternoon more than thirty years ago when Nanao came home from school crying because the parents of a girl in her class were divorcing is still a sharp memory. The whole class had cried. The entire school was shaken.

Billy never talked about divorce. Never once suggested it. It was anathema to him. That his first marriage ended in divorce was a lasting painful experience. It was the main reason he hadn't wanted to marry me.

Dr. R listened. I no longer thought she was cold and aloof. She told me she didn't think I wanted a divorce, but if there were insurmountable problems in my marriage, if my children or I were being abused, for example, she would advise me and help me end the marriage.

"Billy would never hurt me or the children," I said, letting out a dismissive laugh. *How could she even think such a thing?*

"Then you love your husband and believe he loves you?"

I nodded yes.

"So please. Tell me what's wrong."

I started to cry.

When I began to see Dr. R in the late eighties, I never thought that I had tears that I hadn't cried yet. I didn't think that mother-lessness, something I had long ago "accepted," had to be addressed. It didn't even occur to me that I'd be discussing my mother, that is, the pain of not having a mother that I've felt as long as I've had a memory.

I thought I had mourned my father and my brother. I was not aware incomplete grieving over two dead relatives was a problem I had. I didn't even think I was exceptional because two people I loved had been murdered. There are untold others. We're the victims left by the victims. Others survived. I would, too.

At the end of my first session, Dr. R said, "Look. I'm a psychi-atrist and I'm trained as a Jungian therapist. I can do dream analysis and all the rest. You can lie down on that couch if you want. We can do this slowly, the traditional way, or we can get right into it."

Dr. R was on the staff at a Tokyo counseling service. I was thankful they had a sliding scale that made the sessions afford-able, but just getting to and from Tokyo was expensive, and the arrangements I needed to make for the children so I could be out of town half a day were practically Byzantine. She told me she was willing to see me for double sessions. "I think we can get right into it," she said again. "You're obviously ready."

Yes, I was ready. There was so much I'd avoided, hid, buried.

In the years leading up to my sessions with Dr. R, I'd learned, become adept, at burying feelings. She explained it was a survival tactic that had no doubt helped me get through the pain of a motherless childhood. She also explained that this same tactic, employed in my adult life, could only harm me and any intimate relationship I hoped to have.

Considering we only met five or six times, it's hard to believe the impact my sessions with her had on me. I learned to *feel*. No matter what we talked about, I knew she was never far away from me as a woman, as a person. Compassionate, her gaze was both warm and direct and said, *We've got to do this.*

I had to deal with murder.

I've murdered no one. But for many years I dreamed I had. I could feel the hard handle of a knife as its steel blade plunged deep into resistant flesh. I'd wake up thankful, again, that I hadn't killed anyone, only to have the dream again. And again. And again.

"Of course I know I'm not responsible," I told Dr. R.

"Your rational mind knows that. But you are not only your rational self," she said.

"But I know I couldn't have prevented it. Even if I'd been there, there was probably nothing I could've done."

"Right. But you *wish* you could have. Of course you do. You loved your father and your brother. It's hard to lose a close family member. You lost two. Brutally."

Dr. R sat in her chair, composed. She always wore silk blouses, and that day her blouse was a pale blue. I focused on the tiny pearl buttons as she leaned forward and told me I could tell her anything, essentially saying that she could take it. I unlocked my gaze from the buttons and had my eyes on her when I described what happened to my father. When I went on, to tell her about my brother, I saw her flinch. It was almost imperceptible, but she couldn't help it. Still, she let me do it— unburden myself of anguish that could not admit it had a name.

And so, at last, I cried those tears that had not been shed at my father's hospital bedside, where he'd lingered for three days before succumbing to his wounds. I had not cried those tears at my brother's funeral, where, looking in the casket, I thought for a brief hopeful moment, *It's not him. They got the wrong person.* I didn't, I couldn't, recognize him. The bullet that tore through his brain left no trace of him.

Oh, these tears now were more than relief. I finally managed to lose self-possession. I could feel unashamed grief. Pure pain. It had taken me years, but at last I could feel the pain that exhausted me had been excavated and was finally leaving me.

That session with Dr. R was followed by a dream in which I was in a dark tunnel. I couldn't get out of that tunnel even though I could see the exit ahead, large and light. I bumped into the walls and kept losing the path.

"It's all right. Just go through," I heard the voice of my father say. *"You're almost there."*

I never had the Dream of the Murderer again.

· · ·

Still, unlike most people, I suppose, my thoughts can suddenly and for no ostensible reason be interrupted and invaded by awful visions of my eighty-year-old father being attacked and stabbed to death with an ice pick. I wrote about it, as vividly as I could, in my novel. I revised endlessly in an effort to "make it real."

I haven't written about my brother's murder. I would not commit to paper the details I learned from the police. Still, it is those details that have the power to invade my visual mind and force it to shut down. I have to always know. I don't have a choice. It's not possible to write it away.

Some people, the few who know about this part of my past, have suggested that the reason I've settled in Japan is because it's "so safe" and America "so dangerous." But settling in Japan was not part of a plan. We were not escaping America. But I guess we did escape, because we live in a country where we never experience fear that we, or our children, are in imminent danger. Japan is not a fantasyland where no bad thing ever happens, but that it happens seldom and violent crime is rare means you don't have to be vigilant. It's a country where getting your hands on a gun is discouragingly difficult, no schools have metal detectors, and no child has ever been shot.

Although my father's murder was an "incident" never reported in the news, my brother's murder never investigated, just common everyday "occurrences," there was never a place in my consciousness where I could conceive of my family members becoming crime statistics.

I don't know anyone in Japan who knows anyone who's been murdered. Imagine, if you can, being embarrassed that you have two family members who've been murdered. It hurts me that my Japanese friends might regard America with negative circumspection not because of reports in the news, but because they know me.

• • •

The night before leaving for America to go to Mollie's bedside, I saw my father in a dream. He was trying to get into the room where Billy and I lay sleeping but I wouldn't let him. He said he only needed a blanket to cover the baby, my baby sister. I handed it to him.

Before I reached Mollie, before I saw the face that no longer belonged to her, distorted by the destruction of her blood-flooded brain, I knew she wouldn't live.

"Don't leave me," I cried at her bedside. "I don't want to be the last one."

But I am.

When I returned home after Mollie died, depression and gloom enveloped me like a shroud. I needed reassurance—I wanted someone to tell me I was not going to lose everyone close to me. Everyone I loved.

My sessions with Dr. R had stopped months before, but in the immediate aftermath of Mollie's death, I wanted desperately to talk with her. Telephoning her office to make an appointment, I was unprepared to hear the receptionist tell me Dr. R was no longer in Japan. She'd returned to the Philippines permanently.

When it hit me I wouldn't be able to see her, could not talk to her, would not be able to feel her empathy, I was desolate. I put my head down and cried until my tears dried up on my desk.

It was dusk in my room when I finally looked up. I saw then that Dr. R had never presented herself as something, a person, to lean on. She believed I had the answers, and although it might be difficult, I'd find a way to face those days that started out heavy with grief. I would figure out how to get over that feeling of overwhelming weariness at the thought of living. Resilience would replace despair.

During our last session, she'd told me, "You know you're strong, but you don't know just how strong you are. You don't think it's unusual because you've done it, but most people do what's familiar, what's easy, they certainly don't stray far from home. But you have, and built a family and a life, not just in a foreign country, but in a country as culturally foreign as Japan. Courage is your central characteristic. You will be all right, Karen."

I'd lost my family of origin. But I had the one thing that mattered to me, the family I'd created. Their love would sustain me.

23

We still have our American citizenship.

That the laws of nationality are universally arbitrary is highlighted by the fact that if a Japanese couple had children born in the United States, those children would be American. But Mie, Mario, and Lila, born in Japan, are not Japanese. Nanao, born in Denmark, is not Danish.

It took us fifteen years to acquire permanent residence status in Japan. Although we were gainfully employed, paid taxes, had broken no laws, and could be considered upstanding members of our community, our application for permanent residence was turned down several times. The immigration authorities didn't have to give us a reason for the rejection, and they never did.

Then, without explanation, we were granted permanent resident status, and Billy and I made the major decision—not to settle down, but to commit our bodies to staying in the same place for a foreseeable number of consecutive years. It's a fact that we never said, "Let's live in Japan." We just let it unfold.

In 1990, as Billy and I prepared to move out of the home in Hamamatsu where we'd lived for eight years, everything I packed was a reminder it had been the place we'd both lived the longest since leaving our respective homes in New York City at age eighteen. He'd left his Greenwich Village childhood home on MacDougal Street (long before the advent of falafel and gelato shops) to go to university in upstate New York. I'd left Washington Heights (long before the neighborhood became Dominican) to uncover the world beyond 159th Street. Not so much nomadic as not rooted, we would later live on both the East and West Coasts in the United States, and several countries in Europe. Since coming to Japan, we'd had four addresses.

Looking back now, it's hard to believe we arrived in this country with one child and one bag each. When we moved into our current house with our four children, a cat, and a dog, a moving van was required to move our possessions. Evidently, we had settled down.

"Settled down" were dreaded words to Americans whose sixties credentials include being on hand for the Beatles's first concert in the United States. We were around when Bob Dylan was just another folk singer with a guitar playing at Greenwich Village coffee houses. "I was there" we can say, among the throng of 200,000 when Dr. King spoke in Washington about his dream, and when the small town of Woodstock, New York, was declared a nation.

Deciding to buy land in Japan, the first question we had to answer was, "Will we have to continue to pay in the Afterlife for a plot of land as big as a postage stamp?" The second was, "Where?"

Where could we find a place we could get more of a view than the back of a ramen shop, a view that does not include utility poles, where the commute to work doesn't take more time than the time at work itself? And where is that place we won't have to look out our kitchen window into Suzuki-san's bathroom?

Most people can't grasp what a crowded, densely populated country Japan is. It's not just that the population of Tokyo is almost exactly half of all the people who live in Canada, one of the largest countries in the world. Japan's population of 125 million are crowded on to a land mass roughly the size of California. And of that, fully 70 percent is mountains, forests, rivers; with no access to sewage systems, water or electricity, it's not suitable for residential or commercial development. So we are thrown in with that 125 million, sharing the space as best we can. Even here in the countryside, we can expect, and have to accept, crowded conditions. Sure, there is more space to be had further out in the country, but we'd already been there, done that.

We scoured the area looking for land and quite naturally returned to the Atago area of Tenryu. We found that a mountain that had only been a mountain when we'd lived nearby was under development for single-family housing. Forty-five minutes from the city of Hamamatsu, and about the same distance from our old farmhouse on Breast Pocket Mountain, the location seemed just right.

The familiarity of the area was one of the best things about moving there, and the moving van had hardly left before our old village neighbors were at our door with fresh vegetables, dried shiitake, and azalea bushes. On my first trip to the local supermarket, I ran into Nanao's first-grade teacher, Yoshibayashi-sensei.

The plot of land we chose is at the top of a hill, high enough so that on occasion we can see helicopters fly by at eye level.

The view is magnificent. From my desk I can see the Tenryu River and the horizon of the Pacific Ocean.

Our address, in translation:

117 Blessed Verdure Plateau
Heaven's Dragon, Tranquil Hills
Origin of the Sun

Our architect, Sybille Schnabel, had just moved to Japan from Germany when we first met at a UNESCO event in 1980. On her first visit to our farmhouse, she'd pronounced, "The woodshed should be closer to the bath."

With her architect's eye for functionality, she immediately saw what made sense. "You won't need to turn the light on in the kitchen in the daytime if you take out those bushes on the north wall." According to Sybille, most people had no idea how much of their energy (physical and electrical) they wasted because their homes didn't function efficiently. She'd studied Japanese architecture and was familiar with the rusticity of the traditional lifestyle, but she could see the many ways the farmhouse could be made both convenient and comfortable. Just a few weeks after that first visit, she came again, this time with five possible floor plans to renovate and remodel—the farmhouse was in need of both.

Sybille told me then that I should think about what kind of house I'd like, because the day would come when I'd want to build a house, and it'd be useful to know, in broad outlines and detail, what kind of house I wanted. At the time I thought it odd she thought I might actually own a house one day. I still had my Vermont mindset: owning a house is something other people do. There was no place in my imagination for such an idea as building a house. But when the day came, ten years later, I was prepared, and could talk with her about the kind of home I wanted. By that time, she'd designed several houses in Japan, and I knew and liked her style. Designing our house would be the most challenging project of her career, she told me, saying, "I'll be using my European sensibility to try to satisfy the expectations of an American couple while directing Japanese carpenters and a Japanese construction team."

Comfort and function were her basic guidelines, and she said, "If I design a house for someone I want it to fit their lifestyle. And I want to improve on that." While splitting chores and responsibilities fifty-fifty might be the ideal, there are few homes where that's true. Particularly attuned to the many roles women play in the home, Sybille emphasized, "You should be able to accomplish your tasks efficiently, and if the house is well run, you'll have the time and energy for your other pursuits."

That hit home, because goodness knows I worked for our farmhouse, it didn't work for me. At the end of some days I was too exhausted from chores to engage in anything other than a little active wall gazing. Whether it was having a suitable place to wash my calligraphy brushes and inkstones, or whether it was the never-ending battle to keep insects out of the food, the general inefficiency of the farmhouse made every task doubly difficult. Sybille's house design centered around order, which I thrive on, and I could expect order to be maintained because there'd be a place for everything.

With a thousand things to decide during the building of our house, I came to understand why some of my friends told their architect "*omakase*" (I leave it to you) and kept quiet until they were handed the key. Japanese architects prefer that, and many will not discuss design details with their clients. That wouldn't work for me and Sybille knew it. We met and talked often. We went over different designs and sketches, and each new design she presented me with I thought was better than the last. She was adamant in reminding me that no doubt I was accustomed to the lifestyle I'd had, makeshift—but now that I had an opportunity to customize my house, I should take the time and pay attention to do just that.

Happily, we shared the same architectural and interior design aesthetic. I wanted the house to incorporate the best aspects of Japanese and Western design. We were both admirers of the Folkcraft Museum in Matsumoto, which I'd seen when Yoshida-sensei took me there on that first trip out of the dojo. There, handcrafted furniture, textiles from Ghana and Indonesia, could be seen side by side with Korean ceramics and Native American pottery. Traditional Japanese *tansu* (cabinets) and apple baskets woven in Aomori in Japan's far north all harmonized to create a living environment that was simple, functional, and beautiful.

Modern Scandinavian and Italian furniture would complete my design wishes.

After the builders put the last beam of the frame in place, they hung the Shinto *bonten*. Hanging beside it is the *Richtkrone*. Sybille made this "crown" Germans traditionally put in their new homes from pine boughs and ribbons.

Japanese and Western talismans for good fortune, they still hang side by side under the eaves.

24

K aren! Hey! How're you doing?"
   "Fine, fine. And you? It's been a long time."
   "You're telling me. It's been about fifteen years. But I've heard all about you."
   "Oh, really—what've you heard?"
   "That you married a millionaire, have seven children, and live in China."
   "!!??!!"
   That was part of a telephone conversation with my old friend Gloria during a visit to the States. I had to set the record straight, on all counts.
   "So, when are you coming back?" she wanted to know.
   We used to hear that all the time. No one asks anymore.
   Having lived here forty-five years, quite naturally, I call Japan home.

Arriving in Japan at age thirty, I can't say that I grew up here—but this is the country where I've matured. And I see now that living in Japan during these defining years has greatly affected how I perceive Japan, myself, and the rest of the world.

Japan has changed me, and although I wouldn't call it a metamorphosis, I can say that I am simply not the same person who came here all those many years ago. Considering some of the difficulties I've faced, it's not that the question "What am I doing in Japan?" never crossed my mind—it's just that it doesn't anymore.

No one is more surprised than I am how comfortable I became in this country. I wouldn't have imagined in a thousand years that I'd find in Japan so much that reflects my deepest sensibilities.

There was a lot I didn't understand about Japan and its culture when I first came here. It is sometimes disconcerting to think of the many times I must have crossed the invisible lines of decorum and behavior that rule Japanese society. Still, I did see early on that there were cues, and that I could learn by showing a measure of humility and paying attention, that I'd benefit by being a self-reflective and careful observer.

But I could not have guessed that on this small island that sits on tectonic plates, where people eat their fish raw, scald themselves in their baths, and don't think much of verbal communication, I would make a niche for myself. I wouldn't have thought that in this ancient country with all its old customs and formalities and daily obligations, its many written and unwritten rules, I would develop feelings of such deep attachment.

Quite frankly, I'm surprised myself that I didn't leave once I found out the Japanese don't dance at parties.

I no longer live in that isolated hamlet in a farmhouse perched on the side of a mountain.

Still, the *danchi* (residential subdivision of single-family homes) where we built our house is not a cosmopolitan place. None of my neighbors speak English (or, if they do, they keep it to themselves). I can still say, without exaggeration, Billy is the only foreigner I see and speak English with on a regular basis.

That time he returned to the States to do his master's degree, some days I'd speak out loud to myself just so I could hear a voice, period.

I have exactly two American friends, both an hour's drive from me. Often months pass before we meet. Although I've now had half a lifetime of living in environments where I see few people and interact with even fewer, I am no recluse—I enjoy the company of people.

There were times in the past when I'd already been living here for many years when I thought I didn't have any friends. Those were times when I wanted badly to have that special friend, a friend I could laugh and cry with, complain about my husband to, discuss my children with, tell everything.

Then one day I thought about the many people I knew, especially women, who had befriended me since I came to Japan. I thought about women who came to my house and gave me gifts of pickled food I couldn't identify. I thought about people who were kind to my family and who were generous and thoughtful in ways I could've never imagined. I think they would've been hurt if they knew I didn't think of them as friends. For me to think of them as friends, for them to be worthy of my bestowing on them the honored word *friend*, they had to be like my American and European friends. To be eligible for my good-friendship seal of approval, they'd have to be people who, in fact, they weren't.

I had my own ideas of what a friendship was, what form it could take, and I'd decided that, failing to fit into that, these perfectly good and friendly people were not friends. Over time, I realized it wasn't necessary for me to replicate my Western experiences of friendship in this country. In the process I learned I could live anywhere, among any people, and that I would always look for an opportunity to create friendship.

In the process of embracing a culture so different from my own, and opening myself to new experiences, I discovered myself. And I discovered that cultural behavior is learned, and nationality is something named on your passport. Early on I understood no one is going to know much about me, my husband, or our children by our being labeled American, and surely not by the various colors of our skin.

At the time I could still be called a young mother, open-school day, PTA meetings, parent-teacher conferences, traffic monitoring, and associated responsibilities and activities in the community were at the center of my external mothering life. Although far from anything I'd call socializing, it was on these occasions that I'd meet and talk with other mothers. This all came to an end when my children were no longer in Japanese schools. It became clear to me then how central to my interaction with other women the presence of my children had been.

That party with disco dancing mothers is now a thing so far in the past it's hard to believe it actually happened. But it did.

A few years back, I ran into one of the disco mamas, Ogo-san. Knowing all my children lived far away, she looked at me sympathetically and said "*Samishii desu ne*" — "You must be lonely."

I could hardly hide the smile on my face when I answered, "No."

I was prepared for this moment.

Yeah, no young kids around means Billy and I linger over candle-lit wine-infused dinners while listening to our favorite jazz pianists—Bill Evans, Kenny Drew, and Tommy Flanagan. That's just not something we did during the days we were overseeing kids' homework, filling out school forms, making sure the dog was walked, and that the kids got in the bath.

Whereas Friday and Saturday nights used to regularly be dominated by preparations for some school event the following day, now we set aside those nights for Latin dancing and reggae. If we put on the oldies but goodies, it's 1968 all over again as we get carried away by "I Heard It Through the Grapevine."

We didn't travel when the children were young and I never felt it was a sacrifice, because we didn't even think about traveling. Our funds went for visits to the U.S. so the kids could have exposure to English at summer camps, and next up were boarding schools and colleges. Now regular trips to Tokyo and our favorite places in the north, Matsumoto and Takayama, define my post-active-mothering lifestyle.

Travel in Asia has taken us to Vietnam, Bali, Taiwan, Malaysia, and Singapore. When Billy went to New Zealand, I went to China, and now one of my favorite places in the world is Xi'an. I loved seeing the Terracotta Army so much I will definitely make a second trip. And Xi'an is a calligraphy lover's heaven as it is famous for the "Four Treasures of Calligraphy"— brushes, inkstones, ink, and paper.

We took a road trip with Sybille and her husband Horst through eastern Germany not long after the Berlin Wall fell. The only countries in Western Europe we haven't visited are Portugal and Greece. We've been to all the Baltic countries including Estonia, Lithuania, Latvia, and Poland. Most recently we visited South Africa and Ireland. Since we live in a place that's practically a nature reserve, I love visiting cities like Dublin for the bookstores and Cape Town for the restaurants. But "finally" getting to the Grand Canyon, and hiking in Hawaii to see the lava eruption at Kilauea are marvels of nature I would not want to have missed.

During an extended trip to Russia, we got lost on the Moscow subway as we searched for and found the chess center where International Grandmaster Mikhail Botvinnik played. We weren't sure how things were going to turn out when we were trapped in a subway in Budapest. The train stopped in a tunnel and all the lights and engines were turned off when we noticed there was no one around but us. After some yelling and banging on the doors, a conductor came to our rescue, informing us we'd missed the last stop.

About every other year I go to see my friends Nini, Genia,

Kate, and Carol in Copenhagen, my preferred place to be in summertime. If I plan it right, I can be there for not just the Midnight Sun but the Copenhagen Jazz Festival. Aside from wandering around visiting old hangouts from when I was a twenty-year-old discovering that city for the first time, I love joining in the dancing in the park, where people of all ages do swing, tango, mambo.

The day I ran into Ogo-san, we'd just returned from Finland and the Czech Republic.

"You're really smart to enjoy yourselves doing the things you like, like traveling. We Japanese [Japanese often speak of themselves in the first person plural] could do these things [could afford it] but we just don't have the mentality."

Certainly she made it sound as though the Japanese as a population are genetically incapable of enjoying themselves, especially after they reach their mature years, but I think she was just stating a fact. While I can imagine many of my older friends here sitting around planning their funerals (a popular activity), I'd have great difficulty imagining any of them doing the mambo in the park.

Our children were born with an international outlook, so it's not surprising Nanao studied in Mexico, Mie in China, Mario in Ecuador, and Lila in Ghana.

Up until a few years ago, we had four children living in four different time zones. Nanao was at her home in Sag Harbor, on the U.S. East Coast. Mie was living and working in Stockholm. Mario lives in Kyushu, an island southwest of us. And after living in New York City, Lila came to a stop in Los Angeles. (At this writing, both Mie and Lila have moved with their families to Tokyo.)

Since I lost my parents relatively early, I never got to find out that parenting doesn't end, it just becomes different. What your children want and need from you changes as they, and you, age.

The days of applying Band-Aids to scraped knees and my worrying that they'd drink soda are way past. And while I worried that they'd be forever ruined by the twin threats of manga and television, I might have lost my mind completely if the Internet had been around when they were growing up.

These days I may be consulted on life-changing, future-shaping concerns. Sometimes they may just want someone to listen, someone to be there as they wrestle with decisions. I have had more than one occasion to tell them that they have options, and what a privilege that is. And while I've reminded them they have choices, it hasn't always been easy to accept they must make their own choices, and mistakes.

Mainly, I want them to know there is someone who cares and will always support them. While I expect them to be independent, living in Japan's openly interdependent society has taught me that not only is it all right to depend on others, but interdependency is natural, supports the smooth functioning of society, and is crucial for our species. My children, independent adults, know they can always come home.

Since they were very young, I've always also wanted them to know that it is not only their parents who support them. Even when they were babies, it was important to me that they knew there were other laps and arms to hold them, others who could soothe their tears. I have encouraged their building and developing meaningful loving relationships with others, and it makes me happy to see they've done that.

Billy and I regularly have extended visits with them in their widespread outposts. It's a time we can catch up with them and their families, meet and hang out with their friends. All of their homes are cheery, welcoming places where people from all over the world come to stay, gather to eat and talk, drink, and, yeah, dance.

My kids think my pancakes are the best in the world, and whether we're in California or New York or Austria or at home here in Tenryu, there is sure to be one morning when I'm flipping pancakes for an ever-expanding family that now includes spouses and grandchildren. Our all-family gatherings, when and wherever we can make them happen, are our family's treasured moments.

Although we've been separated by distance, that's been alleviated by modern communications technology. Seldom does a day pass when I am not in touch with one or all of them. I answer their messages within seconds—it makes me think I'm carrying on a conversation. And it lets me reaffirm I'm available to my children, always.

When I saw Ogo-san again recently (this time at the hospital; we were both there for routine checks, I'm happy to add), she told me her youngest son, thirty-six, had "finally" gotten married.

"One worries about one's adult children until they get married," she said.

I knew what she was talking about—although years ago I would have balked at this old-style, played-out way of thinking.

But now, although we've had our struggles, Billy and I can say we have found so much contentment and fulfillment in marriage. Especially in having and being part of a family. Naturally, we want that for our children, too.

More than anything, we've wanted them to experience a shared life.

EPILOGUE

I still call myself a New Yorker, though it's not making much sense anymore.

I haven't lived in New York City for fifty years and must ask directions when I visit, and coming out of the subway, I'm not sure if I'm facing uptown or downtown, the east side or the west. Familiar landmarks that would've guided me have disappeared. I no longer recognize neighborhoods where I could've told you where to find the fish store, dry cleaner, Chinese laundry, bodega, and five-and-dime stores.

Being an un-New Yorker was brought home to me when I realized I've now learned to follow rules—such as pedestrian rules. In Japan everyone waits for the light to change before crossing the street. Finding myself doing that in New York appeared to be deviant behavior. One day while I waited to cross the street in Manhattan, I looked around and saw the other people who'd been waiting on the corner with me were now well on their way to their various destinations. Not jaywalking singled me out as not being a New Yorker.

So imagine this: the next time I stood on the corner, I pretended I'd dropped something and looked around on the ground until the light changed, just so I wouldn't look weird because I was obeying the rules and waiting for the light.

A friend from Boston who used to live in Japan was annoyed that people cross on the light here, even when there are no cars coming. When he saw me do it, too, he repeated that worn-out line, "You've been here too long." He regularly made disparaging remarks about Japan being "a nation of fish all swimming in the same direction" and that "people don't think for themselves."

I understood his disapproval because I too used to look askance at so many people adhering to law and order. But I've lost my taste for chaos. I came to see that if nothing else, the rules work, and the reason they do is because everyone follows them, instead of making them up as they go along, which of course could be called "thinking for themselves." Following the rules means you can count on your lost phone or passport being returned to you within the day, and your lost wallet will be returned with the cash and cards.

In Japan, no cars have bumper stickers advertising your religion, political affiliation, or stance on abortion. No one has ever seemed to care or want to know if I "have faith" or "been saved." While religious indoctrination of children is absent, moral education starts early. I'll never forget overhearing Mario (then in kindergarten) telling Lila (who was in nursery school), *"Usotsuki wa dorobou no hajimari"* (a liar is the beginning of a thief) when she didn't fess up to taking a cookie from the pantry!

I'm not poor, but years ago I realized I'd be willing to live in Japan if I were, because I could still live in a good neighborhood, my children could go to good schools. The national public healthcare system that provides for everyone would provide for us, too. I've always been happy knowing my neighbor has access to the same healthcare I do, and that the taxes I pay ensures this system is maintained.

. . .

Billy and I still party.

We have friends here and there who come for our regular shindigs. Sometimes these are proper sit-down dinner parties, and I'll call Nanao to ask her to tell me, again, how she makes Pollo al Vino Cotto.

Some of our parties are potluck, and I can count on Momo to bring a delicious array of fresh breads. Her husband Jukka, whose family we love visiting in Finland, will bring a couple of bottles of carefully selected wine. Linda will bake a carrot cake, wrapping it so prettily I don't want to open it.

Akiko brings prosciutto and salami with truffles for the antipasti. Akiko's husband, the late Franco D'Angelo, was one of my best friends. They met at one of our dinner parties, not long after he moved to Hamamatsu from Florence. That time when Billy and I "ate our way from Como to Sicily," it was under Franco's direction. He not only told us what restaurants to go to, but which waiter to ask for—and how to choose a restaurant when we didn't know where to go.

A master chef, Franco taught me everything I know about Italian cuisine. Taking over my kitchen, I'd be by his side as he turned out Risotto alla Milanese, frittata, and Fritto Misto—telling me all the ways this deep-fried dish was different from tempura.

I made the bean dish Pasta e Fagiole as Franco had taught me, at the home of our friends Celia and Salvatore, in Italy's Abruzzo region, which is where these beans come from. The guests at that dinner party, which included a prince, were amazed. An American woman, from Japan, had mastered this local dish?! "*Applausi!*" the pleased diners said after the first taste, actually applauding at the table.

Gatherings of friends and family around the table are my happiest and most satisfying moments. Good appetites enhance the experience. I may seat guests according to the language they speak, and at our table it may be English, Japanese, Finnish, French, German, Italian, and Spanish.

There is always a moment when I feel quiet inside as I cast my eyes over those around me and remind myself to be thankful for all my good fortune.

And oh, how fortunate I've been. I have love. I've created a family. I have a home.

I've looked for what is good in people, and I've always found it.

At some point in my journey, on a day I never noticed, I found that golden thread, a thing of beauty that, though it cannot be seen, connects us all.

END

ACKNOWLEDGMENTS

While writing this book, I could hardly wait for the pleasure of publicly acknowledging those people who've befriended, supported, and encouraged me over the years. There are so many I am grateful to, and I hope I have not overlooked anyone.

Tamar Cole, longtime friend and confidante, shared in some of the experiences I recount. Embarking on the project of writing my memoir, I was thankful that at every stage I could avail myself of her sagacity, wit, and willingness to talk over matters big and small. My gratitude to her is immense.

I had a draft but not a clear idea of what I would do with it when I sought the editorial assistance of my good friend Veronica Chambers. She actually responded "Anything for you" as she generously made room for me in the middle of her many writing projects. I am sincerely grateful for her generosity and expert guidance.

Ronit Wagman, editor extraordinaire, helped me tell my story. With attention and care, she lined up her sensibilities with mine, asking the questions I needed to answer. The clarity she insisted on helped give structure to an expansive life.

I am grateful to Kathryn Guare who said, "We want to get your book in front of readers," assuring me she'd lend her expertise and assistance until that happened. I thank Susannah Noel for the curiosity, enthusiasm, and detail she brought to her work as copyeditor. Vicki Beyer and Diane Walsh Sasaki were kind to give their time as early readers of the manuscript.

To all who have given the gift of friendship, you have been an inspiration, and your warmth and welcome have moved me: Mal Adams, Felix Arts and Sue Sproule, Momo Asamoto and Jukka Rimpinen, Genia Barosin Bergmann, Annie Bliss and Tom Ickovic, Patricia Carlin, Akiko D'Angelo, Roberta Flack, Stim and Takayo Harriman, Neil and Marie-Thérèse Hausig, Rika Houston, Keiko Ishikawa, Kiyoko Izuka, Nini Jensen and Charles Scawthorn, Yukiko Komatsu, Linda Laddin, Regge Life, Richard MacLean, Yukiko Ogasawara, Masahiro Ōmura, Kuniko Ono, Celia Owens, Tom Pedersen, Marianne Robin-Tani, Erin Sakakibara, Sybille and Horst Schnabel, Anna Stephenson and Alan Leigh, Bob Tobin, Steven Ward and Ximena Elgueda, Galen Williams, Kate Wolin, and Linda and Hideki Yamada.

I see my sister reflected in the faces and characters of my dear nephews: Jonathan McChriston, Scott Dowling, Almasi Dowling, Kenyatta Ribeiro, and Nigel Wright. I am happy to have among my extended family: John Anton and Renee Schwalberg, Glenna Anton and Amir Buchbinder, David Johnson-Igra and Kelly Earls, Mary Ruth Byrd, and Eric Justice Abayaa.

I count myself fortunate that my children married people I love, and love to hang out with: Erling Hope, Christian Fedorczuk, Sari Takano Anton, and Christopher Dalton Shaw. They are all outstanding individuals and their varied backgrounds, interests, and experiences enrich my world.

To my grandchildren, each and every wonderful one of you–Isaiah, Soren, Luka, Umi, Waho, Claire, Leah, Kazuma, Enzo–please know it is my great joy seeing you grow and learn, and I thank you for giving me a glimpse of future generations.

Acknowledgments

I owe everything to my children
Nanao 奈々緒
Mie 美枝
Mario 眞理雄
Lila 璃羅
who are the core of my being

And to Billy Anton from the Village, whose love and companionship I count on as he continues on this journey with me.

ABOUT THE AUTHOR

Karen Hill Anton, formerly a columnist for *The Japan Times* and the Japanese newspaper *Chunichi Shimbun*, is a cross-cultural competence coach. She lectures widely on her experience of cross-cultural adaptation and raising four bilingual, bicultural children. Originally from New York City, she's achieved second-degree mastery in Japanese calligraphy and has lived with her husband William Anton in rural Japan since 1975.